HOLOCAUST STUDIES ANNUAL
1991

GARLAND REFERENCE LIBRARY
OF SOCIAL SCIENCE
(VOL. 787)

HOLOCAUST STUDIES ANNUAL
1991
General Essays

edited by
Sanford Pinsker
and
Jack Fischel

GARLAND PUBLISHING, INC. • NEW YORK & LONDON
1992

© 1992 Sanford Pinsker and Jack Fischel
All rights reserved

ISBN 0–8153–0393–9
ISSN 0738–0739
LC   88–648983

Printed on acid-free, 250-year-life paper
Manufactured in the United States of America

CONTENTS

Contributors vi

Preface vii

"Unreliable" and "Unfit": The Reich Chamber of Culture and the Expulsion of Jews and Other "Dangerous Elements" from German Cultural Life, 1933-1945
by Alan E. Steinweis 3

Hitler's Poland: The View From a Nazi Press in America
by Sidney H. Kessler 23

Nazi Determination and the Destruction of Dutch Jewry
by John A. Leopold 35

The Impact of the Holocaust on Herbert Hoover
by Rafael Medoff 53

Bureaucracy and the "Jewish Question" in Prewar Nazi Germany: The Nuremberg Legislation of 1935 as a Case Study
by Howard Margolian 69

An Estate of Memory: Women in the Holocaust
by Lillian Kremer 99

Sylvia Plath and the Reporting of the Holocaust in the Popular Press
by Gary M. Leonard 111

The Holocaust and the Shaping of the New Germany
by Frank Buscher 135

Writing After: Literary and Moral Reflections of the Holocaust
by Efraim Sicher 147

CONTRIBUTORS

Frank Buscher is Professor of History at Christian Brothers University.

Sidney H. Kessler has appeared previously in the pages of *Holocaust Studies Annual*. He is Professor of History at Glassboro State College.

Lillian Kremer is author of *Witness Through the Imagination* and Professor of English at Kansas State University.

Gary M. Leonard is Professor of English at the University of Toronto.

John A. Leopold is Professor of History at Western Connecticut State University.

Howard Margolian works for the Canadian Department of Justice.

Rafael Medoff is Professor of History at Ohio State University. He is the author of *The Deafening Silence: American Jewish Leaders and the Holocaust*, and was selected as a 1988-89 Hoover Scholar.

Efraim Sicher is Professor of English at Ben-Gurion University.

Alan E. Steinweis is Professor of History at Florida State University.

PREFACE

This volume of *The Holocaust Studies Annual* includes essays which range from an account of the first efforts to expel Jews from German cultural life to a contemporary Israeli critic's survey-assessment of writing after the Holocaust. As such, *From Efforts at Expulsion to Efforts at Moral Reflection* is an appropriate title. The essays were collected from the recent Holocaust Conference held at Millersville University, as well as from material submitted directly to the editors. And while it is true that the nine essays of *Holocaust Studies Annual: 1991* do not orbit around a single, organizing theme, they continue our ongoing concern with how the nightmare of the Holocaust began, what efforts were made, or were not made, by way of "rescue," and how major figures--in literature, theology, and politics--responded, or failed to respond.

These questions and others have been raised in previous volumes of *Holocaust Studies Annual*. No doubt they will be raised, in new combinations and with newer emphases, in future volumes. Perhaps nothing characterizes the post-Holocaust world more than our painful obligations to remember and to document, to search for deeper, more appropriate ways of understanding that which may well lie beyond our capacity for "understanding."

This volume begins with Alan E. Steinweises account of how the Reich Chamber of Culture sought to expel Jews and other "dangerous elements" from contaminating German cultural life and ends with Efraim Sicher's assessment of how a wide range of poets and fictionists responded to the Holocaust.

Between these poles lie Sidney H. Kessler's continuing investigation of the Nazi Press in America, John A. Leopold's account of the destruction of Dutch Jewry, Rafael Medoff's discussion of Herbert Hoover's response to the persecution of the Jews, Howard Margolian's case study of the 1935 Nuremberg Legislation. Taken as a group, these essays talk about the Holocaust in its historical context.

They are followed by a grouping of essays that concentrate on varieties of "aftermath"--including Lilian Kremer's analysis of Ilona Karmel's *An Estate of Memory*, Gary M. Leonard's study of Sylvia Plath's encounter with the Holocaust as it was depicted in popular magazines such as the *Ladies' Home Journal*, and Frank Buscher's critical assessments of the response of the New Germany to the Holocaust.

We owe a great debt to the Annual Holocaust Conference held at Millersville University. In addition, the editors remain grateful to many people whose various contributions make this volume possible. Specifically, the administrations of both Millersville University and Franklin and Marshall College continued to encourage the work of *Holocaust Studies Annual*. The editors would particularly like to thank Millersville University President Joseph Caputo for his continuing and generous support of the Conference, Reynold Koppel for his wise counsel, Cookie Faust, Margaret Eichler and Lori Read for their practical assistance that made this volume feasible, and the academic grants committees of both institutions for their help in funding the project.

Sanford Pinsker
Jack Fischel

Holocaust Studies Annual
1991

"Unreliable" and "Unfit": The Reich Chamber of Culture and the Expulsion of Jews and Other "Dangerous Elements" from German Cultural Life, 1933-1945

Alan E. Steinweis

The historiography of the Holocaust has recently entered a new phase. After a long period during which the attention of Western historians was devoted almost exclusively to the Jewish victims of Nazi persecution and genocide, the last several years have witnessed a spate of publications examining the fate of other victimized groups. Poles,[1] homosexuals,[2] Gypsies,[3] and the mentally ill[4] have provided foci for much fruitful research, the net result of which has been not so much a relativization or diminution of the catastrophe that befell Europe's Jews, but rather a more nuanced understanding of National Socialism's destructive capacities. We now realize that the basis for Nazi persecution extended well beyond its biological-racist core to encompass assumptions about the inferiority and even malignancy of foreign cultures, anxieties about alternative forms of sexual conduct, and traditional notions of order, cleanliness, and productivity.

When attempting to explain patterns of persecution and disenfranchisement in the Third Reich, the Nazi regime's purge of German artistic and cultural life constitutes a natural topic for investigation. This article will show how the systematic purge of the German cultural establishment during the Nazi era reflected a differentiated Nazi conception of ideological unacceptability. The regime saw cultural enemies almost everywhere, but nonetheless distinguished between categories of enemies and modulated its cultural purge measures according to those distinctions.

The Nazis took culture seriously, devoting a good deal of rhetoric and money to it. Since the early 1920's, Nazi propaganda had aggressively and successfully exploited the widespread mystification engendered in German society by the efflorescence of artistic modernism. New modes of artistic expression, such as left-wing revolutionary theater, atonal music, abstract expressionism, and Bauhaus architecture, seemed to flourish, despite the fact that they seemed to appeal only to a minority of the population. The Nazi explanation for this phenomenon possessed the advantage of an alluring simplicity: an alliance of Jews, Marxists, foreigners, sexual perverts, and other enemies of the German *Volk* had conspiratorially infiltrated the cultural establishment in order to propagate its decadent, anti-German world view. Few who paid attention to Nazi propaganda during the years before 1933 could doubt that the promised German "awakening" would feature a purge of the arts.

In the spring and summer of 1933, the Nazi regime employed a variety of methods to carry out the so-called "purifications." The earliest purges were, ostensibly, intended to preserve public order, and were implemented with the help of police emergency powers rooted in the Reichstag Fire Decree of February 1933. For example, in March, Bruno Walter was prevented from conducting the Berlin Philharmonic on the grounds that "it had been impossible to provide security for the concert." The threat to the concert's "security," of course, came primarily from mobs of Nazi Stormtroopers egged on by Berlin *Gauleiter* Joseph Goebbels. Such improvised measures were targeted primarily at Jewish or Marxist cultural figures of some prominence. The Civil Service Law of 7 April provided the basis for a far more sweeping purge. April and May 1933 witnessed massive dismissals of Jewish employees from public theaters, orchestras, museums, and other civil service institutions.[5]

From the regime's point of view, these actions were transitional and far from perfect. Neither the emergency decrees nor the Civil Service Law provided a mechanism for long-term, routine official controls over access to participation in the nation's cultural life. A new system, more permanent and more deeply institutionalized, was required. The regime began to set this new system in place in the summer and autumn of 1933. Ultimately, it took the form of the Reich Chamber of Culture and its seven sub-chambers for music, theater, the visual arts, literature, radio, film, and the press, which formally came into existence in November 1933, and which effectively began to function in the following year. Joseph Goebbels, the Propaganda Minister, played the leading role in the creation of the chamber system, and became its first and only President. The principle upon which the Chamber system was erected was the old German concept of the *Stand* or "estate," an idea which had enjoyed great currency among conservative-nationalist advocates of economic reform during the economically turbulent Weimar Republic. In the context of cultural policy, application of the *Stand* concept amounted to the creation of a single, large, officially recognized organization of artists, in which membership would be a pre-condition for artistic activity on a professional basis. Exclusion from the chamber was tantamount to a professional ban (*Berufsverbot*). Acting as a modern-day guild, a major goal of which was to ameliorate the financial and social hardships chronically confronted by German artists, the chamber system would monitor and regulate fees, wages, salaries, and working conditions, and would establish and enforce minimum educational and professional standards for membership.[6]

As a complement to its economic-professional mission, the chamber system would carry out crucial political-ideological tasks as well. Chamber membership policy was governed not merely by considerations of professional qualification, but also by those of political, social, and, above all, "racial" background. In essence, chamber policy amounted to a form of cultural eugenics. It promoted the interests of ideologically acceptable artists through programs of work-creation, expanded art education, and social insurance measures. Simultaneously, it identified and eliminated from German cultural life so-called "dangerous elements."

In carrying out the purge dimension of its responsibilities, the chamber system could rely on a flexible and potent weapon. Paragraph 10 of a 1 November 1933 Implementation Decree provided as follows:

> Admission into a chamber may be refused, or a member may be expelled, when there exist facts from which it is evident that the person in question does not possess the necessary reliability and aptitude for the practice of his profession.[7]

Paragraph 10 explicitly identified neither Jews nor any other group as specific targets for exclusion from the chambers. This vague phraseology was significant. Paragraph 10 allowed for the exclusion of practically anybody, but did not specifically mandate the exclusion of any single group or individual. It provided a legal foundation for the systematic exclusion of Jews and other supposedly "dangerous elements," yet preserved a high degree of discretion, enabling the chamber system to carry out its purge function in response to fluid economic and political conditions, as well as to evolving conceptions of racial and ideological acceptability. From late 1933 to the end of the Nazi regime, administrative interpretation of Paragraph 10 served as the primary mechanism for the ongoing "purification" of the German cultural establishment.

THE SCOPE OF THE PURGE

Fragmentary surviving documentation does not allow for precise quantification of the cultural purge in all its dimensions, although for some categories of victims, in particular cultural sectors, our information is relatively complete. This is true especially for the Chamber's Jewish victims, as well as those who were "half-Jewish" and those married to "full Jews," all of whom were registered on comprehensive expulsion lists, several of which have survived. The comprehensive systematic purge of Jews from the Chambers took place in 1935. Consulting lists deposited at the Bundesarchiv in Koblenz, Volker Dahm of the Institute for Contemporary History in Munich has placed the figure of Jewish and Jewish-related expellees from the Literature Chamber at around 2,000.[8] On the basis of further lists recently discovered in the Berlin Document Center, the author of the present article estimates that the Theater Chamber expelled about 550 Jews,[9] the Music Chamber about 2,200,[10] and the Chamber of the Visual Arts about 1,700.[11] These numbers reflect an almost total purge of Jews from the Chambers. A small number of Jews and Jewish-related received "special dispensations" (*Sondergenehmigungen*), which allowed them to remain professionally active after the massive purge of 1935.[12]

Although no such comprehensive lists exist for other categories of victims, the evidence does clearly reflect the wide diversity of reasons for which the Chamber issued the *Berufsverbot*. By the early war years the Chamber's purge had come to encompass a vast sweep of victims purged for racial, political, and social reasons. Particularly illustrative is a 1942 Security Police analysis of the Reich's cultural policy, which provides specific data for the Literature Chamber's purge in the year 1941.[13] According to the report, the Literature Chamber had turned down "about half" of the "around 800" applications either for membership or for non-member publishing licenses (*Befreiungsscheine*) submitted during 1941. The grounds for rejection were as follows:

Number	Reason
16	"Jewish extraction" or "Jewish related"
4	"Former Marxists and other enemies of the state"
150	Strong "confessional connection" ("clergy, nuns, pastors' wives")
18	"Members of Christian sects and occult groups"
47	"Previously convicted" and "seriously criminally tainted"

29	Persons "not seen as mentally normal," "drunkards," "elements with an aversion to work," "mental patients," "elderly people from whom culture-creative activity is no longer to be expected"
100 (approx.)	Persons whose "aptitude for positive cultural activity" is "doubtful"; "Foreigners" for whom "cultural activity in the service of German cultural policy" is doubtful (e.g. Americans, Danes, Poles, Czechs)

Several of these classifications will be analyzed in some detail below. Deserving of emphasis at this point is that the relatively small number of "Jews" and "Jewish-related" listed in the chart reflects the simple fact that most persons in these categories had been purged from the Chamber much earlier in the regime. By 1941, most knew better than even to attempt application for admission or re-admission. The relatively high number of church-related victims arose from the regime's crackdown on Catholic autonomy and refractory Lutheranism during the early 1940's. The presence on the list of the "criminally tainted," the "elderly," "drunkards," and "mental patients" further suggests that the Chamber's conception of cultural purification reached far beyond the familiar and oft-cited purge of Jews and Marxists. The variable of racial-ideological "reliability" became combined with more traditional notions of efficiency, social conformity, and order. A category not reflected in the chart consisted of persons guilty of serious violations against one or more of the myriad of economic and professional regulations issued by the Chamber. Systematic sampling of Chamber membership files in the Berlin Document Center suggests that this last category was not large; the Chamber preferred to levy monetary fines and issue warnings to such regulatory scofflaws, reserving the last resort of expulsion only for multiple repeat offenders.

THE RACIAL PURGE: JEWS, GYPSIES, AND POLES

A close look at the purge process reveals a good deal of administrative improvisation on the part of Chamber functionaries. Yet pragmatic considerations affected the speed and details of policy implementation, rather than the overall direction of policy, for which the determining factor remained basic Nazi ideological assumptions about racial, political, and social fitness. Once branded a "racial" undesirable, exclusion was a virtual certainty, though the timing and circumstances of exclusion could be adjusted in response to circumstances. Political-social ostracism was somewhat more subject to case-by-case interpretation, and was therefore more arbitrary, as well as potentially more lenient.

The case of Paragraph 10's Jewish victims provides an illuminating example of how a flexible administrative process could be employed in the service of a rigid goal. In February 1934, as the chamber system was still taking shape, Chamber President Joseph Goebbels publicly declared his intention to exclude Jews from membership:

> If someone must be regarded as unreliable or unfit for specific reasons, he can be refused membership in the [chamber], and in my opinion and experience a Jewish contemporary is, in general, unfit to be entrusted with German cultural goods (*Kulturgut*)![14]

The operative words here, aside from "unfit," are "in general." Jews "in general" were to be denied participation in German cultural life.[15] Exceptions could be, and, in fact, were permitted. The influence of Hjalmar Schacht, President of the Reichsbank and, beginning in 1934, Economics Minister, was pivotal here. Schacht was no philo-Semite but rather a technocrat economist who feared that a sudden and complete elimination of Jews from German economic life might seriously damage an already devastated economy. Schacht's influence with Hitler retarded the implementation of anti-Jewish policies in the early years of the regime. Hitler, whose first priority was to turn the German economy around, on several occasions promised Schacht that even the regime's anti-Jewish policies would not be allowed to stand in the way of economic recovery.[16] In regard to the cultural sector, Schacht feared that inflexible implementation of a ban on Jews would disrupt or close down Jewish-owned business establishments, such as publishers, cinemas, and art dealerships. This result would not only exacerbate the problem of unemployment, but might also adversely affect Germany's balance of trade and reserves of foreign currency, since many of the firms in question carried on extensive business abroad.[17] Indeed, it is likely, although not demonstrable from the available documentation, that it was Schacht who had prevented the inclusion of an explicit "Aryan paragraph" in the Chamber of Culture's membership regulations.

An instruction issued by Goebbels to the chambers in June 1935 summarized what had become official chamber policy in view of Schacht's interventions:

> Jews, non-Aryans, and those related to Jews (*jüdisch Versippte*) who are still members of the Reich Chamber of

Culture are to be gradually eliminated; new members are not to be admitted in principle. Should weighty artistic, domestic political, foreign policy, or economic disadvantages that affect public life arise from this, each case should be reported specifically. The implementation of the rejection or expulsion orders must temporarily occur in such a fashion that economic assets not be lost on a large scale and that a loss of jobs can be avoided as much as possible.[18]

Nevertheless, the vast majority of Jews active in the culture professions remained ineligible for the "special dispensations" issued as the result of Schacht's interventions. By late summer 1935, all but a tiny handful of Jews had been purged, and most of the exceptions had been eliminated by the outbreak of war.

In contrast to the Jews, who had been targets of the cultural purge from the very beginning, Gypsies came under attack only in 1939. During the first six years of Nazi rule, Gypsies were usually classified among Germany's "asocial elements," along with "beggars, tramps, prostitutes, and persons with infectious diseases." But only in December 1938 did the Reich government officially designate the Gypsies as a race. This was accomplished by the Decree on the Battle against the Gypsy Menace, which was issued by Heinrich Himmler in his capacity as Chief of the German Police. In March 1939 Himmler elaborated upon the nature of this "battle": "the aim of the measures taken by the state must be the racial separation once and for all of the Gypsy race from the German nation."[19] The chamber most directly affected by Himmler's decree was the Music Chamber, which contained several dozen Gypsy musicians. The President of the Chamber, Peter Raabe, vowed in May 1939 that the Music Chamber would act in the "spirit" of the decree.[20] Between February 1940 and the end of that year, the Music Chamber published lists of expelled Gypsy members in its official newsletter.[21]

Two observations are in order: first, the Gypsies remained in the Chamber for several years beyond the point at which most Jews had been expelled; and, second, the Chamber's expulsion of Gypsies came not on its own initiative, but, in effect, as a response to policy formulated elsewhere in the regime, specifically in the SS. Few in number, lacking in prominence, and active mainly in a narrow range of "entertainment" musicianship, the Gypsies quite simply had not been worthy of Music Chamber attention until pressure came from the outside.

The annexation of over 90,000 square kilometers of Polish territory in October 1939 presented the Chamber of Culture with a new task: the cultural Germanization of the territories. Hitherto, the relatively small culturally Polish minority in the Reich had *not* been targeted for exclusion from the chamber. Ironically, from the viewpoint of the Chamber of Culture, which generally employed the racial definitions prescribed by the Nuremberg Laws, the Poles were, technically, "Aryan." The acquisition of several million Polish subjects in late 1939, however, necessitated a functional, if not theoretical, redefinition of the Poles.

At the end of December 1939 the authority of the Chamber was formally expanded into the newly annexed areas.[22] A transition period of one year was anticipated, during which the individual chambers would review applications for membership. In early 1940 the Propaganda Ministry instructed the chambers on how to handle applications from Poles.[23] The goal of Chamber membership policy was that "within this year the new eastern regions will have a purely German character in the intellectual sphere." Consequently, because "Poles as a general principle do not possess the necessary reliability for the practice of activity that would require membership in the Reich Chamber of Culture," Poles were "not to be admitted." Poles living within the borders of the Reich were, in other words, now to be treated as German Jews had been treated since 1934: as a racial group to be eliminated "in general."

Two complications delayed completion of the task. First, there was the inevitable problem created by applications received from persons of uncertain or mixed descent. This problem was especially acute in West Prussia, where the Nazi authorities had divided the population into the three categories of "ethnic German," "Poles," and those falling into an "intermediate layer" of so-called "West Prussian Germans." The sorting-out of the population would naturally take some time, especially since ancestry documents had to be secured by all new applicants.[24] The Music Chamber in West Prussia decided to admit applicants who could clearly prove that they were "ethnic Germans," but had to defer deciding in other cases until applicants had received official word of their racial status.[25]

The second complication was a shortage of qualified Germans in some cultural fields, especially the book trade. In May 1940 the Literature Chamber informed the Propaganda Ministry of an "urgent need" for "qualified German book trade assistants." Until an adequate supply of Germans could be made available, Poles would have to remain on the job.[26] It was, consequently, impossible to complete the cultural purge in the annexed territories by the target date of 31 December 1940. As late as April 1941, a large proportion, in some areas 50 percent, of book trade employees in the annexed Polish territories were ethnic Poles.[27]

The Chamber's bureaucratic strategy for dealing with such Poles who "must still remain active" in the cultural sphere for purely practical reasons provides yet another illustration of the Chamber's opportunistic use of Paragraph 10. The Poles in question would be neither accepted nor rejected into the Chamber. Instead, consideration of their applications was to be "postponed" until their services were no longer required, at which point the rejections on grounds of Paragraph 10 would be issued.[28]

THE SOCIAL-POLITICAL PURGE: "MARXISTS," FREEMASONS, AND THE CLERGY

Turning from the Chamber's "racial" to its social and political victims, we encounter an altogether different method of operation. Because behavior, rather than blood, provided the basis for exclusion, the facts of each individual case had to be investigated by chamber functionaries. This allowed for far greater latitude--and arbitrariness--in the interpretation of Paragraph 10.

The surviving chamber documentation on purge policy toward persons with Marxist connections is, unfortunately, very fragmentary. What *is* available makes clear, however, that in evaluating the "reliability" of Marxists the chamber took under consideration such factors as length of membership in the Communist or Socialist party, whether the person in question had been an active or passive member, and whether he or she exhibited any propensity for "treasonous" activity against the National Socialist state. Not surprisingly, a communist background constituted a far greater liability than did a socialist one. The surviving chamber membership personal files in the Berlin Document Center contain numerous cases of ex-Socialists who were permitted to remain in the chamber. Artists with Communist connections had been a much smaller group to begin with, and had also been subjected to mass arrest and summary incarceration in the spring of 1933, months before the Chamber of Culture came into being. By the time the Chamber of Culture took up its work, therefore, the police and the SA had already completed much of the dirty work involved in eradicating these so-called "art-bolshevists."

Although no document explicitly outlining the principles applied to Marxists has survived, guidelines for the treatment of ex-Freemasons reflect the same logic that seems to have been employed for Marxists. In 1936 the Reich Ministry of the Interior had issued regulations governing the employment of former Freemasons in the civil service. The chamber soon adopted these guidelines for use in its own membership decisions. The guidelines fundamentally differentiated between ex-Freemasons who had left their lodges after 30.1.33 and those who did so before the Nazi seizure of power. Persons in the former category were to be considered highly suspect. Those in the latter category were to be evaluated on the basis of whether they had joined or "deserved well" of the Nazi party prior to the seizure of power, whether they had held leading positions in their lodges, whether they had attained a high "Degree" in the Masonic organization, and whether they had continued connections with the Masons since their departure. In *all* cases, "prior membership in a lodge *alone*" was not to "be viewed as a deficiency of the reliability necessary for practice of the profession," but rather "the condition of unreliability" had to be proven by the "existence of broader circumstances."[29]

The Chamber's treatment of persons with Communist pasts could be remarkably flexible. In 1935, the 39-year-old illustrator Carola Gärtner was convicted of treason as a consequence of her activity in the illegal Communist Party in 1934. After serving a three-year sentence, Gärtner proposed to resume her artistic career, for which she required membership in the Chamber of the Visual Arts. No less a personage than Reinhard Heydrich, chief of the Gestapo and the Security Service, signed a letter on Gärtner's behalf, testifying that she had been rehabilitated during her incarceration, and that she possessed "talent, taste, diligence, and the necessary artistic ambition." The Chamber admitted her in 1941.[30] Although Gärtner's case was exceptional in that it involved the intercession of an extremely powerful official, it was by no means the only instance in which the Chamber granted membership to a convicted "traitor."[31] Such cases serve to illustrate the Chamber's belief in the possibility of rehabilitation for political offenders, an option that was unavailable to persons of the wrong "race."

Whereas Marxists had been subjected to close scrutiny from the very beginning of the regime, clergymen became a major target of chamber purge policy only in the early war years. The Nazi attempt to destroy the traditional power of the churches had intensified gradually between 1933 and 1939, only to subside at the outbreak of war out of concern for maintaining unity on the home front. Nonetheless, during the first half of 1941, the Reich leadership unleashed a new wave of measures designed to destroy what still remained of clerical autonomy, especially in Catholic Bavaria.[32] Goebbels and his assistants in the Chamber of Culture Central Office, especially Nazi "old fighter" Hans Hinkel, ensured that Chamber membership policy would be brought into line with the crackdown.

Before the war had begun, the Literature Chamber in particular had been frustrated by its inability to exclude clergymen. The frustration stemmed from the legalistic tendency within the chamber hierarchy to abide precisely to the provisions of Paragraph 10. "The admission of writers can be rejected," the Literature Chamber complained to the Propaganda Ministry in August 1939, "exclusively on account of insufficient reliability and aptitude." But for most applications from clergymen, "grounds for exclusion" could not be identified.[33] Christianity, after all, was not illegal.

The general anti-church crackdown of 1941 provided an environment in which Chamber functionaries were emboldened to apply Paragraph 10 more aggressively. We have particularly good documentation for how this was done in cases involving members of the so-called Confessing Church (*Bekennende Kirche*), the refractory wing of German Lutheranism in the Third Reich. The regime regarded this entire movement as hostile, but, aside from leading church personalities, such as Dietrich Bonhoeffer,[34] no technical-legal basis existed for systematic exclusions from the Chamber. Indeed, Goebbels, himself, had insisted that the stipulations governing the application of Paragraph 10 be taken seriously. Chamber officials, therefore, sought a "loophole" in order to "exclude these people in all cases." Since the vast majority of such cases concerned applications to the Literature Chamber, a convenient loophole was, indeed, at hand: The Chamber leadership resolved that "during the war the rejection of admission into the [Literature Chamber] . . . should be justified on grounds of paper shortage."[35] As far back as October 1939, Reinhard Heydrich, in a memorandum for Hitler, had suggested paper rationing as a tactic to be employed in a wartime campaign against the church press,[36] and by the summer of 1941 paper allocations were being routinely denied to religious publishers of all denominations.[37] Now the pretext of paper shortage was employed to reject applications for Literature Chamber membership as well.

Much as the anti-church offensive of early 1941 had supplied the Chamber with the opportunity to institute a more restrictive membership practice, subsequent developments in the broader political context forced the Chamber again to readjust its attitude toward the clergy late in 1941. Indignation over the so-called "euthanasia" action, and Catholic resistance to secularization measures in Bavaria, forced the Nazi leadership to employ more moderation in its dealings with the churches. The need to maintain public support for the war effort required an at least partial ideological retreat on the home front. In October 1941 the Chamber decided that measures against the clergy "are to be postponed in order to avoid the appearance of persecution of the church under present wartime circumstances."[38] Several months later, Goebbels wrote in his diary, "it won't do to get started now, in wartime, on so difficult and far-reaching a problem," and added that "the Führer, too, expressed that viewpoint."[39]

THE PURGE OF HOMOSEXUALS

During the Weimar years, Nazi propagandists and other cultural conservatives had repeatedly pointed to the decadent influence exercised by supposed cliques of homosexuals in the art and entertainment fields. From the Nazi standpoint, homosexuality represented a highly threatening form of social deviation, negating as it did the bourgeois norms prevailing in both party and society. Equally important, homosexuality constituted a serious offense against Nazi racial doctrine, resulting in many instances in severe eugenicist solutions, as current research into sterilization measures is in the process of establishing.[40]

In the Third Reich, (male) homosexuality was a crime prosecutable under Paragraph 175 of the Reich Criminal Code. For its part, the Chamber of Culture treated homosexuals much in the same way as it did other categories of criminals. Generally speaking, the Chamber took no drastic measures against members who were merely suspected of homosexual activity, though Chamber functionaries did meticulously record for possible future reference reports of *alleged* homosexual encounters received from the SD or the Gestapo.[41] The Chamber took action on the basis of Paragraph 10 only *after* it had received confirmation of a conviction on the basis of Paragraph 175.[42]

Subsequent to conviction, numerous so-called "175ers" were expelled from the Chamber. But conviction did not *automatically* mandate exclusion. The Chamber instead seems to have employed a system of disciplinary measures modulated according to the seriousness and circumstances of each case. For example, in 1936, the painter Egon Adam was convicted under Paragraph 175 and sentenced to 4 months in prison. The Visual Arts Chamber nonetheless permitted him to retain his membership, albeit with a clear warning that recidivism would result in certain expulsion.[43] In 1937, ballet director Edgar von Pelchrzim received a 2 month sentence for his Paragraph 175 conviction. The Theater Chamber permitted him to keep his membership, issued him a warning, and, for good measure, fined him RM 300. As the result of a new conviction in 1944, the Chamber kept its word and revoked his membership.[44] In 1939, opera singer Boris Greverus, who had received a nine-month sentence, retained his Theater Chamber membership, but was forbidden by the

Chamber from participating in entertainment programs for German army troops.[45]

The Chamber's approach to homosexuality seems to have conformed to the general pattern of gay persecution in Nazi Germany that has been described by Richard Plant: hard-core "libidinal felons" were treated more severely than were persons for whom homosexual encounters were deemed aberrational. The Chamber showed little mercy for persons convicted on multiple counts, and for those whose convictions involved "seduction" or "attempted seduction" of a minor. Both sorts of behavior reflected an incorrigibility that could not be tolerated. Moreover even the tolerance initially granted by the Chamber to first offenders who had received short prison sentences seems to have evaporated during the later stages of the war. Infractions that probably would have provoked warnings in 1936 regularly resulted in speedy expulsions in 1944.[46]

The well-known case of Gustaf Gründgens and the "Gründgens circle" in Berlin is an exception that proves the rule. The Chamber of Culture took no action against Gründgens or those around him only because Hermann Göring had personally interceded with Goebbels. High officialdom in the Chamber of Culture Central Office was incensed at Göring's protection of these supposedly incorrigible perverts at the center of German theater life.[47] Most gay targets of the cultural purge possessed neither the talent nor the good fortune of a Gründgens.

CONCLUSION

In the cultural sphere, as in other influential professional and economic sectors, the Nazis were driven by a highly developed anti-Jewish paranoia. This paranoia had been fueled by the conspicuous success of persons with Jewish backgrounds in German cultural life prior to 1933. Although Jews constituted a small minority of the population professionally active in cultural affairs, they were sufficiently prosperous and numerous to become a preoccupation for Nazi cultural theoreticians and propagandists. The same would not hold true for the other groups examined above, with the exception of left-radical cultural figures, for whom the iron logic of Nazi racial doctrine did not apply as it did for Jews.

The Nazi obsession with Jewish influence in the cultural sphere came to be particularly personified in the figure of Joseph Goebbels, who as President of the Chamber of Culture exercised ultimate authority over Chamber membership policy. The recently published authoritative scholarly edition of the first half of Goebbels' personal diaries evince the intensity of the Propaganda Minister's anti-Jewish sentiment. Believing the "de-Jewification" of German cultural life to be a "grandiose achievement,"[48] Goebbels pledged to himself that he would "not rest" until the Chamber was completely "free of Jews."[49] He complained bitterly about the equivocations of Finance Minister Hjalmar Schacht, who favored the issuance of special dispensations to "non-Aryan" cultural entrepreneurs on financial grounds, and in the late 1930's ranted almost hysterically against the continued membership in the Chamber of even a miniscule number of "half-Jews" and persons with Jewish spouses.[50] In regard to no other category of targeted persons did Goebbels exert such extreme and persistent pressure for exclusion.

Without diminishing the personal tragedy that befell all victims of Paragraph 10, we may conclude that the purge of the Jews was the most thorough and inexorable. With the exception of the Gypsies after 1939 (at any rate a very small group), ostracism of persons in the non-Jewish categories was subject to case-by-case interpretation, whereas Jews were regarded as *a priori* unacceptable and were eligible for special dispensations in only a tiny number of cases. The purge of Jews was prosecuted more vigorously and was undertaken from the very beginning of the regime with a greater sense of urgency than was the elimination of the clergy, Marxists, gays, Gypsies, and Poles. We ought not lose sight of this plain fact at a time when historiography is, justifiably, shifting more of its attention to non-Jewish victims of National Socialist persecution.

NOTES

1. For Poland see especially Richard Lukas, *The Forgotten Holocaust: The Poles under German Occupation, 1939-1944* (Lexington: University of Kentucky Press, 1986).
2. Though too general and at times highly superficial, the standard work on the Nazi persecution of homosexuals remains Richard Plant, *The Pink Triangle: The Nazi War against Homosexuals* (New York: Henry Holt, 1986).
3. An excellent discussion of the place of the Gypsies in Holocaust historiography is Sybil Milton, "The Context of the Holocaust," *German Studies Review* XIII (May 1990), pp. 269-83.
4. A cogent analysis of the Nazi regime's murder ("euthanasia") of "lives not worth living" is provided in chapter 7 of Robert Proctor, *Racial Hygiene: Medicine under the Nazis* (Cambridge: Harvard University Press, 1988).
5. Especially useful for the earliest phase of the purge of Jewish artists is Comite des Delegations Juives, *Die Lage der Juden in Deutschland: Das Schwarzbuch-Tatsachen und Dokumente* (Paris: Comie des Delegations Juives; Frankfurt: Ullstein, 1983). The Bruno Walter case is documented on pp. 409-10, 416.
6. For general observations on the origins and institutional goals of the Chamber see Volker Dahm, "Die Reichskulturkammer als Instrument kulturpolitischer Steuerung und sozialer Reglementierung," *Vierteljahrshefte für Zeitgeschichte* (Heft 1, 1986), pp. 53-84.
7. "Erste Verordnung zur Durchführung des Reichskulturkammergesetzes," 1 November 1933, Paragraph 10, in *Das Recht der Reichskulturkammer: Sammlung der für den Kulturstand geltenden Gesetze und Verordnungen, der amtlichen Anordnungen und Bekanntmachungen der Reichskulturkammer und ihre Einzelkammern*, First edition: 5 vols., ed. by Karl-Friedrich Schrieber (Berlin: Junker und Dünnhaupt, 1935-37) (=RdRKK-1), Second edition: 2 vols., ed. by Karl-Friedrich Schrieber, Alfred Metten, and Herbert Collatz (Berlin: de Gruyter, 1943) (=RdRKK-2), first ed., vol. 1, pp. 2-8.
8. Volker Dahm, "Das jüdische Buch im Dritten Reich. Teil 1: Die Ausscahltung der jüdischen Autoren, Verleger und Buchhändler," *Archiv für Geschichte des Buchwesens* XX (1979), p. 53.
9. Untitled lists, 21 pp., accompanied by letter, Theater Chamber to Propaganda Ministry, 2 July 1938, identifying lists as "drei Listen über die aus der Reichstheaterkammer ausgeschlossenen Juden,

18   Alan E. Steinweis

jüdischen Mischlinge und mit Juden Verheirateten," in unlabeled file, Berlin Document Center (=BDC).
10. Leitz Ordner, "Liste der aus der Reichsmusikkammer ausgeschlossenen Juden und jüdischen Mischlinge," 379 pp., (approx) 1936, BDC.
11. Untitled list, 61 pp., accompanied by letter, Visual Arts Chamber to Propaganda Ministry, 8 June 1933, identifying list as "Liste sämtlicher bisher aus meiner Kammer ausgeschlossenen Juden, jüdischer Mischlinge und mit Juden Verheirateten," in unlabeled file, BDC.
12. The dispensations were usually granted for economic reasons, or to persons with powerful patrons. Excepting a handful of economically significant entrepreneurs in the Visual Arts Chamber (e.g., art and antique dealers) and the Film Chamber (e.g., cinema operators), the dispensations almost never went to "full Jews." For lists see the file "Entjudung der Einzelkammern," BDC.
13. "Meldungen aus dem Reich (Nr. 273)," 2.4.42, in Heinz Boberach, ed. *Meldungen aus dem Reich: Die geheimen Lageberichte des Sicherheitsdienstes der SS, 1938-1945*, 17 vols. (Herrsching: Pawlak, 1984), vol. 10, pp. 3571-72.
14. Speech of 7.2.34, DNB release of 8.2.34, in Bundesarchiv-Koblenz (=BAK) R43II/1241. The German terms used by Goebbels were "unzuverlässig oder ungeeignet," a direct reference to language contained in Paragraph 10.
15. On 24 March, Goebbels took the step of formally directing the chambers to exclude Jews as a matter of general principle. Volker Dahm, "Das jüdische Buch im Dritten Reich. Teil 1: Die Ausschaltung der jüdischen Autoren, Verleger und Buchhändler," *Archiv für Geschichte des Buchwesens* XX (1979), pp. 60-61.
16. Uwe Dietrich Adam, *Judenpolitik im Dritten Reich* (Düsseldorf: Droste, 1972; Athenäum, 1979), pp. 88, 122-24; Avraham Barkai, *From Boycott to Annihilation: The Economic Struggle of German Jews, 1933-1943*, translated by William Templer (Hanover, N.H.: University Press of New England, 1989), pp. 59-63.
17. Dahm, *Jüdisches Buch*, pp. 46-49, Adam, *Judenpolitik*, p. 172. Schacht's pragmatic position reflected fears that existed also on the grass roots level in some Nazi circles. In June 1933, for instance, the NSBO cell in the Ullstein publishing house, a Jewish-owned enterprise, appealed to Hitler, requesting that Ullstein not be subjected to a party-led boycott. The writer could "not believe that the party desires that 19,000 brave German workers and employees (not counting family members) should be eliminated in order to affect three

Mr. Ullsteins." Nationalsozialistische Betriebszelle des Verlags Ullstein to Reichskanzlei, 21.6.33, BAK R43II/600. Note also the indication at the top of the first page that Hitler had been made aware of the substance of the document.
18. Goebbels to chambers, 27.6.35, BAK R56V/102.
19. Donald Kenrick and Grattan Puxon, *The Destiny of Europe's Gypsies* (New York: Basic Books, 1972), pp. 72-74.
20. *Amtliche Mitteilungen der Reichsmusikkammer*, 1.5.39, Records of the Reichsministerium für Volksaufklärung und Propaganda, National Archives Microfilm Publication T-70 (=T-70), reel 109, frames 3632755-6.
21. The lists begin with the issue of 15.2.1940, T-70/109/3632796-8.
22. "Verordnung des Reichsministers für Volksaufklärung und Propaganda und des Reichsministers des Innern über die Einführung der Reichskulturkammergesetzgebung in den eingegliederten Ostgebieten," 29.12.39, RdRKK-2, RKK, I, 20.
23. RMfVuP to Presidents of Chambers, 9.3.40, BAK R55/1426.
24. In January 1940 the RSK warned new applicants in the annexed territories that "according to experience, the production of ancestry documents is very time-consuming. It is therefore necessary to begin therewith immediately." "Eingliederung des Schriftums der eingegliederten Ostgebiete in die Reichsschriftumskammer," 27.1.40, RdRKK-2, RSK, I, 70.
25. RMK-President to RMfVuP, 29.7.40, BAK R55/1426.
26. RSK-President to RMfVuP, 18.5.40, BAK R55/1426.
27. RSK-President to RMfVuP, 30.4.41, BAK R55/1426.
28. RMfVuP to Chamber Presidents, 5.12.40, BAK R55/1426.
29. RSK (Gruppe Buchhandel) to RSK (Berlin), 3.6.38; "Aktennotiz" (signed by Ihde), 18.6.38; "2. Nachtrag zu der Handakte: Grundfragen der Kammerzugehörigkeit und der Berufsausübung," 1938; "Zugehörigkeit von Beamten zu Freimaurerlogen..." (copy of RdSchr. d. RuPrMdJ, 2.9.36), all in Captured German Records Filmed at Berlin (AHA), National Archives Microfilm Publication T-580, reel 939, file 1.
30. BDC/RdbK/Carola Gärtner.
31. See also, e.g., BDC/RbdK/Alfred Gravenhorst.
32. John S. Conway, *The Nazi Persecution of the Churches* (New York: Basic Books, 1968).
33. RSK (Ihde) to RMfVuP, 31.8.39, BDC/RKK/Ihde-"Preisbildung." A different sort of problem, discussed in an SD report ("Meldungen aus

dem Reich," (Nr. 200), 7.7.41, Boberach, *Meldungen*, vol. 7, p. 2491), was that some clergymen and theologians, confident that they would be turned down for membership or *Befreiung* by the RSK, simply failed to apply at all, yet continued to publish. According to the SD, these writers were taking advantage of a loophole in RSK membership regulations that exempted authors of small brochures (*Kleinschriften*) from compulsory membership. (See "Amtliche Bekanntmachung Nr.88 (Neufassung)" ("Bekanntmachung über die Erfassung der schriftstellerisch Tätigen durch die Reichsschriftumskammer"), 21.11.38, RdRKK-2, RSK, I, 37.) The SD report cited here suggests that this loophole had been closed by July 1941, although no such measure is indicated in the RdRKK compendium. The Reich, in the SD's view, was flooded by "hundreds of thousands" of such religious brochures.

34. Dietrich Bonhoeffer, the Lutheran pastor and theologian, was ultimately murdered in a concentration camp for his opposition to the regime. Bonhoeffer had published several theological works in the late 1930's even though he had not applied to the Chamber either for membership or for a non-member's license to publish (*Befreiung*). In November 1940 the Chamber fined Bonhoeffer RM 30 for unauthorized publication as far back as 1937, and ordered him to submit an application to the Chamber. Bonhoeffer paid the fine and forwarded his application, only to receive a rejection on grounds of Paragraph 10 in March 1941. Bonhoeffer did not accept the decision complacently. He protested that his theological works were "scientific" (*wissenschaftlich*) and therefore did not fall under Chamber jurisdiction. The Literature Chamber dismissed this objection, claiming that guidelines for "scientific" works applied only to authors with appointments at educational institutions, and in the clearest of terms reminded Bonhoeffer that "this rejection has the effect of an official professional prohibition on literary activity." As to Bonhoeffer's astonishment that the Chamber had waited so long to inform him of his obligation to apply for membership, the Chamber agreed to refund the RM 30. RSK-President to Bonhoeffer, 17.3.41, RSK-President to Bonhoeffer, 19.3.41, Bonhoeffer to RSK-President, 22.4.41, RSK-President to Bonhoeffer, 22.5.41, in Dietrich Bonhoeffer, *Gesammelte Schriften*, ed. by Eberhard Bethge, vol. 2 (Munich: Chr. Kaiser, 1959), pp. 367-72.
35. "Arbeitssitzung der RKK," 23.5.41, BAK R56I/94.
36. Conway, *Persecution of the Churches*, pp. 235-37.

37. "Meldungen aus dem Reich," (Nr. 200), 7.7.41, Boberach, *Meldungen*, vol. 7, p. 2492. The report notes that religious publishers were often able to circumvent the rationing by relying on their own reserves of paper.
38. "Reichskulturrat-Sitzung," 2.10.41, BA R56I/94.
39. *The Goebbels Diaries*, ed. by Louis P. Lochner, (New York, Doubleday, 1948), entry for 21.3.42.
40. For example, the unpublished papers on systematic mass sterilizations, presented by Geoffrey Giles and John Fout at the Annual Meeting of the German Studies Association, Milwaukee, October 1989. The best single work on the subject remains Richard Plant, *The Pink Triangle: The Nazi War against Homosexuals* (New York: New Republic Books, 1986).
41. For example, the membership file of Werner Kelch, a Dramaturg in Essen, contains an index card with the following remarks: Der Chef der Sicherheitspolizei und des SD-IV C 4 c--B.Nr.1275/42--gibt auf Befragen bekannt (am 14.1.43): "Dr. Kelch ist unbestraft." Abschliessend wird von dort noch bemerkt: Obwohl über die Angefragten u.a. Dr. K. in gleichgeschlechtlicher Hinsicht nichts bekannt geworden ist, wird ihnen eine derartige Veranlagung zum Vorwurf gemacht. BDC/RTK/Dr. Werner Kelch.
42. That is not to say, however, that employers exercised the same restraint. In one case in 1944 in Erfurt, a theater invalidated the contract of its intendant, who had been arrested, but not convicted, on sodomy charges. The Theater Chamber approved of this measure, and instructed the theater to reinstate the intendant with back pay in the event of an acquittal. BDC/RTK/Joachim Poley.
43. BDC/RdbK/Egon Adam.
44. BDC/RTK/Edgar v. Pelchrzim.
45. BDC/RTK/Boris Greverus. Presumably the desire was to keep persons with homosexual "predispositions" away from the German armed forces which were themselves busily attempting to root out homosexuals in their own ranks. See Plant, *Pink Triangle*, pp. 145-48.
46. For example, opera singer Nino Eckert was expelled from the Theater Chamber within eight weeks of his conviction in May 1944, for which he received a one-year prison sentence. BDC/RTK/Nico Eckert.
47. "Aktennotiz, Betr: Besprechung mit SS-Oberführer Hinkel," July 1938, BAK R58/984.

48. *Die Tagebücher von Joseph Goebbels: Sämtliche Fragmente. Teil I: Aufzeichnungen 1924-1941*, 4 vols., ed. by Elke Fröhlich (Munich: Saur, 1987), entry for 3.2.37.
49. *Tagebücher*, entry for 5.5.37.
50. In addition to the two previous entries, see those for 2.7.36, 11.12.36, 5.6.37, 21.9.37, 9.10.37, 24.11.37, 15.12.37, 16.12.37, 13.1.38, 9.2.38, 18.5.38, 27.7.38, and 26.1.39.

Hitler's Poland:
The View From a Nazi Press in America

Sidney H. Kessler

Some historians have described Hitler's occupation policies as developing piecemeal; they were secondary to his main objective of military conquest. The reorganization of defeated nations under the Nazi "New Order" would come later, according to this view.[1] This theory fails to integrate the dictator's brilliance at fusing words with swords, ideology with action. Hitler made this clear on the first page of *Mein Kampf*--"One blood demands one Reich!" One of his most consistent objectives was to unite, at any cost, all Germanic people into an expansive Greater Reich.[2]

With the invasion of Poland, on September 1, 1939, actions were begun which were later condemned as war crimes by the International Military Tribunals at Nuremberg: shooting of civilians, forced labor, ghettoization of Jews, mass migration of people according to racial concepts, starving of the defeated populace. In 1945, Polish authorities estimated the total civilian dead between 1939 and 1945 as 5,384,000 persons, including 3,200,000 Jews.[3] Hitler summarized his Polish policies which produced these deaths barely a month after he initiated the Second World War. This speech, given in Berlin on October 6, 1939, was titled by wary journalists as another of the Fuehrer's "peace" speeches--this was the last demand the dictator would make, and the West should accept "peace" on his terms.

This important statement, as well as many other pronouncements by Nazi leaders, was translated into English and reprinted in the most important voice of Nazidom in America, *Facts In Review*. *Facts*, a slick, 8 to 16 page news bulletin in the English language, was cleverly edited by George Sylvester Viereck, a man who was a German agent in both World Wars. *Facts* was published from August 16, 1939 to June 7, 1941, when all agencies of the Third Reich were closed due to American-German naval incidents. Distributed free to educators, journalists and politicians, it achieved a circulation of 320,000 a month. It was truly "Goebbels' American Proxy."[4]

Americans, had they been perceptive enough, could have learned a great deal about the unfolding tragedy of Poland had they correctly absorbed the implications of Hitler's "peace" speech, published in the October 14, 1939 issue of *Facts In Review*. The Fuehrer's five "guide posts" for the occupation of a nation he despised as an "abortion" of the Versailles Treaty were being transformed into actions as he spoke:
1. Boundaries for the Reich which will do "justice to historical, ethnographical, and economic facts";
2. "Pacification" and "peace and order";
3. Security for the Reich and its "entire sphere of interests";
4. Reorganization of economic life and development of "culture and civilization"; and
5. The "most important task," Hitler emphasized, was a "new order of ethnographical conditions" which would involve "resettlement" of nationalities.

The first "guide post," ethnographical boundaries, was clearly captioned in *Facts* as early as October 3, 1939: "Ravished Provinces Return Home To The Reich." Hitler decreed that 20,000 square miles of territory in western Poland, granted by the Versailles Treaty, containing a large German minority or *Volksdeutsch*, should be incorporated into the Reich. All persons in Danzig, West Prussia, Posen and Eastern Upper Silesia having at least some "German Blood" were citizens of the Third Reich as of November 1, 1939. Poland as a nation existed now only in the heart.

The central portion of Poland, including Warsaw, Krakow, Radom, Lublin, and later Eastern Galicia was not incorporated into Germany, but named the General Government. It was placed under the rule of a civilian, the Nazi party lawyer Hans Frank, assisted by the Austrian party figurehead, Arthur Seyss-Inquart. After Nuremberg War Crimes Trials, both were hanged for committing war crimes and crimes against humanity. In his Nuremberg testimony, Frank revealed that Hitler's order was to exploit the General Government as the "first colonial territory" of the Greater Reich and to make it serve as its booty. The Poles were to be reduced to drones, learning only how to count a little, and how to obey Germans. The Catholic Church was to be a tool of the Nazis. The task of the priest was to keep the people submissive or face arrest. Ultimately, thousands of priests were arrested, of whom 850 died in Dachau.[5] Two months after the war began, crammed trains of Poles and Jews were forced into the General Government. In *Facts* of April 22, 1940, Frank described his realm as including more than 110,000 square kilometers with approximately 14,500,000 inhabitants, of whom 12,000,000 were Poles, 2,000,000 Jews, from 400,000 to 500,000 were Ukrainians, and 60,000 to 70,000 were Germans.

To justify his first "guide post," just boundaries for the Reich, Hitler warned, in his "peace" speech, that the Poles' ambitions were to draw the Polish-German boundary on the Elbe River. This line, well west of Berlin, would have encompassed most of what is today East Germany. The next issue of *Facts*, October 19, 1939, included a small map which was highlighted as a sample of similar ones for sale in Poland before the war. "Poland's Dreams of Aggrandizement" was the caption. This map of Polish "aggression," however, drew a boundary east of Berlin beginning at Szczin, but moving southwest to encompass all of Czechoslovakia. Yet another map of alleged Polish expansionist threats appeared in *Facts* of July 8, 1940. This one was supposed to have been reproduced from a Posen newspaper, *Dziennik Poznanski*. Now the Polish-German border was drawn on a line south from Bremen to Hannover to Gottingen and Fulda, to Nuremberg, slicing Germany into a sliver of a nation, without its capital, squeezed between an imperialist Greater Poland and the low countries. The heading to this was "Polish Delusions of Grandeur," and a question was posed: "Who Started The War?" Hitler's fright at imagined Polish territorial ambitions was commented on in his conversation of January 23, 1942: "As regards the Pole, it's lucky for us that he's idle, stupid and vain."[6]

The readers of *Facts* were informed of Hitler's pacification policy, his second "guide post." The successful German military campaign was illustrated with a map in the January 15, 1940 issue. The 1939 and 1940 news weeklies were replete with details on how a primitive Poland, for its own good, was being provided with the fundamentals of modernization--sanitation, food, bridge and rail rebuilding, education, and medical care. Summarizing an occupation that was presented as benign, Seyss-Inquart was quoted on February 13, 1940 in *Facts*: " . . . This does not look as if we wanted to exterminate the Polish population." Furthermore, the postal service, railroads, courts, police, and banks were staffed by Poles, he assured.

Regarding Catholic matters and pacification, *Facts* had to be read carefully to glean the truth. All church holidays were declared to be legal holidays by Frank, who was himself a Catholic. Poles and Germans were photographed praying together in *Facts* of October 28, 1940, and it was also claimed that church property was untouched, new seminaries opened, and churches built. Still, the edition of February 13, 1940 carried a different message. In presenting the Archbishop of Warsaw's rejection of charges by Cardinal Hlond that the Germans engaged in religious persecution, revelations were made that twenty-two priests were arrested for distributing political leaflets. *Facts* of February 19, 1940 carried an item discussing a statement by an American nun, Sister Bogumila, also denying the Cardinal's accusations. Another report, in *Facts* of May 13, 1940, citing the official *Deutsche Diplomatische Korrespondenz* admitted that clericals were removed when they engaged in "chauvinistic activity." "Action taken against individual agitators cannot be construed as action directed against the churches as such," *Facts* maintained on September 9, 1940. One of the last editions of the weekly, printed April 21, 1941, contained an article on "Religious Life in the Government General." This discussed a spiritual tour in the region made by Father Krawczyk of Gross-Strehlitz in Upper Silesia. Typical of such reports in *Facts*, no mention was made of the religious life of Jews. The priest noted that the Catholic Church was flourishing, but also observed that "some clerics had to be arrested" because of espionage, possession of illegal weapons, and "rumor-mongering." *Facts* added the notion that these arrests were "comparatively rare." The same issue of *Facts* disagreed with the Portugese newspaper *Avoz* which had recently published a report that 700 Polish priests had been shot and 3,000 more were held in concentration camps. Except for a "few isolated cases," commented *Facts*, "in which priests were killed as members of the Polish fighting forces, or were executed during military operations as snipers shooting at German troops from ambush." Bishop Fulman, it was revealed, was pronounced guilty of concealing weapons and assigned the city of Neusandez as his residence.

Another aspect of Hitler's pacification policy was its approval by the international community; most notably by the American Red Cross. Early in the occupation, Ernest J. Swift, its foreign division director, gave an account of conditions in Warsaw to the Washington *Times-Herald* which was cited extensively in *Facts* of January 22, 1940. Swift, impressed with German occupation activities, concluded: ". . . The general health conditions in Warsaw are better than before the war." The Germans he observed were courteous too: "At no time did I see anyone being 'pushed around' by soldiers." When he visited Lwow, Swift dismissed as insignificant the ghettoization process then under way: "Except for the labelling of Jewish stores," which Swift described as merely a "customary Nazi policy," the market was "normal" with "haggling and bargaining." According to this A.R.C. official, there was no scarcity of food in Poland that winter of 1939/1940.

On April 8, 1940, *Facts* reprinted an appreciative letter by the same Ernest J. Swift, now vice chairman of the A.R.C., to the Reich's Charge d'affaires in Washington, Hans Thomsen. Dated March 22, 1940, the letter mentioned a shipment of $250,000 worth of relief supplies approved by the Allied Contraband Control for the Government General. In connection with relief supplies, other A.R.C. officials, Wayne Chatfield-Taylor and James T. Nicholson made what they termed a "very satisfactory" inspection tour between March 4 and March 14, 1940 of Warsaw, Cracow, Lublin, and other areas in the Government General. Upon returning to Berlin, they cabled their observations to Swift. The two A.R.C. officers reported the distribution of these supplies through what they said were "Polish and Jewish channels," with German authorities extending "complete cooperation." Among the groups distributing these relief goods were the Polish Central Relief Committee, the Polish Red Cross, and Marcele Biberstein, called the "head" of the Jewish community in Cracow. The idea of using Jews to administer forced ghettos for Nazi purposes had been developed before the war by Adolph Eichmann in Vienna, Berlin, and Prague. Yet, to the end of his life in 1969, James T. Nicholson, executive vice president of the A.R.C. took pride in dealing with the Nazis in Poland during 1939 and 1940 because, he believed, relief was distributed "on the basis of need and without regard to race, religion, or politics."[7] In the same issue of *Facts*, April 8, 1940, was a large headline, "American Red Cross Acknowledges German Cooperation In Poland" placed over a photograph of Duke Carl Eduard of the German Red Cross posing with Norman H. Davis, chairman of the A.R.C. during the German's visit to the United States. The report that followed pointed to the close cooperation of the two organizations in Poland. The A.R.C. was able to "pry loose" shipments of relief materials delayed by the Allied governments. The account rejected as "propaganda . . . stories to the effect that Warsaw was on the verge of an epidemic, and that Poles, as well as Jews, were subjected to what was sarcastically referred to as "starvation, persecution, etc. etc. . . . ." These "inventions," as they were described, were denied by the A.R.C. visitors to the Government General, Chatfield-Taylor, and Nicholson. On May 27, 1940, *Facts* reprinted an interview with Nicholson printed in the Washington *Daily News* for April 19, 1940: "I know of no atrocities against Jews in Poland," Nicholson insisted. "The movement of several million non-Aryans into the southern and eastern parts of the country," he asserted, "is simply a solution to the minority problem." According to Nicholson, Jews were "treated with the utmost consideration throughout the Government General." On June 17, 1940, *Facts* printed Nicholson's letter addressed to "Dear Dr. Frank" offering Hitler's appointee "my thanks and my respects" for cooperating with the American Red Cross.

Other Americans involved with relief also were pleased with the Germans in Poland. The *Facts* copy of September 2, 1940 named Gamble and Murray--no first names offered--of the Polish Food Commission, who appreciated the Germans restoring "order" and reconstruction. On February 5, 1940, *Facts* mentioned that the distribution by the American Friends Society's workers of a special donation by the Pope to Polish Catholics was accomplished with Frank's approval.

By the end of the first year of Hitler's policies in Poland, *Facts* quoted a headline from *The Economist*--no date given--"Life in Poland 'Normal' *The Economist*." According to *Facts* of November 18, 1940, the British periodical wrote that the German administration was beginning to work well, and despite wartime destruction and a bitter winter, agriculture was expected to show an upward trend.

Hitler's rationale for his third "guide post" of Polish occupation, security for the Reich and its interests, had long been expressed in his speeches and writings. But now, in his October 6, 1939 "peace" speech, he outdid himself with an attack against the "barbarism of the east" who engaged in a "sadistic persecution" and slaughter of thousands of *Volksdeutsche*, the German ethnic minority in Poland, and were torturing and massacring German prisoners of war. These charges, repeated frequently in *Facts*, amounted to a journalistic license to murder Poles under the guise of "self defense." The October 31, 1939 issue carried an appeal by the German Red Cross to the International Red Cross to investigate the *Volksdeutsche* situation in Poland, but nothing further was written in *Facts* about this plea. A summary of the Third Reich's Foreign Office document, *Official Report on the Systematic Extermination of the German Minority in Poland* was provided by *Facts* on February 27, 1940. Now a new Charge was added--that Poles were assassinating German Protestant pastors and destroying their churches in an orgy of religiously-motivated butchery. Dr. Ernst Schubert, identified only as a "Councillor of the Consistory" estimated that one million Germans who resisted Polonization were forced to flee for their lives. Now that parts of Poland were "re-occupied," according to Schubert, Protestantism would have a "new lease of life." On January 15, 1940, *Facts* reprinted obituary notices in German of nine pastors who supposedly had been murdered. This was one of the few instances of the use of the German language in *Facts*. The editor of the weekly, George Sylvester Viereck, claimed that the "Polish reign of terror," both in its physical and spiritual forms, brought about German intervention. Thus Viereck, in his way, blamed the Poles for causing the Second World War!

Hitler's fourth "guide post" for Poland, the reorganization of economic and cultural life, was carried out according to his early policy directives to Frank. Poland was to be ruthlessly exploited for German interests. All resources, including labor forces, were to be shipped off to the Reich and the local population reduced to minimum level of subsistence. The Polish intelligentsia was to be crushed, and educational institutions closed. In addition, the region was to serve as a dumping ground for "undesirable elements" from the expanded German empire, such as Jews and Poles. They were to be deprived of leadership and reduced to an elementary economic level until their ultimate fate would be decided. "Poland is to be treated as a colony," concluded Frank, "the Poles are to be the slaves of the Great-German World Reich."[8]

While subjugation was Poland's grinding reality, the tone of *Facts* was typified by the copy of December 9, 1940, marking the first anniversary of the Government General. It was touted as "The Land of the Future," with praise for its "unlimited possibilities." Busy with agricultural and industrial growth and reconstruction projects, it was a veritable paradise for its inhabitants. Until its last copy on June 7, 1941, many news items in *Facts* contrasted the backwardness of pre-war Poland with German--sponsored improvements in education, sanitation, roads, industry, agriculture, and the arts. In the issue of February 19, 1940, Frank actually boasted the Nazis were doing their best to promote "life freedom and order" in ravished Poland. Some cultural improvements were mentioned, although a Germanic streak could be detected. On September 9, 1940 *Facts* reported that a new German theater was opened in Cracow, and Dr. Hans Rohr of Munich was reorganizing its orchestra. The library in Cracow, named for Polish King Jagiello, was moved to a new building, noted *Facts* of March 3, 1941, and rechristened the *Staatsbibliothek*, Dr. Abb, director of the Berlin University Library, was given the task of completing the structure, which was described in *Facts* of May 12, 1941 as one of "striking design in the German architectural manner."

The most comprehensive view of Hitler's Poland appeared in *Facts* of April 22, 1940, which devoted seven of its eight pages to the theme "A Nation Rebuilds." Photographs were presented of the reconstruction of roads and bridges, the rebuilding of cities, the improvement of health, the growth of industry, and all due, it was claimed, to the "tremendous job undertaken by Dr. Hans Frank and his German and Polish assistants." Part of a page carried a boxed insert outlining the biography of Frank, with his photograph. The main caption read "Dr. Hans Frank" followed by a quotation in italics: "I wish to be able to justify myself in the eyes of the Polish people too." The entire edition carried excerpts from an address by Frank to the "foreign press" who were not named. He discussed the problems of administering such a large area which was left in a "deplorable" condition due to the backwardness of the Polish nation. "It was Poland's great good fortune," said Frank, "that due to the technical perfection of the German armed forces the war lasted a relatively short time." "The occupying forces," he asserted, "received the command and instructions from the Fuehrer to guarantee to the Polish people freedom, work and the possibility of progress...." For the first time, he maintained, Polish industry experienced a "progressive and socially-minded treatment of labor." Frank referred to newspaper rumors that described him as "the great destroyer of the Polish masses." He dismissed these reports as "senseless," attributing them to the enemies of Germans. No, he insisted, the "Polish nation has never before been so benevolently governed...." Yet, the enemy forces, despite all this Nazi good will, were responsible for Polish resistance centers. "These activities compel us to take certain measures," warned Frank, "which are carried out in accordance with my instructions." Still, everything was "legal." "I am a lawyer myself," Frank soothed, and "when I am told that I have liquidated 13,000 students, that I have killed 880 ecclesiastics, that I sterilized Polish children, drove thousands upon thousands of people into the woods to starve and deliberately fostered starvation--then . . . I can only smile. Nothing is easier than to launch unproven contentions upon the world. . . ." Regarding religion, Frank assured not the "slightest interference" with the activities of priests and laymen. Jews were "unmolested," he contended, although countless pogroms already occurred, and he referred to the Gestapo-controlled Jewish councils set up by Reinhard Heydrich as "the self governing body of the Jews." In italics: "The Jews carry on their activities without interference. . . ." Frank denied the charge that he destroyed the Polish intelligentsia, but admitted--no surprise here--there were certain "troublesome elements" in the academic community. His response to this and other charges was printed in italics: "There is not a single concentration camp in the whole of Poland. . . . I am proud to tell you that the health of the Polish people has never been as good as it is today." Hitler's ruler asked the press to believe that "countless applications were coming in to him from Poles requesting residence in his realm. From 60,000 to 70,000 Germans lived in the region near Lublin, and they would soon be transferred to their "home country." According to Frank, Jews also "wanted" to live in the area, and he was "ready to place the Lublin district at the disposal of world Jewry. . . ." In fact, rumors of a so-called "Lublin Reservation" for Jews persisted, and was an element in the deception of "deportation to the East." In ending his address to the foreign journalists, Frank appealed to those commentators to publicize his desire to cooperate with the Poles to "create a peaceful community." Until the very last issue of *Facts*, the weekly was describing the Government General as "The Land of the Future."

A discerning reader of the weekly might have noticed military implications in the reported economic progress in Poland, such as the rapid opening of coal mines, the repair of railroads, and bridge rebuilding. On April 10, 1941, *Facts* displayed a headline: "Mitteland Kanal Completed." The accompanying map showed how, by a series of connections involving the Oder, Elbe, and Weser Rivers, and the completion of an Oder-Danube canal, Germany was intent on transporting men and material from the English Channel to the Black Sea. Over a month later, Hitler invaded his ally in Poland, the Soviet Union.

In his October 6, 1939 "peace" speech, Hitler labeled "as the most important task," the fifth "guide post" of Polish policy: a "new order of ethnographical conditions." Himmler was placed in charge of repatriating Germans out of foreign lands and into the bulging Reich. Race would be the all-powerful guide to Hitler's Poland. By 1940, 1,200,000 Poles and 300,000 Jews were driven east to the Government General, while 500,000 ethnic Germans were settled in their place in the German-incorporated areas of western Poland, or the Wartheland.

From its first printings, *Facts* offered much information about German repatriation movements; from Brazil, the Baltic countries, Central Europe, and Soviet-occupied Poland. The attractions were jobs, new housing, and a vast new area to be developed. Great improvements were described in agriculture, mining, soil conservation, drainage, industry, and commerce. On March 3, 1941, *Facts* reported that Upper Silesia's mines were being reconstructed according to the Reich's Four Year Plan. In one district, 4,000 textile factories were modernized, according to *Facts*. This was part of a "Home Coming of Germans" from Galicia, Bessarabia, and Lithuania. In thirty days, 92,000 people passed through ports on the Danube with all their possessions and were received in camps. Optimistic reports were frequent. *Facts* of March 3, 1940 bragged about Bromberg, formerly Bydgoszcyz, calling it the "Garden City of the East," neglected by the Poles, but now being renewed with housing, jobs, a town hall, museum, public swimming pool, a women's health center and a park system along the Weichsel River, formerly the Vistula. Culture too was offered. As early as the November 15, 1939 issue of *Facts* was the claim that from the border with France to the "reconquered territories" from Poland, concert halls and theaters flourished. "Germany is not at war with Shakespeare's England" proclaimed *Facts*. Hitler took a special interest in Posen, where an old pre-Versailles German theater existed. The September 2, 1940 issue of *Facts* stated that the Fuehrer ordered a complete remodeling of Posen, including civic buildings, Posen Castle, and the theater. The front cover of *Facts* for April 28, 1941 displayed a photograph of the theater, a Greek temple type of structure, on the occasion of is gala opening. *Facts* of December 28, 1939 announced the creation of a new college in Posen, soon to become a full university. One year after the invasion, over sixty new high schools and colleges were opened; fifteen near Kattowitz, according to *Facts* of September 9, 1940. Agricultural schools and folk schools were created as well. The National Socialist Welfare Organization of Germany extended its varied activities to the eastern provinces of Germany with mother and child organizations, kindergartens, nurse stations, and country vacations. *Facts* of November 30, 1940 unwittingly revealed a bitter irony, in view of what was really occurring throughout Poland, with its claim that "one of the most notable achievements was the lowering of the infant mortality rate."

More information was given about the *Volksdeutsche* than any other group. Still, a close reading of *Facts* disclosed what was happening to other people. A compulsory labor decree, which Frank announced for all Poles, went into effect on April 20, 1940, a date which was also Hitler's 51st birthday. Poles of "German descent," informed *Facts* of June 24, 1940, could avoid forced labor by enlisting in the German armed forces. The "new order" was described by *Facts* of April 1, 1940 as a "boon" for Polish farm workers, 800,000 of whom were toiling in the Reich. "Contrary to hostile propaganda there is no compulsion of any sort involved," asserted the weekly, and the workers were enjoying better wages and conditions than in

Poland. Still, on May 27, 1940, *Facts* denied an account from the Polish Information Bureau stating that young girls were being kidnapped and sent to Germany as prostitutes.

Facts of April 8, 1940 carried one item with the headline "Polish Atrocities Against the Ukranian Minority," using words such as "extermination" which was "not yet well known to Americans." Allusions were made to British comments in 1921 and 1930 which appeared in the *Manchester Guardian* and the *New Statesman*, but no exact dates were given. Ukrainians were finally achieving what *Facts* termed "complete self government in cultural, economic and church affairs." In Lublin and Cracow, the Greek Orthodox Church was given official status. The cathedral at Chelm and fifty other churches it alleged were taken by the Poles but were returned. It was also stated that a Ukrainian press was "permitted to develop," but gave no further information.

In 1939, Poland's 3,250,000 Jews made up 10 percent of the population. *Facts* dealt with Jews obliquely; either to deny rumors of "persecution" or by omitting any mention of Jews while discussing Poland. Both tactics were used in an issue for November 30, 1939, which quoted with approval the "Americana Annual for 1939": Nazism guaranteed "freedom of conscience," one read, to Protestants, Catholics, and "those of other faiths. . . ." However, "restrictive legislation relating to the Jewish population is solely a racial question and in no respect a matter of religion." On February 27, 1940, *Facts* denied British accounts of large-scale shooting of Jews in Lodz. *Facts* of April 8, 1940 stated that Jewish laborers "also live at home with their families during their term of service," implying that Jewish and Polish workers were treated equally, and there was a time limit for slave labor. The same issue assured that religious life in the area had "practically returned to normal," but writing only about churches. An item from the magazine *International Goodwill*, volume XI, number 2, April, 1940 was favorably quoted in *Facts* of September 16 the same year. The American press had charged Hitler with conducting a "campaign" against Jews and Christians; however, the periodical soothed, "there has been no apparent interference . . . with the ritual or devotional exercises of either denominations." *International Goodwill* agreed with Nazi government's statement that "never before has a government in Germany better served the true interests of the church. . . ."

Typical of how Jews were omitted in print was the item "Winter Relief Reports" in *Facts* of May 27, 1940. The National Socialist Welfare Organization, aided by the Quakers and the American Red Cross, was "extremely active" in the occupied Polish territories, claiming to have cared for 1,171,000 persons. This figure was broken down to Poles, Polish refugees, Polish workers going to the Reich, the German minority, and "other smaller groups"--no mention of Jews. No word about Jews was written in a story carried by *Facts* on May 27, 1940, which denied reports from "Polish information circles" regarding mass shootings in Chelm. Chelm, fabled in Yiddish folklore for its innocent fools, contained 15,000 Jews in 1939, and the community had existed since the 12th century.

The last entry in *Facts about Jews* was on May 12, 1941. The Jewish councils were mentioned as necessary to give the Jews "specific tasks" which would be fulfilled under the control of the "German authorities," which was in reality the Gestapo. A new tax was to be used for "philanthropic purposes," and "new veterinary regulations" included the "supervision of slaughter and inspection of meat." Read correctly, this meant the Germans extracted more profit from Jews, and kosher meat was further restricted or taxed. One month later, Germany invaded the Soviet Union, and hundreds of thousands of Jews would suffer the same fate as those of Chelm, whose last remnants were deported to the Sobibor death camp beginning in May, 1942. Today, Chelm still exists, east of Lublin, near the Soviet border, but no Jews live in that small city, for Poland is a land without Jews.

Between the invasion of Poland and the preparations for the attack on the Soviet Union, a perceptive reader of *Facts In Review* could have learned a great deal about Hitler's Poland. Hitler's goals were clearly stated and ardently pursued from the beginning of the war. Racial ideology was inseparable from occupation policies: oppression of Poles and Jews, ghettoization for Jews, mass shootings, slave labor, forced migration of people, and Germanization. Still, resistance was revealed beneath the glowing reports of modernization which benefitted the Reich and supported its military objectives in the east. The pacification of the Poles received approval by international agencies, most notably the American Red Cross. Jews were directly ruled by the Jewish councils, which were described as "self-governing bodies" but which were in actuality controlled by the Nazis. Many of the key elements of the Holocaust were already in place before the spring of 1941 when the decision was made to murder all the Jews within the grasp of the Third Reich.

On February 27, 1940, *Facts In Review* published an article, "The Same Old Method," comparing British propaganda of the First World War with that of the war then raging. It mocked a report from London that executions of a large number of Jews had been carried out in Lodz, Poland. The article concluded with a statement the editor of *Facts* hoped would disparage any contentions of the British because of its "impossible" exaggerated figures: ". . . 5,000,000 Poles died of starvation or exposure, or killed in battle, or were shot by German firing squads. . . ." Although this 1940 figure, given in sarcasm by *Facts* to deflate an enemy account, greatly understated the figure of the future dead; it represented an omen and a warning to the civilized world. Death was the very essence of Hitler's Poland, . . . but also the elementary substance of a Nazi victory anywhere.

NOTES

1. Gordon Wright, *The Ordeal of Total War, 1939-1945*. NY, Harper and Row, 1968, p. 107. A differing view, that Hitler consistently mixed words with deeds, and was guided primarily by race and ideology, is contained in: Norman Rich, *Hitler's War Aims*. NY, Norton and Co., 1973/4, 2 vols.
2. Adolf Hitler, *Mein Kampf*. Boston, Houghton Mifflin Co., 1943, p. 1.
3. *Statement of War Losses and Damages of Poland in 1939-1945*. Warsaw, Presidium of the Council of Ministers, War Indemnity Office, 1947, p. 43. Cited by Nora Levin, *The Holocaust: The Destruction of European Jewry*. NY, Schocken, 1973, p. 163.
4. Sidney H. Kessler, "Goebbels' American Proxy: *Facts In Review*," *Holocaust Studies Annual*, vol. III. Greenwood, FL, Penkevill Publishing Co., 1987, pp. 165-175.
5. Robert E. Conot, *Justice At Nuremberg*. NY, Carroll and Graf, 1983, pp. 212-213.
6. H.R. Trevor-Roper, ed., *Hitler's Secret Conversations 1941-1944*. NY, New American Library, 1961. (January 23, 1942), p. 237.
7. *Who Was Who In America*, vol. V. Chicago, A.N. Marquis Co., 1973, p. 533.
8. Frank's comments from his diary and from the International Military Tribunal are cited in: Norman Rich, *Hitler's War Aims: The Establishment of the New Order*, vol. II. NY, Norton and Co., 1974, pp. 86-87.

Nazi Determination and the Destruction of Dutch Jewry

John A. Leopold

By 1945 the Nazis had killed over 104,000 Jews from the occupied Netherlands.[1] In a country with such liberal traditions, how could this happen?

Numerous testimonies preserved in Yad Vashem praise the heroism and liberality of Dutch rescuers; the Avenue of the Righteous Gentiles in Jerusalem and the statue of the Docker on Mejer Square in Amsterdam recall the bravery of Dutch resistance.[2] The German monopoly of power, however, isolated the Jews from their countrymen and the threat of violent death caused most to retreat into passivity. Without the strong protection of government authority, Jews hoped for survival in Holland through an unwilling acquiescence to Nazi force. Alongside heroic resistance stood the treachery of a small number of Dutchmen who for either ideological or financial reasons supported the deportation of Dutch Jews. Calculatedly, the Germans exploited their power to divide and rule the country so well that by 1944, the Nazi rulers could boast to Berlin that they had eliminated Jews from the "body of the nation."[3]

Before 1940, Amsterdam was for many Jews the Jerusalem of the West. Two large synagogues bordered the Jonas Daniel Meier Square and testified to the religious freedom which Sephardic and Ashkenazic Jews had enjoyed in the Netherlands since the sixteenth century. In Dutch society, Calvinists and Catholics lived side by side with over 110,000 Jews who enjoyed the full and equal protection guaranteed by the country's constitution. Racist antisemitism which had flourished in central and eastern Europe and even in France did not develop a significant following in the Netherlands. Radical parties which emulated fascism and Nazism remained political fringe groups. At its foundation, the largest of these right wing parties, the National Socialist Movement (*National-socialistische Beweging,* NSB) strongly asserted the rights of

Jews to join. Some did. Later when the movement emphasized racial antisemitism, it lost votes.[4]

Amsterdam was not quite Jerusalem. Traditional antijudaism persisted among some Catholics. The church forbade Catholic girls to work in the homes of Jews and perpetuated a prayer for the "perfidious Jews" in its Good Friday liturgy.[5] Similar medieval attitudes persisted in Protestantism, especially in some rural areas.[6] During the last half of the 1930's, the influx of 30,000 German, Austrian and eastern Jews fleeing the terrors of Nazism taxed the tolerance of Dutch society. In Amsterdam, some Dutchmen began to mock and envy the wealthy German Jews who moved into the southern part of the city.[7]

The Nazi conquest of Holland changed the entire framework within which relatively liberal Netherlanders had lived. In four traumatic days, they witnessed the invasion of their country, the bombing of Rotterdam and the flight of the queen and her cabinet into exile. Having enjoyed neutrality and peace since the Napoleonic wars, the Dutch now found themselves dominated by a foreign power.

Attempting to woo the Netherlanders, Adolf Hitler sent Arthur Seyss-Inquart, the man who had helped subvert Austria and unite it with Germany, to rule the Dutch. His goal for the new *Reichskommissar* was to reconcile the nine million Dutch to the new order and to reverse the three hundred year history which had separated the Lowlands from the German Reich. Seyss-Inquart offered a friendly hand to the "blood related Dutchmen."[8] His rule began not by dissolving parties but by organizing his regime to mesh with the roles filled by the secretaries general who had remained in the country to administer traditional cabinet responsibilities.[9] The violence and persecution which followed in the wake of Hitler's defeat of Poland did not characterize the low keyed introduction of German rule into the Netherlands.[10] Seyss-Inquart's Commissar for Administration and Justice assuaged the anxieties of government officials, who knew the Nazi hatred of the Jews, by noting that there was no "Jewish question" in Holland.[11]

Without strong support, the Germans moved slowly in their introduction of antisemitic measures. On 29 June 1940, Prince Bernhard's birthday, so many Netherlanders expressed their loyalty to the royal family by wearing flowers and placing bouquets at royal monuments that they surprised the Germans who had portrayed the queen as a delinquent who had fled her country in its time of need. Obviously, Jews whom the House of Orange had traditionally protected, joined in this silent protest. The Nazis used this as an excuse to drive all Jews from the air raid service.[12] The question immediately arose--how is one to know who is a Jew?

In the fall of 1940, the *Reichskommissar* responded by demanding that all civil servants, over 200,000, file an Aryan declaration detailing their ancestry. The Dutch secretaries general objected and emphasized the constitutional provision which allowed all citizens to hold government office. Seyss-Inquart refused to honor their objections.[13] Several lawyers argued this decree would lead to violations of the Hague Convention which required an occupying power to respect local law. On a technicality, the Dutch Supreme Court voted 12-5-1 in favor of complying with the decree because no statute explicitly forbade making such a declaration.[14]

Once the Nazis had this information, they demanded that the 2,535 Dutch Jewish civil servants leave government service.[15] On 15 November 1940 the secretaries general again objected and argued that at most they could only tolerate that Jews continue to be paid, but that they "be temporarily relieved from the fulfillment of their duties." Seyss-Inquart demanded the removal of the word "temporary" and the Dutch officials complied.[16] Deprived of government support, how would society accept this decree?

The major Protestant churches, for the first time in their history, formed a joint committee and officially filed an objection with the *Reichskommissar*.[17] Students at the University of Delft went on strike and the SS closed the school. At the nation's oldest university, Leiden, the Dean of the Law Faculty, E.R. Cleveringa, took the most heroic stance and appealed to the conscience of his countrymen. On 26 November when the Jewish Professor E.M. Meyers would normally have lectured, Cleveringa stood in his place. In an auditorium filled to overflowing, the Dean praised "this Netherlander, this noble son of our people ... this scholar whom the foreigner, who now hostilely rules over us, has 'relieved from his duties.'" He concluded with the hope that Meyers would once more resume his position. Students immediately went on a wild cat strike. The SS closed the university and arrested Cleveringa.[18] Germans complained that the Dutch with their liberal, humanistic orientation could not understand racism.[19] In reality, the vast majority of Netherlanders understood Nazi racism very clearly and they rejected it.

Over the winter months a new series of antisemitic measures including the decree requiring all Jews to register increased tension between Nazis and the ordinary Dutch citizen. When one of Seyss-Inquart's commissars encouraged the *Weerafdeeling* (WA), the paramilitary group of the NSB, to act like the German SA and "rough up" Jews in Amsterdam, confrontation sharpened. Forays into the traditional Jewish quarter aroused the ire of the residents. Jews in this area had strong ties with their Dutch compatriots who lived side by side with them. Together, they organized *knockploegen,* literally knuckle squads, to meet force with force. On 11 February during one of the WA's sorties into the area H. Koot, a Dutch Nazi, received such a beating that he died three days later.[20]

This incident shocked Seyss-Inquart's deputy in Amsterdam and he hurriedly tried different responses. First he closed off the area and wanted to establish a ghetto, but almost as many non-Jews lived there as Jews. Ghettoization created too many difficulties.[21] He called in the chief rabbi of the Ashkenazic community and the president of his congregation, Abraham Asscher, the diamond broker, and demanded that they form a commission to help pacify the area. Under pressure, Asscher agreed.[22] He and his colleague, David Cohen, a professor at the University of Amsterdam, organized mass meetings at the Diamond Bourse and urged Jews to turn in their weapons. No one complied.[23]

Meanwhile in the southern part of the city other Jews had begun to organize *knockploegen.* One such group met at Koco's ice cream parlor. When the Nazis learned of this they raided the place. The owners, two German emigres, E. Cahen and A. Kohen, had filled one of the spigots with ammonia and when the German police came in they sprayed them with this so that their fellow conspirators could escape. Hanns Rauter, the Commissar for Security and the Chief SS and Police Leader in the Netherlands, raged at this "renewed Jewish impertinence." In this relatively pacific country Jews dared to fight back. He agreed with his superior, SS *Reichsfuehrer* Heinrich Himmler, that Germans should seize 425 Jewish hostages.[24]

On Saturday afternoon, 22 February 1941, 600 heavily armed German police moved into the traditional Jewish quarter and brutally seized young men between the ages of 20 and 35. To reach their quota, they repeated the raid on Sunday. The publicly vicious treatment and arbitrary arrest of fellow citizens shocked the Dutch.[25] Leaders of the underground Communist party in the Netherlands used this incident to ignite the powderkeg of frustration in the city. In circulars hurriedly mimeographed, they urged a general strike and headlined their appeal with a call to "protest the horrid Jewish persecutions."[26]

On Tuesday morning, 25 February 1941, the strike began. From trolley car drivers, to dockers, to factory workers, to the store keepers in the central city, people walked off their jobs. All Amsterdam went on strike and neighboring communities began to do the same. Once more Rauter conferred with Himmler. The SS leader raged; no other Nazi occupied country had dared to act with the boldness that the Dutch manifested in this strike. Take a thousand hostages, if necessary, the Reich Leader urged. The German military commander, Air Force General Friederich Christiansen, declared martial law in the province of North Holland. Armed SS divisions moved into Amsterdam and used grenades as well as machine guns to disperse groups of citizens. Before the strike ended the next day, the Nazis killed nine people, wounded over 40 and arrested 200 others.[27]

On 3 March, Cahen, one of the owner's of Koco's, became the first victim of a German firing squad in the Netherlands; 18 others followed ten days later. On 14 May after other incidents of sabotage and resistance angered the Germans, the SS went out to round up at least 300 other Jewish males from Amsterdam.[28] These young men eventually went to Mauthausen Concentration Camp. Shortly after their arrival, families began receiving death notices citing a variety of illnesses; for a minimum fee Germans offered to send home cremated remains.[29] For Dutch Jews Mauthausen beame synonymous with death; they dubbed it Mordhausen.[30]

The February strike forced Seyss-Inquart to alter his policy. He still offered the option of collaboration to the Dutch, but he made clear that opposition would meet "the strength of our bayonets." Praising the "uniqueness" of Dutch "Germanic blood," he offered the Netherlanders a choice place in the "new order," but they had to choose "with us or against us"--there could be no other alternative. Repeatedly the *Reichskommissar* emphasized, "The Jews are for us not Netherlanders. They are enemies with whom we can come neither to an armistice nor to a peace. . . . We will beat them where we meet them and whoever goes with them has to bear the consequences." Prophetically he warned, "All Europe will go into ruins before Germany gives up the battle" and certainly "the occupied territories would go to ruins before the enemy comes to Germany."

At a time when only England remained at war with Hitler, the message to the vulnerable land of dikes could not have been clearer. He concluded, "We are filled with a true religious fanaticism. Adolf Hitler, the *Fuehrer* of the great German Reich, the leader of all Germanic peoples in the new order of the west, has given us the mandate. We have begun; we may fail; he will triumph."[31]

For the Jewish community, the Reich Commissar's words spelled continued persecution. Despite constitutional guarantees, the Dutch secretaries general could or would do little to frustrate German policy toward the Jews. Resignation or determined resistance, they feared, would open the way for Dutch Nazis to control the entire bureaucracy and thus make things worse for all Netherlanders including the Jews. As death reports from Mauthausen mounted, Asscher and Cohen appealed to the secretaries general, but nothing happened.[32] In The Hague, the Netherlands Zionist Federation had encouraged the formation of a Jewish Coordinating Committee to develop a united front and represent Jewish concerns to the secretaries general. Under the leadership of Ludwig Visser, the forcibly retired president of the Dutch Supreme Court, these leaders believed that any direct contact with the Germans would undermine the legal position of Jews as Dutch citizens. Visser sought to influence the Dutch governmental leaders and then as a private citizen he tried to see Rauter. The SS leader refused to meet with him. All that Secretary General K. Frederiks could tell him was that the Nazis remained "irrational" on this issue.[33]

Meanwhile in Amsterdam, the Germans encouraged Asscher and Cohen to develop their organization into a Jewish Council for Amsterdam and then for the entire country. From its inception this group invited controversy because Germans and not Jews demanded its existence. The twenty man *Joodse Raad* hardly reflected the diversity of the Jewish community and certainly did not represent the large number of working class Jews in Amsterdam. Visser and his colleagues on the Coordinating Committee criticized Cohen and Asscher noting that the the Jewish Council had gotten itself into a "hellish circle" with no way out. Visser minced no words in stressing that many Jews objected to the council's servile manner in dealing with the Germans. Cohen could only respond that in an occupied country where the Germans had power to work their will, the position of the Jewish council was not heroic but only realistic.[34]

In 1941 most Dutch Jews could not envision mass deportations, let alone gas chambers. Some form of accommodation, council members believed, could appease German fanaticism. Strikes, protests, sabotage had not helped the Jews. Life was not so intolerable that one could not hope to wait for better times. In the meanwhile the Jewish Council could help the community survive by cushioning the demands of the Nazis and serving as a philanthropic board dispersing help wherever possible to persecuted Jews.

Just as the secretaries general acquiesced to German decrees "in order to avoid worse things," so the Jewish Council followed suit.[35] When the Nazis demanded that Jews have special permits to travel, the Council set up a procedure to help people move whenever necessary. When the *Reichskommissariat* demanded that all Jews attend separate schools, Asscher and Cohen hastened to set up an efficient system to guarantee proper education. When the Germans confiscated savings and aryanized businesses, the *Joodse Raad* used the meager funds placed at its disposal to subsidize Jews and to employ as many as possible in its own burgeoning bureaucracy. When the Germans demanded that unemployed Jews be sent to work camps in the Netherlands, Asscher and Cohen insisted that Jewish doctors give them a physical examination first.[36] Unfortunately, the Nazis never kept their promises and continually tightened the circumference of the "hellish circle."

As the winter of 1941-42 passed, Jews quietly cheered the entrance of the United States into the war and the chilling setback which the Germans encountered in Russia. They hoped the allies would soon liberate the Netherlands and the nightmare would end. The "religious fanaticism" of Seyss-Inquart and the SS dashed that hope. During this same period, the Nazis gradually, but consciously and deliberately circumscribed the Jewish community with more and more social and economic limitations. Special decrees barred Jews from movie theaters, parks, bath houses and museums; other mandates forced Jewish artists, writers and musicians out of professional life. The Nazis required Jews to purchase groceries late in the day and then only at certain stores. Jews had to turn in their radios; gentile women could no longer work in Jewish homes.[37] Obviously the Germans expected that social isolation would cut Jewish ties with the Dutch and prepare the way for making the country *judenrein*. Most Netherlanders, however, had little sympathy with these measures and frequently conspired with Jewish colleagues to circumvent these decrees.[38]

In the tight war time economy, the Nazis demonstrated their fanatical determination to persecute the Jews by deliberately robbing them of any sense of economic freedom. In the Netherlands, the majority of Jews were not wealthy. Even of the 22,000 Jewish firms forced to register with the occupation government, the Nazis determined that about 9,000 small family stores and enterprises did not warrant an Aryan "administrator" but only rapid liquidation. Two thousand others were sold and the remainder came under Nazi control. The famous diamond industry of Amsterdam included some Jewish firms like Asscher's and these the Nazis secured for themselves through the naming of *Treuhaender* who supervised the administration of such companies.[39]

German persecution of Jews, however, did not aim at making money. The stakes were much higher. Key leaders in the *Reichskommissariat* clearly understood this as early as the spring of 1941. At that time, the Reich Central Security Office of Reinhardt Heydrich, Chief of the Security Police, sent Erich Rajakowitsch to Holland to establish a *Zentralstelle fuer juedische Auswanderung*, a Center for Jewish Emigration.[40] Rauter and Seyss-Inquart also discussed establishing a fund to secure "the financing of the emigration and the coming final solution of the Jewish question in Europe."[41] In the same period, the SS security police formed a special office, *Sondereferat J*, for resettlement.[42] Obviously the Nazis had a clear strategy for dealing with the Jews of Holland. By concealing their "final solution," the Germans deceived both the Dutch secretaries general and the Dutch Jewish Council and led them to believe that they were avoiding the worst by accepting lesser compromises.

In the summer of 1941, Seyss-Inquart decreed that any Jew with a bank account of 10,000 guilders or more and an annual income of 3,000 guilders would have to use the firm of Lippmann-Rosenthal on Sarphati Street, an old Jewish bank which the Germans now controlled. By March 1942, the bank had to administer all Jewish accounts and no one could withdraw more than 250 guilders per month. In May, Jews had to turn in all valuables including art work, tapestries, gold, silver and precious stones to this firm. Meanwhile the special *Einsatzstab Rosenberg* confiscated significant Jewish collections such as the *Bibliotheca Rosenthaliana* and sent them off to Berlin.[43] The Dutch secretaries general could do nothing to stop this blatant theft of Dutch Jewish property.

German economic persecution created great unemployment in the Jewish population and the Nazis capitalized on this by offering young Jewish males under the age of 30 the opportunity for relief by earning minimal wages in work camps. Members of the Jewish Council and the Secretaries General knew of Dachau and Ravensbrueck, not to mention Mauthausen. In a spirit of "compromise," the Germans agreed that Jews would go only to camps in the Netherlands.[44] Once more the Nazis deceived the Dutch. The age limit rapidly moved up to 60 and Rauter viewed the camps not merely as places to confine men for work, but as assembly grounds organizing a ready pool of Jews for ultimate deportation.[45] At Vught, the Nazis used confiscated Jewish funds to help build the largest of these work camps. The Germans rightly calculated that Dutch Gentiles would provide for Dutch Jews machines that they would not turn over to their conquerors.[46] Thus workers at Vught included skilled laborers in the diamond industry, the confectionary business and the Philips electrical corporation. The Nazis fostered the illusion that good production in Holland would prevent deportation.

Despite the diabolical circumscription of civil and human rights, Dutch Jews continued to hope for liberation and the vast majority of their Gentile countrymen continued to sympathize with their plight. Grocers saved produce for their Jewish patrons.[47]

People in the large cities circulated freely and the adventurous could ignore some of the Nazi laws.[48] After all, the Germans could not stop every Netherlander to check identity papers for the large black J which labeled Jews. The Jewish Council's expanding bureaucracy provided jobs for many middle class Jews and the forced transition of the *Hollandse Schouwburg* to the *Joodse Schouwburg* provided the opportunity for actors and musicians to entertain their fellow Jews.[49]

In April 1942, the "fanatic" Germans tightened the noose and snuffed out even this little glimmer of freedom. Seyss-Inquart decreed that all Jews had to wear a large yellow star labeled with the work *Jood*. Asscher and Cohen argued against this decree but then they had to tell people where they could purchase these badges.[50] Sympathetic Netherlanders wore similar stars or yellow flowers; others demonstratively walked arm in arm with Jewish friends. The underground newspaper, *De Vonk*, circulated thousands of paper stars of David with the inscription, "Jew and non-Jew one in the fight" and opponents of the Nazis threw paper stars from the roof of the *Bijenkorf*, the large department store near the palace in Amsterdam.[51] With a keen sense of gallows humor, Jews nicknamed a main street in the old Jewish quarter, the "Milky Way" and Waterloo Square surrounded by large synagogues became the Place d'Etoile.[52] The Nazis, however, saw no humor in Dutch attitudes. They required the *Telegraaf* to publish an editorial noting, "For the German occupying power, the Jewish star is no joke, but bitter earnestness. The inhabitants of this country are through this divided into two camps: friend and foe." German authorities, the article claimed, had great patience, but

> To all patience there is an end. With the continuation of such behavior which the occupying power observes as unsuitable and undesirable in the highest degree, severe measures shall follow. . . . Netherlanders who cannot decide to cease their friendly association with Jews or who defy the occupying power through their conduct run the danger of being themselves handled as Jews with all the consequences that flow out of that. . . .[53]

With the star Seyss-Inquart had effectively achieved his goal--"the economic, cultural and personal separation of the Jews from the non Jews."[54] He had carefully set the stage for the "final solution."

At the end of June 1942, the *Reichkommissariat* announced that Jews would go whence they came; they would leave Holland for work details in the East. Stunned, Asscher and Cohen objected; the secretaries general objected.[55] Christian churches began preparing a joint declaration to be read from all pulpits. Seyss-Inquart hastily began negotiations for exempting baptized Jews and in the process cleverly separated Protestants and Catholics. The result was that only Catholic church goers heard priests read the bishops' pastoral letter objecting to the unjust and unmerciful policy instituted against the Jews.[56] An irate *Reichskommissar* retaliated by ordering the SS immediately to arrest the hundred or so Catholic Jews, including the Carmelite nun, Edith Stein, and send them immediately to Poland. Like Cohen, many Dutchmen must have asked, if the powerful Catholic church could not protect its own Jewish members, who could help the Jews?[57]

Exploiting the dreadful image of Mauthausen, Germans required the *Joodse Weekblad* to publish an announcement that Jews who did not voluntarily report for work in the East would go to Mauthausen.[58] No one knew where Auschwitz was but Jews preferred work to death. The first group left Amsterdam on 15 July. When Cohen objected to the use of freight cars, the Germans agreed to use passenger trains.[59] Despite threats, most Jews refused to comply with their summonses. Police had to surround Jewish areas and forcibly collect people to fill the trains to Westerbork. The imposition of a curfew sought to make arrests easier for the Nazis who came at night to haul away their victims.[60]

The Westerbork transit camp in Drente housed Jews until their turn came for transit to the East.[61] According to Adolf Eichmann's scheduling, one or usually two trains came each week to collect about two thousand passengers for the three day trip to Auschwitz or Sobibor.[62] Conditions in Westerbork remained relatively good.[63] Dr. Fritz Spanier presided over a hospital barracks which very efficiently treated the sick until they were well enough to go on "work detail" to Poland.[64] No wonder the Dutch and Jews who heard in late 1942 and in 1943 about exterminations and gassings tended to dismiss these reports as grisly war propaganda.[65] Everyone knew conditions in the East would be hard; the Germans publicly stated that. Mauthausen, however, seemed worse and the Germans proclaiming that they were not barbarians promised to keep together families going to Poland.[66]

By the end of 1942, resettlement to the East shifted from a work detail to total expulsion. To fill the trains, the Nazis spared neither the infirm nor the aged. Secretary General K.J. Frederiks tried to save some 500 prominent Dutch Jews from deportation; the Germans agreed to let them stay together at Barneveld.[67] The Jewish Council strove to prevent the expulsion of Jewish leaders whom they considered essential for the restructuring of the community when, as they hoped, the deportees could return after the war.[68] Neither group succeeded. The Nazis sent the Barneveld group to Theresienstadt and in September 1943 rounded up the Jewish Council itself.[69] The Germans could boast that they had resolved the Jewish problem in the Netherlands.[70]

The vast majority of the nine million Dutchmen did nothing to help the 140,000 Jews in their country. Between May 1942 and April 1943, the Nazis forced over 163,600 Netherlanders to leave the country for work in Germany and some people in the provinces probably noted little difference between their fate and the plight of Dutch Jews.[71] Trolley car drivers, railway engineers and even policemen fearing for their own security continued working for the machinery which harassed, arrested and deported Jews. The vast majority of the Dutch also did not support the Germans. Soldiers had valiantly fought against the invasion and the overwhelming majority of ordinary citizens refused to join the Nazi movement. Over 25,000 young men did, however, volunteer for the *Waffen* SS and fight on the eastern front. Others joined the government in the highest and lowest ranks to take the place of secretaries general, mayors and policemen who refused to collaborate with the Germans.[72]

At the same time 20-40,000 Jews found refuge in the homes of Dutch Christians. At least one out of three of these *onderduikers*, divers as they were called, got caught, but thousands of people like Corrie ten Boom and Hannes Bogaard risked their lives, went to concentration camps or even died for helping others.[73] At the *Hollandsche Schouwbourg*, the holding center for the Jews of Amsterdam, Walther Suesskind, a German Jew, smuggled children out of the hands of the Nazis and saved them from resettlement.[74] Others such as a group of Chalotzim, Palestine pioneers, training in Holland received the aid they needed to escape across the border and ultimately reach freedom in Switzerland, Spain and Palestine.[75] All this occurred before the resistance flourished in Holland.

When in April 1943, the Germans sought to send about 300,000 Dutch veterans into captivity for labor details in Germany, another massive strike galvanized larger numbers to join resistance groups. Leaders then banded together to destroy census records, steal ration cards and set up an elaborate system for hiding fugitives from the Nazis.[76] Unfortunately all this began after the Nazis had already deported 58,000 Jews and had thousands of others trapped in transit camps or registered and labeled in Amsterdam.[77] One resistance worker noted that the Jews came on the market one year too early. Perhaps, however, he noted the need for greater resistance one year too late.

Had people known of the gas chambers at Auschwitz or Sobibor, Dutch reactions might have changed dramatically. The Germans, however, did everything possible to conceal the ultimate fate of the Jews. Not even the *Begleitkommando* which accompanied the train to Auschwitz could enter the camp. Hundreds of postcards and letters from the deportees rallied hope and contradicted reports of mass murder.[78] After the death of scores of young men in Mauthausen, Dutch officials and Dutch Jews did not view resettlement as a worse mortal threat. Isolation, pauperization and terror prepared the way for the final deception.

Judging the reaction of nine million Netherlanders to the persecution of the Jew in Holland from 1940 to 1945 allows for no easy generalization. Certainly the minimal antisemitism before 1940 and the general strike of 1941 in Amsterdam underline a lack of sympathy for Nazi policy. Germans complained that in contrast to other countries, measures against the Jews in the Netherlands had to be born by occupation forces "all alone" because the average citizen did not understand racism and was *judenfreundlich*.[79] On the other hand, Berlin's representative from the Foreign Office reported that "the Dutch people completely oppose the deportations, but still manifest an overwhelming apathy (toward them)."[80]

Accustomed to a peaceful bureaucratic state, the Dutch traumatized by the bombing of Rotterdam and the violent conquest of their country did not rush to establish resistance. Bereft of arms and confronted with a series of Nazi triumphs in Belgium and France, the majority of citizens passively accepted the status quo. Only Nazi decrees against the Jews mobilized an early passive resistance in the Amsterdam strike of February 1941. However, the harsh suppression of this uprising once more demonstrated the powerlessness of the ordinary citizen and frustrated immediate prospects for any civilian confrontation with the occupation. The Nazis calculatedly exploited their control of the state bureaucracy and the media to isolate the Jews. Unable to change German policy, the non Nazi Dutch secretaries general sought to mitigate the impact of German aggression; the German organized Jewish Council followed the same policy. Asscher and Cohen never encouraged resistance and never urged people to go underground; salvation, they believed, would come through compliance. Still Jews joined the resistance and over 25,000 went into hiding; three to four times that number participated in the attempt to save men, women and children from deportation. These rescuers, who hid people in their attics, cellars, chicken coops and all sorts of ingeniously devised places, ultimately saved more Jews than the Danes brought to Sweden.[81]

Surely the fact that the Netherlands suffered the loss of 75 percent of its Jewish population--the highest percentage of any occupied state in the West and one of the highest percentages for all of Europe--did not spring from any indigenous anti-Semitism in Holland.[82] Germanic ability to implement the final solution in the Netherlands depended not so much on the cooperation of a few or even the "apathy" of most Dutchmen, but on the religious fanaticism of the *Reichskommissariat*.[83] Hitler viewed the Netherlands as part of a great German Reich and he determined to make the entire area *judenrein*. The dedication of men like Seyss-Inquart and Rauter to his ideals sealed the fate of Holland's Jews.

NOTES

1. Joods Historisch Museum (ed.), *Documents of the Persecution of Dutch Jewry 1940-1945*, (Amsterdam, 1979), 174. For a brief and excellent analysis of the Holocaust in Holland, see Louis de Jong, *The Netherlands and Nazi Germany*, (Cambridge, MA., and London, 1990), 3-25.
2. Jerusalem, Yad Vashem Archives, Ball-Kaduri Collection and Wiener Library Collection; and Jan Stoutenbeek and Paul Vigiveno, *Wandelingen door joods Amsterdam*, (Weesp,1985), 30.
3. Amsterdam, Rijksinstituut voor Oorlogsdocumentatie (henceforth referred to as RIOD), 20 Stab Wimmer 12/7, Seyss-Inquart to Bormann, 28 February 1944.
4. See Lawrence D. Stokes, "Anton Mussert and the N.S.B.1931-45," *History*, (Vol. LVI, October 1971), 487-507.
5. Stoutenbeek and Vigiveno, 22. The Good Friday Liturgy used throughout this era included a series of orations, one of which began, "Oremus et pro perfidis Judaeis..." in The New Roman Missal, (New York et al., 1952), 484.
6. See Louis de Jong, "Jews and Non-Jews in Nazi Occupied Holland," in Michael Marrus (ed.), *The Nazi Holocaust: Historical Articles on the Destruction of European Jews*, (Westport,CT and London, Meckler, 1989), 129-30.
7. See Louis de Jong, *Het Konigrijk der Nederlanden in de tweede wereldoorlog*, (The Hague, 1969), I, 459-92.
8. Arthur Seyss-Inquart, *Vier Jahre in den Niederlanden: Gesammelte Reden*, (Amsterdam 1944), "Aus Anlass der Uebernahme der Regierungsgewalt," in The Hague on 29 May 1940, 11.
9. See Konrad Kwiet, *Reichskommissariat Niederlande: Versuch und Scheitern nationalsozialistischer Neuordnung*, (Stuttgart, 1968), 55-109.
10. See Gerhard Hirschfeld, *Fremdherrschaft und Kollaboration: Die Niederlande unter deutscher Besatzung 1940-1945*, (Stuttgart, 1984), 22-28.
11. de Jong, IVb, 747.
12. de Jong, IVa, 282-88, and J. Presser, *Ondergang: de vervolging en verdelging van het nederlande jodendom 1940-1945*, (The Hague, 1965), I, 18-19; the latter has been translated by Arnold Pomerans as *The Destruction of the Dutch Jews*, (New York, 1969). All references here are to the original edition.

13. See the correspondence in RIOD, Stab Wimmer 5, e.g., General Secretaries to Wimmer, 24 February 1941.
14. Hirschfeld, 102 and de Jong, IVb, 765.
15. de Jong, IVb, 780.
16. de Jong IVb, 766-80 and Presser, 26-54.
17. See the text of the protest in H. Wielek, *De ooorlog die Hitler won*, (Amsterdam, 1947), 18.
18. For the citation and context see, de Jong, IVb, 785-800.
19. See RIOD, HSSPF 16/30a, Meldungen aus den Niederlande, 3 December 1940, 3. "The regulations against the Jews are the subject of lively discussion among the widest circles of people and are almost always sharply rejected. A whispering campaign throughout the entire country seeks an opportunity to stand up for the 'poor Jews.'"
20. See B.A. Sijes, *De februari staking: 25-26 februari 1941*, (Amsterdam, n.d.), 62-87 and Ben Barber, *Zelfs als wij zullen verliezen: Joden in verzet en illegaliteit*, (Amsterdam, 1990), 57-63.
21. See Jerusalem, Yad Vashem, Joodsche Raad voor Amsterdam, Vol II, "1941: Onderzoek naar de gevolgen van ghettovorming te Amsterdam."
22. RIOD, Cohen, Memoirs, 19.
23. Wielek, 38.
24. Presser, I, 85-86.
25. de Jong, IVb, 890-92.
26. See Sijes, 110-135.
27. RIOD, HSSPF, Rauter's report on these events to Christiansen, Himmler and Seyss-Inquart, 4 March 1941.
28. de Jong, IVb, 926-41.
29. See a copy of such a notice in New York: Yivo Institute for Jewish Research, Netherlands Collection, II,6.
30. To his fellow SS men, Rauter commented that "Asiatic type Jews" sent to Mauthausen "died like flies in the fall." Rijksinstituut voor Oorlogsdocumentatie (ed.), *Het Process Rauter*, (The Hague, 1952), 37.
31. Seyss-Inquart, Speech on 12 March 1941, 37-66.
32. de Jong, Va, 551-65.
33. See J. Abel Herzberg, "Kroniek der Jodenvervolging," in J.J. van Bolhuis and C.D.J. Brandt (eds.), *Onderdrukking en Verzet: Nederlands in Oorlogstijd*, (Amsterdam, n.d.), III, 144-45; de Jong, Va, 550-53. For an examination of the importance of Zionism for Dutch Jewry see Jozeph Michman, "The Jewish Essence in Dutch Jewry," in his edited

work, *Dutch Jewish History*, Vol. II, (Van Gorcum et al., 1989), 1-22.
34. See J. Melkman, "De briefwisseling tussen mr. L.E. Visser en prof. dr. Cohen, *Studia Rosenthaliana*, (Vol. VIII, 1974), 107-30 and "The Controversial Stand of the *Joodse Raad* in the Netherlands," *Yad Vashem Studies* (Vol. X, 1974), 9-68.
35. K.P.L. Berkley, *Overzicht van het onstaan, de werkzaamheden en het streven van de Joodse Raad voor Amsterdam*, (Amsterdam, 1945), 15.
36. Presser, I, 135-202, and Herzberg 143-96. In 1942 the Jewish Council even took an ambivalent pride in its work. See Rene Kok, "Een foto reportage van de Joodsche Raad van Amsterdam," *Oorlogsdocumentatie '40-'45: Tweede jaarboek van het Rijksinstituut voor Oorlogsdocumentatie,* (Zutphen, 1990), 134-51.
37. Herzberg, 54-55.
38. Wielek, 129.
39. de Jong, 7a, 419-20.
40. B.A. Sijes, *Studies over jodenvervolging*, (Assen, 1974), 113.
41. Cited in Sijes, *Studies*, 67.
42. Ibid.
43. de Jong, 7a, 419-24.
44. Berkley, 53.
45. See Rauter to Himmler, 24 September 1942, in *Het Process Rauter*, 29-30.
46. Berkley, 82.
47. Presser, I, 237.
48. Etty Hillesum, *An Interrupted Life: The Diaries of Etty Hillesum 1941-1943*, (Trans. Arno Pomerans), New York, 1983, 61 et passim.
49. Presser, I, 154-59.
50. RIOD, Cohen, Memoirs, 61.
51. Hans Galesloot and Susan Legene, *Partij in het verzet: De CPN in de tweede wereldoorlog*, (Amsterdam, 1986), 128.
52. Presser, I, 229.
53. As cited in Wielek, 128.
54. RIOD, HSSPF, 114/185a, Seyss-Inquart to General Commissars et al., 25 November 1941.
55. Presser I, 233-55; Wielek, 140-41.
56. S. Stokman (ed.), *Het verzet van de nederlandsche Bisschoppen*, (Utrecht, 1945), Pastoral Letter of 20 July 1942, 249-51 and see 114-17.
57. RIOD, Cohen, Stukken von Overtuiging, 10 January 1949, 28.
58. *Het Joodsche Weekblad*, 7 August 1942.

59. RIOD, Cohen, Notes in his Defense, 11 November 1948, 70.
60. See Presser, I, 248-387.
61. See Jacob Boas, *Boulevard des Miseres: The Story of Transit Camp Westerbork* (Hamden, CT., 1985).
62. See the dates of trains, the number of deportees and destinations in *Documents of the Persecution of Dutch Jewry*, 115-22.
63. Philip Mechanicus, *In Depot: Dagboek uit Westerbork*, (Amsterdam: Polak and Van Gennep, 1964).
64. Boas, 50.
65. Herzberg, 161 and RIOD, Cohen, Stukken von Overtuiging, 10 January 1949, 47.
66. Berkley, 72.
67. Presser, I,439-47.
68. See Sijes, *Studies*, 141-42; Presser, I, 287-98 and RIOD, Cohen, DI 294c, Meyer de Vries in "Huldigung van prof. dr. Cohen" which contains testimonials for Cohen's sixtieth birthday on 31 January 1942.
69. de Jong, VIIa, 310-11; and see K.J. Frederiks, *Op de Bres*, (The Hague, 1945), 75.
70. RIOD, HSSPF, 113/183f, Rauter to Himmler, 2 March 1944, " The essential Jewish problem in Holland can be viewed as resolved."
71. See N.K.C.A. in'T Veld, *De SS in Nederland: documenteen uit SS Archiven 1935-1945*, (The Hague, 1976), I, 807.
72. See de Jong, passim and B.A. Sijes, *De arbeidsinzet: De gedwongen arbeid van Nederlanders in Duitsland 1940-1945*, (The Hague, 1966 and 1990), 208.
73. de Jong, VIa,348-51 and VIIa, 441 n., 472. See also Corrie ten Boom (with John and Elizabeth Sherrill), *The Hiding Place*, (New York, 1974) and Andre Stein, Quiet Heroes: *True Stories of the Rescue of Jews by Christians in Nazi-occupied Holland*, (New York, 1988).
74. RIOD, Cohen DI 294e, "How Holland Helped the Jews."
75. See Jerusalem, Yad Vashem, 01, Ball-Kaduri Collection, 115, "Vom Ringen des hollaendischen Hechaluz."
76. See P.J. Bouwman, *De April-Mei stakingen*, (The Hague, 1950).
77. See Yad Vashem, Eichmann Trial, #589, Zoepf to RSHA, IVB4, 27 April 1943.
78. RIOD, Cohen, DI 294e, Postal analyses sent to the Jewish Council on 4 December 1942 and 12 April 1943.
79. RIOD, HSSPF, 111/118A, "Entwicklung der Judenfrage in Niederlanden" (bis zum Jahreswende 1942).

80. Yad Vashem, Eichmann Trial, #725, Bene to Foreign Office in Berlin, 25 June 1943.
81. See Leni Yahil, "Methods of Persecution: A Comparison of the 'Final Solution' in Holland and Denmark," in Marrus, Vol. 4, 189-90; and J.C.H. Blom, "The Persecution of the Jews in the Netherlands in a Comparative International Perspective," in Michman, *Dutch Jewish History*, II, 273-89.
82. Judith Miller's conclusion that "Holland's record during the war is ... appalling" stems less from an evaluation of the historic context than from an isolated review of statistics. Her description of the country as filled with a "collective sense of shame over the destruction of the Jews" seems to contradict her view that the Dutch value the hiding of Ann Frank as general absolution of responsibility. She rightly notes the rich literature dealing with these problems--especially the treasury of works produced by the RIOD, the Netherlands State Institute for War Documentation, under the aegis of Louis de Jong and his colleagues,--but her journalistic chapter on Holland does not analyze this extensive historiography and its continuous attempt to sensitize the present generation to the horrors of the occupation. See her publication, *One by One by One: Facing the Holocaust*, (New York et al., 1990), 93-111. For a more insightful view see Henriette Boas, "Commemorating the Holocaust in Holland: Positive and Negative Aspects," in Michman, *Dutch Jewish History*, II, 309-21.
83. The situation in the Netherlands confirms Michael Marruses conclusion, "In the implementation of the Final Solution, the crucial factor was always the extent to which the Nazis determined to do the job." See his work, *The Holocaust in History*, (Hanover and London: University Press of New England, 1987), 57.

The Impact of the Holocaust on Herbert Hoover

Rafael Medoff

Sympathy for refugees formed the cornerstone of Herbert Hoover's public life. Hoover successfully organized relief efforts for the tens of thousands of American nationals who were trapped in Europe by the outbreak of World War I. He subsequently led the massive campaign to feed the population of German-occupied Belgium, paving the way for his appointment, in 1917, as U.S. Food Administrator, a post that ultimately paved his way to the White House.

It may be presumed that Hoover's occasional contacts with Jewish refugee matters during those years encouraged his sympathy for the establishment of a Jewish national home in Palestine, although he displayed no special interest in the plight of Jewish refugees, and his support for Zionism was passive.

An episode involving Polish Jewish pogrom victims in 1919 illustrates the limited impact that such incidents had on Hoover's thinking. Familiar from his Belgium experience with the unreliability of wartime atrocity stories, Hoover responded with skepticism when the local press (he was based in Paris at the time) reported a massacre in Poland of fifty Jews. His doubts multiplied after he "sent one of our staff to investigate and found there was really not much truth in the story"; nonetheless, Hoover decided, some sort of further U.S. action was necessary because stories about the pogroms "still raged in the American press and began to threaten our relief work." He therefore persuaded President Woodrow Wilson to establish a commission to investigate the matter. The three-man commission, which was headed by the former U.S. ambassador to Turkey, Henry Morgenthau, documented eight separate anti-Jewish outbreaks that took place in Poland between November 1918 and August 1919, in which a total of 280 Jews were said to have been murdered. Despite the commission's findings, Hoover's initial skepticism seems to have remained unshaken. Years later, in his memoirs, Hoover still claimed that the commission "did a fine service by exposing falsity."[1] It may be that Hoover paid less attention to the facts of the violence than to the "mitigating circumstances" cited by the commission, such as the absence of premeditation; the involvement of only "uncontrolled troops or local mobs," rather than government-authorized forces; and the Poles' irritation over what they perceived as "the 'alien' character" of the Jews, a perception allegedly reinforced by the fact that the Jews "speak a language of their own" (the reference is to Yiddish) which was derived from German--and Germany "still is looked upon by the Poles as an enemy country."[2] In any event, the significance of the episode for the present study lies in Hoover's evident failure to regard the Jewish pogrom victims as requiring any extraordinary solution to their troubles.

The same may be said for Hoover's reaction in August 1929, when Palestinian Arabs massacred 59 Jews in Hebron. Declining to take any specific political action on the Palestine question, Hoover issued a statement--which was read aloud at a Zionist protest rally in New York--declaring his "profound sympathy with those who have been bereaved and who have suffered through these disturbances." The "immediate and pressing question," Hoover asserted, "is the relief to those who are suffering," and he therefore recommended to all Americans that Palestine relief efforts "should receive the most generous support." Political intervention, however, was out of the question; Hoover was not prepared to step on the toes of the British, who, he said, had already taken "vigorous action" and thereby "restored a large measure of protection" to Palestine and Jewry.[3]

It was only with the rise of Nazism that Hoover's approach to the Jewish question was slowly transformed from passive sympathy to active intervention. The change was not evident during the first years of the Hitler regime, however. Strongly opposed both to any American interference in European conflicts and to increased immigration to the United States, Hoover was not inclined to lead the rhetorical charge against Germany. Domestic political affairs occupied most of Hoover's attention. He was an outspoken critic of the Roosevelt Administration's New Deal policies, and devoted much of his time to exploring the possibility of seeking the 1936 Republican presidential nomination.

Hoover's reluctance to advocate specific American action on behalf of Europe's Jews persisted during the years leading up to World War II. This is not to suggest that Hoover was indifferent to the plight of Hitler's victims. Indeed, shortly after Germany's absorption of Austria, in March 1938, Hoover specifically denounced "the heart-breaking persecution of helpless Jews," and he, the former president, included "persecution of Jews" as one of the seven "forces or factors" that had made for "an alarming and disheartening picture" of life in Europe. Yet in the same address, Hoover emphasized that "I am not here tonight to tell governments or nations abroad what they should do. It is not the right of any American to advise foreign peoples as to their policies."[4] Later that year, Hoover denounced the Kristallnacht pogrom as "an outbreak of brutal intolerance which has no parallel in modern history," but he again refrained from urging concrete U.S. action on behalf of German Jewry.[5]

Hoover's position on the German Jewish situation was consistent with his conviction that the U.S. should refrain from any steps that could drag it into a conflict with Germany. He criticized the Lend-Lease Act for edging America towards war, and feared that if Roosevelt's proposal for American convoying of arms shipments to Great Britain was accepted, "we shall be at war the moment our Navy is put into action."[6] Considering the charged atmosphere that enveloped the prewar debate between isolationists and interventionists, it is no surprise that Hoover was sometimes assumed to be part and parcel of the extreme isolationist camp, and the cheers that greeted the mention of his name by a speaker at a pro-Nazi rally in New York's Madison Square Garden in 1939 could only have served to underline that perception.[7] Hoover's suggestion that Americans with "old, diverse national origins and sympathies, with their conscious or unconscious propagandas" might encourage the U.S. towards wars based on "old world ideologies" inflamed Stephen Wise, who as president of the American Jewish Congress, co-chairman of the World Jewish Congress, and longtime leader of the Zionist Organization of America, was arguably the most important Jewish leader of the era. Wise charged that any American who dismissed the German annexation of Austria as the product of "old world ideologies" "has ceased to be an American."[8] Unlike the hardline isolationists, however, Hoover favored the provision of American arms to England.[9] Furthermore, he refused to join the America First movement, whose ranks, he acknowledged, included many unsavory "extremists."[10]

Hoover departed most dramatically from the political line of the America First group when he publicly endorsed the 1939 Wagner-Rogers bill to admit 20,000 German refugee children into the United States.[11] Hoover's stand on Wagner-Rogers marked the first time that his sympathy for Jewish victims of Hitler had translated into a recommendation for substantive U.S. action on their behalf. Hoover was no doubt aware of the political risks inherent in favoring increased refugee immigration; he still entertained hopes of being drafted as the 1940 Republican presidential nominee, and public opposition to immigration was overwhelming. Silence on Wagner-Rogers would have been the politically prudent course of action. Yet the torrent of reports about Nazi atrocities against the Jews aroused Hoover's humanitarian instincts and compelled him to brush aside ordinary political considerations.

At the same time, Hoover was involved in behind-the-scenes discussions with Bernard Baruch, the financier and Roosevelt confidante, about the idea of creating a homeland for European Jewish refugees in an African region comprising portions of Tanganyika, Belgian Congo, Kenya, and northern Rhodesia. Convinced that the region was blessed with a soil and climate "upon which ten to twenty millions of white civilization could be [sic] builded," Hoover volunteered to help organize the new country's transport, communications, and development of its natural resources.[12]

Hoover's interest in a Central African homeland for the Jews did not constitute a repudiation of his previous expressions of support for Zionism. As president he had praised the Zionist development of Palestine as an "inspiring enterprise" and declared his hope that "the steady rehabilitation of the [sic] Palestine" would result in the establishment of "a homeland so long desired by the Jews."[13] Yet Hoover was also well aware of the intense Palestinian Arab opposition to Zionism, which had been manifest during his term office in the Hebron massacre, and had found expression since then in numerous other waves of anti-Jewish (and anti-British) violence. Arab protests had influenced the British to whittle down their original promise to facilitate the creation of a Jewish national home in Palestine; on May 15, 1939, London issued a White Paper that severely restricted Jewish immigration for the next five years--precisely the period of greatest Jewish need. Hence the suffering of Jews in Europe and the inaccessibility of Palestine constituted, in Hoover's view, "an immediate call," and an African homeland would be "aid to those who are today evicted."[14]

Hoover's reasoning mirrored that of the "territorialists" of the early Zionist movement--Theodor Herzl most prominent among them--who at the Zionist Congress in 1903 argued that the anti-Jewish pogroms in Czarist Russia and the political difficulties involved in gaining Jewish access to Palestine necessitated the establishment of a temporary Jewish refuge in what today comprises Uganda. Proponents of the Uganda plan maintained that they were not permanently abandoning Zion, but simply seeking a *nachtasyl*, "shelter for a night," for oppressed Russian Jews.[15] For the Uganda faction in 1903, as for Hoover in 1939, Palestine remained the long range goal.

In any event, the Hoover-Baruch plan failed to impress Great Britain, the colonial ruler of the territories in question. When Hoover aide Lewis Strauss arrived in London in July 1939 to promote the plan, he was surprised to discover that it had already received "the kiss of death from some quarter"; Strauss blamed Joseph P. Kennedy, the U.S. ambassador to Britain, who he knew to be "unsympathetic to the [Jewish refugee] problem." The British government officials with whom Strauss conferred came armed with reports denigrating the feasibility of the project. "London seethes with schemes," Strauss reported to Hoover, and the Central Africa project was being taken no more seriously than other proposals to settle a few thousand Jews on "a plantation in Brazil" or to send Jews to "the swamps of the upper Nile in the Sudan where no human life, white or black, exists."[16] Until a more convincing plan for helping the Jews presented itself, however, Hoover stood by the Central Africa proposal. He reiterated the idea at a fundraising dinner for European Jewish refugees that was held in Chicago in February, 1940,[17] and he was apparently still enamored of the scheme in 1943 when, after a three year interval, the 'Jewish question' once again attracted his active attention.

A look at Hoover's agenda during the years 1940-1943 helps clarify his failure to speak out about the suffering of the Jews during that crucial period in which the Nazi persecutions were transformed from sporadic atrocities to organized genocide. During 1940 and 1941, Hoover lobbied actively against American participation in the European war, labored to smooth the way for a deadlocked Republican convention to choose him as its presidential nominee, and--most significant for the purposes of the present study--spearheaded efforts to provide food and clothing to the populations of Finland (occupied by the Soviets), the Low Countries (occupied by the Nazis) and Poland (divided between the two). Hoover's Commission for Polish Relief and its expanded version, the National Committee on Food for the Democracies, found their activities obstructed by Allied regulations barring commerce with enemy-occupied territory; but had they succeeded, they might have brought a significant measure of relief to the Jewish communities of those countries. Ever the man of practical action, Hoover preferred sending a starving Polish refugee a food parcel to making eloquent but toothless speeches about the suffering of Hitler's victims. He regarded "getting food to them before they die" as the best way to help the suffering Jews.[18]

When America entered the war, Hoover stepped back from the public limelight and undertook a variety of literary endeavors, including three volumes of memoirs and a history of U.S.-Soviet relations. He spent much of the first half of 1942 collaborating with Hugh Gibson, the former U.S. ambassador to Belgium, on *The Problems of Lasting Peace*, an analysis of postwar international relations that proved to be a bestseller. Whatever information Hoover may have been receiving during 1942 about the plight of the Jews of Europe, it does not seem to have been startling enough to distract him from his intensive literary pursuits. If one of his primary sources was the daily press, his ignorance is all the more understandable. As Deborah Lipstadt has shown, even after confirmed reports about the Nazi genocide reached American newsmen in the summer of 1942, the American press "did not highlight this news and often omitted from its reports key pieces of information or burdened them with various disclaimers." Those newspapers that did publish Holocaust news "placed the various stories on inner pages and allotted them but a few lines. Consequently, readers were left free to accept this news as valid or to dismiss it as unverified information in which the paper had little faith."[19]

Still, had Hoover been approached by American Jewish leaders for a statement about the intensified persecution of European Jewry, it seems likely that he would have assented; he certainly had not hesitated to speak out on previous occasions when his sympathy was solicited. The failure of Jewish organizations to seek Hoover's aid on the issue during 1941-1942 may be attributed in part to simple political considerations. A fervent Democrat like Stephen Wise, with his antipathy for Republicans in general and the experience of his 1940 clash with Hoover in particular, was not likely to make contact with the former president. In any event, an appeal to Hoover would have gone against the grain of the prevailing political approach of most Jewish leaders. The contemporary Jewish political strategy of seeking the support of congressmen or other politicians to counter the policies of the administration was not commonly utilized during the Holocaust years. Thus when Roosevelt Administration officials asked Wise, in September 1942, to temporarily suppress information regarding the Nazi annihilation campaign, Wise did not turn to senators or former presidents for help; he simply complied with the request.[20]

The one Jewish organization that finally did seek Hoover's aid during the Holocaust, the New Zionist Organization of America (NZOA), was not part of the mainstream U.S. Jewish leadership, but was, rather, a small militant group that had no particular affinity for the Democratic administration and no compunctions about wooing Roosevelt's political rivals. The NZOA was the U.S. wing of the Revisionist Zionist movement, which broke from the World Zionist Organization in 1935 to pursue more aggressive methods of countering Arab violence and pressuring the British Mandatory authorities to facilitate the establishment of a Jewish state. In early 1943, the NZOA created a front group[21] the rather cumbersome name of the "American Resettlement Committee for Uprooted European Jewry" (ARC). Its executive director was Eliahu Ben-Horin, Russian-born journalist who had lived in Palestine for some years before imigrating to the United States in 1940. Ben-Horin probably played a seminal role in the creation of the ARC; the political ideas expressed in the book he had just written, *The Middle East: Crossroads of History*, were almost identical with those of the new organization.

The significance of Ben-Horin's book and the ARC platform lay in their radical new understanding of the relationship between the European Jewish crisis and the Arab-Jewish conflict over Palestine. The traditional position of the Revisionist Zionist movement was that the Jewish historical right to the Holy Land, combined with the immediate needs of persecuted Jews in the Diaspora, necessitated the establishment of a Jewish state in all of Mandatory Palestine. According to this scenario, the Palestinian Arabs would remain in the country as equal citizens of the Jewish state, although they would be reduced to a minority status by virtue of the mass immigration of Jews from Europe and elsewhere. In the wake of the Nazi persecutions, however, Ben-Horin became convinced that this optimistic forecast for peaceful Arab-Jewish coexistence in a single country would not be realized.

In a May 10, 1943 letter to Hoover, Ben-Horin asked the former president to become Honorary President of the Resettlement Committee. To the letter he attached a twelve-page memorandum detailing the group's platform. Jewish life in Europe had long since become untenable, the memorandum argued. Centuries of economic discrimination against Europe's Jews had "foredoomed them to extinction," and the Nazis "accelerated this process" by forcing millions of Jews "into ghettoes and reservations, and cutting them off entirely from any possibility of earning their daily bread." Now, unless a "haven of refuge" were to be found, "millions of Jews under Nazi domination are doomed to extermination." Reconstruction of Europe's devastated Jewish communities was economically impossible and would probably arouse "a terrific wave of anti-Semitism." Massive emigration, then, was the only feasible solution. Where should they go? Sending the emigrants to various countries would result in "the implanting of anti-Semitism" in those lands, and in any event would be "quantitatively impossible." America could not be their destination, since, "we may be certain, (it) will tighten the immigration laws, and further raise the barriers around this country." Most other projected emigration sites had never reached the stage of serious consideration; the memorandum listed thirteen such failures, including the African areas that Hoover had promoted. The only two that had advanced further than the drawing-board, Birobidjan (a region in the eastern Soviet Union) and the Dominican Republic, had proven to be economic "fiascos."

Palestine, then, was the sole solution, according to the memorandum. As the ancient Jewish homeland, it was "natural" that Jewish refugees go there; the Zionist colonization effort had proven itself to be "a remarkable success"; Palestine's Jews had expressed their "unreserved willingness" to welcome European Jewish refugees; and by sending Jewish refugees to Palestine, anti-Semitism would diminish in those countries where they might otherwise have settled.

The significant new point that the ARC made was in its final argument: "Should the Palestinian Arabs persist in their objection to and obstruction of Jewish settlement in Palestine, a sound plan for the transfer of the Palestinian Arabs to Iraq could be evolved." In addition to clearing Palestine for Jews fleeing Hitler, such a population transfer would be "highly beneficial" to both Iraq and the Palestinian Arab emigrants themselves, the memorandum claimed, although it did not elaborate. Interestingly, the ARC buttressed its argument for transferring Arabs from Palestine by citing a passage from Hoover and Gibson's *The Problems of Lasting Peace*, in which the authors argued that in various countries, "the problem of mixed border peoples" could be resolved "by the heroic remedy of transfer of populations," which, while involving "great hardship," was preferable to "the constant suffering of minorities and the constant recurrence of war" (provoked by ethnic conflicts involving "mixed border peoples" such as the Sudeten Germans).[22] The Hoover-Gibson passage does not seem to have been inserted in the ARC memo solely to impress Hoover; Ben-Horin had previously included it in his own book, and it is likely that it was included in the composition of the ARC paper long before Hoover was targeted by the group.[23]

Hoover was intrigued by Ben-Horin's proposal. It was rooted in humanitarian concerns that he shared, and went beyond mere platitudes by formulating a concrete, if unorthodox, plan of action for obtaining a Jewish refugee haven. In a letter to George Sokolsky, a journalist who was friendly with Hoover and served on the ARC's National Committee, Hoover set forth some of his objections and posed a variety of questions about the ARC platform. He complained, first of all, that the ARC activists had "throw(n) overboard" his Central Africa plan simply because it did not satisfy "their ideas of nationality." Hoover also seemed concerned by the company he might be keeping if he linked up with the ARC; he was struck by the absence of "any of the prominent Jews" from the organization's list of officers as well as by the presence of "many of the people" who had "opposed my every effort" to organize food shipments to Europe--evidently a reference to individuals who had supported the Roosevelt Administration's view that such food shipments would constitute unwarranted trafficking with enemy-occupied countries. On the other hand, Hoover pointed out to Sokolsky, he had always been "Both sympathetic and aroused over the present situation of the Jews in Europe"; he had merely believed "that getting some food to them before they die was more important than movements which can only be eventuated after the war is over." The decisive question for Hoover was one of practicality. How could a small organization like the Resettlement Committee "move Arabs out of Palestine"? "(I)s that not too great a job for anybody but governments?" Or was it the ARC's intention "simply to work quietly for a defined purpose to be eventuated at peace," that is, to circulate its proposal in the hope that it would be taken up by the victorious powers at a postwar peace conference?[24]

His hopes buoyed by Hoover's evident interest in the ARC, Ben-Horin quickly composed a reply intended to soothe the expresident's concerns. The ARC would be happy to further "study" the Central Africa plan, Ben-Horin wrote; the absence of "prominent Jews" was no loss, since such Jews were "protagonists of assimilationism" who were "unfit" for the Zionist cause; and temporary "relief" measures" such as food shipments were no substitute for "a permanent solution" to the crisis. As for the actual work of the Resettlement Committee, Ben-Horin envisioned two phases, the first consisting of "research, propaganda, publications and mapping plans," while the second would involve the actual financing of European Jewish settlement in Palestine.[25]

On the same day that Ben-Horin was writing his reply to Hoover (via Sokolsky, their intermediary), Hoover wrote a short note responding directly to Ben-Horin's original letter. He raised a new objection to the ARC plan: the debilitating conflicts between various organizations within the American Jewish community. So long as the war continued, Hoover wrote, proposals such as Ben-Horin's would be a source of "division and conflict" among American Jews. "(T)he different organizations seem to be busy trying to destroy each other," and Hoover was in no mood to become entangled in such battles. Yet the letter was never mailed; instead, Hoover jotted a note to his secretary across the top of the typed draft: "Sokolsky could make an appointment--do not send."[26] Hoover's appointments calendar shows that he did indeed meet Ben-Horin for a half hour on June 2.[27] Ben-Horin's follow-up note to Hoover is the only source of information as to the content of their conversation. It describes the expresident as having shown "interest, good will and desire to help." Hoover expressed unspecified "hesitations" about being able to "find his way in the labyrinth of Jewish realities"--probably a reference to his concerns about Jewish in-fighting. Hoover also stated his intention to discuss the subject with his friend Arthur Hays Sulzberger, publisher of the *New York Times*. Finally, according to the note, Hoover agreed to read over the galley proofs to Ben-Horin's book, *The Middle East: Crossroads of History*.[28]

Hoover's reply to Ben-Horin's note reiterated his mixed feelings. While wanting "very much to be helpful in what I regard as one of the most dreadful of human tragedies in history and one of the worst managed by statesmen," Hoover believed that only "at a later time . . . if we could bring the factions together," would the time be right "for me to enter the picture."

Yet Hoover could not quite bring himself to end his letter on such a disappointing note. Instead, he restated his cognizance of "the great strain you are under, the urgent and poignant problems which must haunt your mind," and, reaffirming his desire "to be of help to you and . . . to work with you," Hoover offered that "we can have another talk" when he returned from his forthcoming trip to California.[29] When Hoover returned to New York two weeks later, he received another letter from Ben-Horin, this time proposing that they discuss the subject with an assortment of twenty politicians, journalists, authors, and congressmen, most of them members of the ARC Executive Committee, at a dinner in the Waldorf-Astoria (where Hoover was living) "at any date suitable to you."[30] This time Hoover's demurral was more decisive. He was on his way to the West Coast again, he wrote; but instead of proposing a mutually convenient date, he urged Ben-Horin to "go ahead with the others," that is, hold the dinner without him. Ben-Horin's purpose in arranging the dinner, of course, had been to secure Hoover's participation in the Resettlement Committee; his reply effectively put an end to Ben-Horin's lobbying efforts. It was no doubt of small consolation to Ben-Horin that Hoover concluded his letter by praising *The Middle East: Crossroads to History* as "a much needed job."[31]

Ben-Horin's initial contacts with Hoover had ended in utter failure from the point of view of the ARC, but for Hoover the discussions marked something of a turning point in his approach to the Jewish crisis. Ben-Horin's innovative association of the European Jewish refugee problem with the idea of encouraging Arab emigration from Palestine meshed two crucial ingredients of Hoover's social philosophy: humanitarianism and engineering. Hoover's remarkable mining successes in far flung regions, from Australia to the Orient, earned him an international reputation as "the Great Engineer" during the early 1900's. His subsequent organization of civilian relief efforts during the First World War won him fame as a friend to the downtrodden, paving the way for his entry into government service and eventually the presidency. When Ben-Horin presented him with a plan that utilized engineering--a mass transfer of population--to effect a humanitarian goal--the creation of a haven for millions of refugees--Hoover's interest was naturally aroused. Although the former president declined to head the Resettlement Committee, Ben-Horin's influence was evident in Hoover's subsequent statements regarding the Holocaust and Palestine.

In a July 25 radio address to a New York conference on the plight of Europe's Jews, Hoover presented his latest ideas on what he called "a great human problem." Both interim and long range measures were necessary, he said. Those refugees who had already escaped to neutral countries should immediately be granted haven in "definite refugee stations" there, while at the same time efforts would be made to transfer them to "other quarters." Furthermore, the quick dispatching of food shipments "would save the lives of thousands of Jews." In formulating a long range solution, Hoover continued, it was necessary to accept the fact that mass migration to "the older and more fully settled countries" was impossible because they "have no longer any land and opportunity" to offer (the similarity between this point and the argument made in the ARC memorandum may not have been a coincidence). Palestine could absorb Jewish refugees, once the way was made clear "by moving the Arab population to some other quarter." But Hoover saw two problems with regard to Palestine: it was capable of holding "only a part of the three or four millions" in need of refuge, and the Arab issue was "impossible to settle during the war." In the meantime, therefore, Central Africa remained the ideal location for the carefully-engineered creation of "an outlet for the persecuted of all lands and all faiths, not Jew alone." From the Jewish point of view, Hoover suggested, the African haven "could be considered sentimentally an annex to Palestine."[32]

By mid-summer, Hoover had all but abandoned the Central Africa scheme. At an August 6 meeting in San Francisco with American Zionist leader Louis Levinthal, Hoover stated definitively that the Palestinian Arabs should be "evacuated to other countries in the Near East," although he did not specify which countries he had in mind. The "evacuation" "cannot be voluntary, but must be compulsory, imposed by the British or the United Nations." Hoover mentioned the Central Africa idea only in the context of employing it as a ruse to facilitate the Arab transfer plan: "he said," according to Levinthal's account, "that Britain will be so fearful about being required to give up the very rich Tanganyika area, that it will much prefer to make a real Jewish State of Palestine, and will even force the Arabs to evacuate to the Arab countries, investing the necessary funds to develop these undeveloped lands so as to receive the Arabs from Palestine."[33]

Hoover's July 25 radio address and his August 6 conversation with Louis Levinthal contained the kernels of the last two ideas that would eventually crystallize into his own formal proposal for solving the Palestine problem. He believed that no transfer of the Arabs could be accomplished during the war, and he expected that funds would have to be invested in undeveloped parts of the Arab world in order to make those areas inhabitable for Arab emigrants from Palestine. Indeed, that was precisely how matters then evolved: shortly after the war concluded, Hoover began thinking about a Palestine solution linked to Western-financed development of Arab lands.

In October, 1945, Ben-Horin, now a staff member of the American Zionist Emergency Council (a coalition of the four major U.S. Zionist organizations), asked Hoover for a general statement endorsing the Zionist goal of a Jewish state. Hoover surprised Ben-Horin by expressing his desire to issue a statement calling for "a transfer of Palestine's *fellaheen* [Arab peasants] to Iraq."[34] Hoover spent the next two weeks poring over fifteen books and an assortment of articles--many of them provided by Ben-Horin--related to the feasibility of agricultural development in Iraq.[35]

The final product of Hoover's studies, issued on November 19 in the form of a 400-word press release, outlined what the former president called "a solution by engineering instead of by conflict" for the Palestine controversy. In view of the need for "settling the Palestine question and providing ample Jewish refuge," Hoover wrote, the time had come for the victorious Allies to finance the development of Iraq's Tigris and Euphrates river valleys "on the consideration that [they] be made the scene of resettlement of the Arabs from Palestine." Thus the Palestinian Arabs would be given land that was "more fertile" than Palestine's, and they "would be among their own race which is Arabic speaking and Mohammedan"; Iraq would gain because "it badly needs agricultural population"; and Palestine would be clear "for a large Jewish emigration and colonization."[36] All sides would profit, Hoover believed. Not everyone agreed; Iraqi newspapers denounced Hoover's plan as "devilish," the Allies ignored it altogether, and within a short time the proposal had faded from public view.[37]

There can be no doubt that the Holocaust was the major impetus in the transformation of Hoover's stand on the Palestine issue. The persecution of Jews in Germany during the 1930's was the major reason for Hoover's original interest in the creation of a refugee haven in Central Africa. The reports of intensified persecution in 1943 compelled Hoover to reconsider his previous resistance to Palestine as a refuge. During the spring and summer of 1945, Hoover, like many Americans, finally grasped the enormity of the Holocaust as newsreel footage of the liberated Nazi death camps and firsthand reports from returning soldiers provided graphic confirmation of the horrifying events that had transpired in Nazi-occupied Europe. When Hoover made reference to the problem of "providing ample Jewish refuge" in the very first sentence of his November 1945 plan for Palestine, he certainly must have been thinking about the hundreds of thousands of Holocaust survivors then languishing in Displaced Persons camps. For Hoover it was, first and foremost, the unprecedented suffering of the Jews that necessitated the establishment of a Jewish Palestine; Arab claims to the territory would have to give way to the unique needs of the persecuted Jews. Yet Hoover the engineer required a practical plan of action just as much as Hoover the humanitarian was moved by the persecution of innocents. The mass transfer of Palestinian Arabs to a newly-irrigated Iraq precisely suited Hoover's lifelong predilection for (in the words of the historian Joan Hoff-Wilson) "view[ing] world peace as more of an economic than a political problem."[38]

NOTES

1. *The Memoirs of Herbert Hoover: Years of Adventure 1874-1920* (New York: MacMillan, 1951), 357-358; "Paderewski Asks American Inquiry," *New York Times* (hereafter NYT), June 2, 1919, 1.
2. "Fixes Blame For Polish Pogroms," NYT, January 19, 1920, 6.
3. Hoover to Zionist Organization of America, August 29, 1929, Presidential Papers-Foreign Affairs (hereafter PPFA): Countries-Palestine, Herbert Hoover Presidential Library (hereafter HHPL), West Branch, Iowa; Naomi W. Cohen, *The Year After the Riots* (Detroit: Wayne State University Press, 1988), 48.
4. Herbert Hoover, *Addresses Upon the American Road: 1933-1938* (New York: Charles Scribner's Sons, 1938), 309, 312, 317.
5. "Texts of the Protests by Leaders in U.S. Against Reich Persecution," NYT, November 15, 1938, 4.
6. "Text of Hoover Speech Opposing Convoying Ships to Britain," NYT, May 12, 1941, 4.
7. "22,000 Nazis Hold Rally In Garden; Police Check Foes," NYT, February 21, 1939, 1. For Hoover's disavowal of the Nazi cheers, see "Hoover Sees Peril of 'Five Horsemen'," NYT, February 24, 1939, 1.
8. "Peace Rally Hears Attack On Clergy," NYT, April 5, 1938, 11; Hoover, *Address upon the American Road: 1933-1938*, 301.
9. See, for example, "Text of Hoover Speech . . .," op.cit.
10. Hoover to Walter H. Newton, May 20, 1941, cited in Richard Norton Smith, *An Uncommon Man: The Triumph of Herbert Hoover* (New York: Simon and Schuster, 1984), 298.
11. "Hoover Backs Bill To Waive Quota Act For Reich Children," NYT, April 23, 1939, 1.
12. Lewis L. Strauss, *Men and Decisions* (Garden City, NY: Doubleday, 1962), 113-116; Henry Feingold, *The Politics of Rescue* (New Brunswick, NJ: Rutgers University Press, 190), 102-109.
13. Hoover to Zionist Organization of America, August 29, 1929, Foreign Affairs: Countries-Palestine, HHPL.
14. "Hoover Envisions Refuge To 10 Million," NYT, February 12, 1940, 3.
15. For a full discussion of the controversy, see Robert G. Weisbord, *African Zion* (Philadelphia: Jewish Publication Society of America, 1968).
16. Memo, Strauss to Hoover, August 22, 1939, Post-Presidential Individual (hereafter PPI): Strauss, Lewis, HHPL.

17. "Hoover Envisions . . .," op.cit.
18. Hoover to Sokolsky, May 12, 1943, PPI-Sokolsky, George, HHPL.
19. Deborah E. Lipstadt, *Beyond Belief: The American Press & the Coming of the Holocaust 1933-1945* (New York: The Free Press, 1986), 163-164.
20. Monty Noam Penkower, *The Jews Were Expendable* (Urban, Ill: University of Illinois Press, 1983), 59-97.
21. The ARC seemed to waver between pretending to be separate from the Revisionists and admitting that it was a Revisionist front. Neither the ARC's stationery nor the full-page advertisement that it placed in the *New York Times* in October 1943, made mention of a Revisionist connection. Yet the address of its "office" was that of NZOA headquarters in New York, the majority of its officers were publicly-known leaders of the NZOA, and the NZOA's journal, *Zionews*, unabashedly referred to the ARC as having been "organized" by the NZOA. (See "Resettlement Committee Launched," *Zionews* 4 [September-October 1943], 3.)
22. Ben-Horin to Hoover, May 10, 1943, and "Memorandum for the Hon. Herbert Hoover on the American Resettlement Committee for Uprooted European Jewry" (12 pp), PPI-Ben-Horin, Eliahu, HHPL.
23. Eliahu Ben-Horin, *The Middle East: Crossroads of History* (New York: W.W.Norton, 1943), 231. Years later, Ben-Horin told Gibson that the entire section in The Middle East that detailed his Palestine-Iraq transfer plan had been "largely inspired" by the "heroic remedy" passages in *The Problems of Lasting Peace*; that claim, however, cannot be verified. (See Ben-Horin to Gibson, June 11, 1952, PPI-Ben-Horin, Eliahu, HHPL).
24. Hoover to Sokolsky, May 12, 1943, PPI-Sokolsky, George, HHPL.
25. Ben-Horin to Sokolsky, May 15, 1943, PPI-Ben-Horin, Eliahu, HHPL.
26. Hoover to Ben-Horin, May 15, 1943, PPI-Ben-Horin, Eliahu, HHPL.
27. Calendar: May-June 1943, HHPL.
28. Ben-Horin to Hoover, June 3, 1943, PPI-Ben-Horin, Eliahu, HHPL.
29. Hoover to Ben-Horin, June 8, 1943, PPI-Ben-Horin, Eliahu, HHPL.
30. Ben-Horin to Hoover, June 22, 1943, PPI-Ben-Horin, Eliahu, HHPL.
31. Hoover to Ben-Horin, June 25, 1943, PPI-Ben-Horin, Eliahu, HHPL.
32. "President Pledges Aid To Save Jews," NYT, July 26, 1943, 19.
33. Levinthal to "Arthur," August 6, 1943, Harold Manson Papers, The Temple, Cleveland, Ohio; Levinthal to Hoover, September 20, 1943, Post-Presidential Subject (hereafter PPS)-Jews, Public Statement 2773, HHPL.

34. "A Brick for the Bridge" (manuscript of the unpublished autobiography of Eliahu Ben-Horin), 184, Eliahu Ben-Horin collection, Metzudat Ze'ev (Jabotinsky Institute), Tel Aviv.
35. Ben-Horin to Hoover, November 1, 1945, PPS-Jewish-Zionist, HHPL; Ben-Horin to Hoover, November 13, 1945, PPS-Jewish-Zionist, HHPL; Hoover to Ben-Horin, November 14, 1945, PPS-Jewish-Zionist, HHPL. In a conversation the following February, Hoover reportedly said that he read "at least thirty other books on Palestine and Iraq before arriving at his conclusions." Fifteen would seem to be a more realistic figure, unless the "thirty" refers to books read during the months (or years) prior to October 1945. (See "Memorandum No. 30--Strictly Confidential," Epstein to Members of the Executive, The Jewish Agency for Palestine, February 19, 1946, z6/2272, Central Zionist Archives, Jerusalem.
36. "Hoover Urges Resettling Arabs To Solve Palestine Problem," *New York World-Telegram*, November 19, 1945, 1.
37. Ben-Horin to Hoover, November 27, 1945, PPS-Jewish-Zionist, HHPL.
38. Joan Hoff-Wilson, "A Reevaluation of Herbert Hoover's Foreign Policy," in Martin L. Fausold, Ed., *The Hoover Presidency: A Reappraisal* (Albany, NY: State University of New York Press, 1974), 166.

Bureaucracy and the "Jewish Question" in Prewar Nazi Germany: The Nuremberg Legislation of 1935 as a Case Study

Howard Margolian

From the moment of its inception, the Nazi party was committed to the denaturalization of German Jewry and to their segregation from so-called "Aryan" Germans.[1] Accordingly, the enactment of the Nuremberg Race Laws in November 1935 represented the culmination of NSDAP efforts to reverse decades of German-Jewish emancipation. Short of deportation, little more could have been done from a statutory point of view after 1935 to remove the Jews from the mainstream of German life. That the Nuremberg Laws therefore constituted a watershed in Nazi *Judenpolitik* (Jewish policy) was acknowledged by no less an authority than Hitler himself. Addressing the session of the Reichstag at which the new initiatives were announced, the Führer ominously referred to the legislation as "an attempt to regulate by law a problem that, in the event of repeated failure, would have to be transferred . . . to the National Socialist Party for final solution."[2]

Despite Hitler's intimation that the state had reached the end of its anti-Semitic competency in November 1935, subsequent scholarship has taken the opposite view. Citing the interior ministry's expertise in key matters relating to the "Jewish Question," its lead role in drafting the Nuremberg Laws, and its creation of a privileged (by Nazi standards) category of persons of Jewish descent--the part-Jewish *Mischlinge*--historians have tended to characterize the year 1935 as the dawn, rather than the twilight, of the bureaucratization of the Holocaust.[3] In view of the discrepancy between historiographical and contemporary interpretations, the purpose of this paper is two-fold. First, the paper provides a much-needed reassessment of the interior ministry's specific contributions to the conception, promulgation, and implementation of the

Nuremberg Laws. Second, it serves as a case study of bureaucratic complicity in the Final Solution.

Between 1933 and 1935, statutory *Judenpolitik* fell almost exclusively under the jurisdiction of the Reich interior ministry. Issues such as German-Jewish citizenship and "race relations" occasionally were handled by other Reich departments, but the work of all responsible agencies was channelled through the office of Bernhard Lösener, the interior ministry's in-house "Jewish expert."[4] Supervised by Hans Pfundtner, the ministry's secretary of state, Lösener initially did little more than process anti-Semitic petitions.[5] Once the persecution of the Jews began in earnest, however, the interior ministry's unheralded "Jewish desk" became the focal point of policymaking on the "Jewish Question."

Based on the thoroughness of their anti-Semitic handiwork, one might be tempted to conclude that Pfundtner and Lösener approached the tasks of Jewish denaturalization and segregation with relish. Owing to the yeomanlike efforts of the two officials, after all, the civil rights of Germans of the Mosaic faith had been all but abrogated during the first two years of Nazi rule. As early as July 1933, for example, *Ostjuden* (Jewish immigrants from Eastern Europe) who had been naturalized after the First World War were stripped of their German citizenship.[6] The status of Jewish citizens of longer standing, moreover, was almost as tenuous. By virtue of the Law for the Reconstitution of the Professional Civil Service, co-signed by Hitler and Interior Minister Wilhelm Frick on April 7, 1933, non-"Aryans" (i.e., Jews) were prohibited from holding public office in Germany.[7] Two years later, even the traditional right of service in the defense of their country was denied to German Jews.[8] Adding to the harshness of this legislative harassment was the indiscriminate manner in which it was meted out. Apparently bent on providing Nazi *Judenpolitik* with as much latitude as possible, the interior ministry agreed to link the applicability of existing discriminatory statutes to an all-inclusive definition of "Jewishness." According to the decree whereby the April 1933 civil service law was implemented, the non-"Aryan" who was its intended victim was any individual descended from one or more Jewish grandparents.[9]

The pre-Nuremberg "race relations" work of the interior ministry suggests that its staff was as eager to segregate Jews from "Aryans" as it was to revoke Jewish citizenship. The only obstacle to segregation, according to Lösener, was the absence of sound methods for "assessing German (racial) stock."[10] To that end, the interior ministry established a Committee of Experts on Population and Race Policy, whose task it was to collect information on the hereditary composition of the German population.[11] Owing to the sheer magnitude of the endeavor, the committee was unable to provide the ministry with estimates of the Jewish-descended population in Germany before April 1935.[12] The resulting delay did not seem to dull officialdom's segregationist impulses. On the contrary, the "Jewish desk" used the interregnum as an opportunity to render existing anti-Semitic statutes more harsh. On August 8, 1933, for example, the interior ministry enacted legislation that extended the "Aryan" racial requirement for civil service employment to the spouses of public officials.[13] Ostensibly a means of shielding the civil service from "indirect" influence by Jews, the law also could be interpreted as a less-than-subtle pronouncement on the evils of "Aryan"-Jewish intermarriage.

Notwithstanding the bureaucratic momentum that seemed to be driving the Third Reich's early *Judenpolitik*, it is the contention of this paper that the anti-Semitic impulses of the interior ministry were rather weak. The basis for such an argument is the ministry's consistently reactive approach to policymaking on the "Jewish Question." The statute whereby *Ostjuden* were deprived of their German citizenship, for example, did not even originate in the interior ministry. Instead, milder versions of the law were proposed by officials from the economics ministry and the Reich chancellery.[14] Indeed, when Interior Minister Frick was apprised of these proposals in cabinet, his initial response was to reject them as being too radical.[15] Anti-Semitism was similarly down-played by interior ministry bureaucrats during the drafting phase of the April 1933 civil service legislation. Despite State-Secretary Pfundtner's contention that the "Aryan paragraph"--the article whereby Jewish officeholders were arbitrarily pensioned off--was the "most significant" of the law's eighteen clauses, none of the ministry's preliminary drafts had contained such a paragraph.[16] Had it not been for Hitler's timely intervention, in fact, the Law for the Reconstitution of the Professional Civil Service might have been enacted without any anti-Semitic content.[17]

By the time of the promulgation of the Nuremberg Race Laws, the interior ministry had become even further dissociated from the uncompromising Judeophobia of the Nazi party. No longer simply reluctant accomplices in the de-emancipation of the Jews, interior ministry officials had begun to actively obstruct the implementation of the Nazi regime's anti-Semitic statutes. For example, in a futile attempt to prevent the insertion of an "Aryan paragraph" into the 1935 conscription law, Pfundtner deliberately exaggerated the number of persons who would thereby have been rendered ineligible for military service.[18]

Cognizant of the importance of terminology in determining the quantitative impact of *Judenpolitik*, the staff of the interior ministry reserved its most sophisticated obstructionist tactics for interpreting the 1933 definition of "Jewishness." In the opinion of the bureaucrats, of course, settling on a definition was an administrative problem, not an ideological one. Accordingly, their handling of the matter was informed by consideration of the broader organizational, fiscal, and political costs of the Nazi regime's anti-Semitic policy. Resistance to the definitional clause of the civil service law was advocated as early as October 1933, at which time Lösener prepared a memorandum that outlined three drawbacks of an all-encompassing definition of "Jewishness." The first, according to Lösener, was that the designation of quarter- and half-Jews as non-"Aryans" rendered the task of investigating racial origins cumbersome and time-consuming. Second, the comprehensive definition increased the number of potential victims of disruptive economic boycotts. Third, the government was undermining the definition by retaining part-Jews in upper-level civil service positions.[19] In the interests of administrative efficiency, economic recovery, and political consistency, then, Lösener recommended that part-Jews be exempted from the non-"Aryan" designation.[20]

Lösener's memorandum became the basis of a bureaucratic policy of conferring "Aryan" status on part-Jews. Though not feasible in every case, the number of part-Jews able to avoid being designated as non-"Aryan" was increased dramatically by this policy. In the years leading up to the momentous Nuremberg party congress of 1935, the interior ministry was to make three adjustments to its methods of investigating the racial origins of current and prospective civil service employees. Crafted along the lines of Lösener's recommendations, each adjustment was calculated to limit the inclusiveness of the existing statutory definition of the term non-"Aryan." The first revised regulation, adopted in January 1934, replaced automatic inquiries into grandparental origins with the honors' system, except in cases where there was a compelling reason to doubt a declaration of confessional status, such as the possession of a Jewish-sounding name.[21] The second regulation, effective as of the end of 1934, unconditionally exempted quarter-Jews from the "Aryan paragraph" of the previous year's civil service law.[22] The last regulation, introduced concurrently, permitted the interior ministry to presume a public official's "Aryan" grandparentage unless conclusive proof of Jewish great-grandparentage could be adduced.[23]

The cumulative impact of these temporizing regulations was two-fold.

By exempting quarter-Jews from the "Aryan paragraph" of the civil service law, the interior ministry had indicated its intention to confer *de facto* "Aryan" status on persons with three "Aryan" grandparents. Furthermore, by relaxing the standards for determining "Aryan" grandparentage, the ministry had made it possible for some half-Jews to claim "Aryan" status as well. A hypothetical example will suffice to elucidate the circumstances under which this could have occurred.

Suppose that a preliminary investigation of a government official's family tree revealed that he was descended from one Jewish grandparent and three "Aryan" ones. Of the three "Aryan" grandparents, two had Jewish-sounding names. According to the bureaucracy's revised regulations, additional genealogical research was called for. Upon further investigation, it was discovered that the grandparents with the Jewish-sounding names were in fact the offspring of mixed "Aryan"-Jewish marriages. Four of the official's eight great-grandparents, in other words--two who were the parents of the lone Jewish grandparent, and the two who had married "Aryans"--were Jewish. However, since it was the policy of officialdom that Jewish grandparentage ought to be predicated on marriages between two Jewish great-grandparents, the part-Jewish grandparents in this case would have to be designated as "Aryans." The second investigation thus would confirm the findings of the first--the bureaucrat in question was a quarter-Jew. As such, he would be entitled to an exemption from the "Aryan paragraph," and, therefore, could continue to hold public office. Despite being fifty percent Jewish in a genealogical sense, then, the official would have been treated as though he was a pure "Aryan."

This kind of bureaucratic inertia and obstructionism was not confined to the realm of Jewish denaturalization. Prior to the promulgation of the Nuremberg Laws, officialdom was similarly reluctant to press the issue of racial segregation. Despite its attempts to discourage mixed marriages among civil servants, two years passed before any comprehensive action was taken.[24] Indeed, it was not until the summer of 1935, when registrars throughout Germany began to deny marriage licenses to interracial couples, that the ministry seriously contemplated an outright ban on "Aryan"-Jewish intermarriage.[25] Even then, Frick delayed the imposition of such a ban--over the strenuous objections of the Gestapo--while he awaited the emergence of a juridical consensus on the legality of the registrars' actions.[26] Only after several courts had rendered judgements favorable to the registrars did the interior minister officially prohibit further marriages between "Aryans" and Jews.[27]

The bureaucracy's tentative approach to the issue of "Aryan"-Jewish intermarriage in July 1935 is noteworthy because it coincided with the culmination of five months of unbridled anti-Semitic agitation. In addition to the defamation, physical abuse, and boycotts that were the stock-in-trade of the NSDAP, the SA and other grassroots party organizations used the arrival of summer as their cue for expanding the anti-Semitic campaign to public baths, swimming pools, and beaches across Germany.[28] Ostensibly, the new tactic was in no way connected to the segregationist activities of the registrars. The targeting of bathing and swimming facilities by Nazi militants was no accident, however. Since it was well known in Germany that such facilities were popular as trysting places, the intention of the militants could not have been anything other than to discourage "provocative" forms of interracial contact.[29]

The interior ministry's measured approach to the "Jewish Question" was thrown into disarray by the Nazi campaign of anti-Semitic terror. Characteristically, it was not Frick, but rather Economics Minister Hjalmar Schacht, who recognized the gravity of the situation. Cognizant of the threat to his own near-dictatorial powers posed by unauthorized anti-Semitic boycotts and demonstrations, Schacht called a cabinet-level meeting for August 20 at which he hoped to air his concerns.[30] No specific remedies were discussed at the meeting, but Frick seems to have come away from it with a greater sense of urgency.[31] On September 3, he wrote a letter to Schacht in which he conceded that only "positive measures to restrict Jewish influence" would forestall the further erosion of the government's authority over *Judenpolitik*.[32] Despite his forceful words, however, the interior minister failed to follow up with any concrete action. On the eve of the promulgation of the Nuremberg Race Laws, then, the ministerial bureaucracy had no new anti-Semitic initiatives in the works.

On September 13, in the midst of the Nazi party congress at Nuremberg, Hitler ordered Frick to produce segregationist legislation within two days.[33] Though the reasons behind Hitler's sudden decision remain shrouded in mystery, the most likely explanation was that the Führer shared the frustration of his subordinates over officialdom's lack of initiative on the "Jewish Question." Significantly, Hitler's order to Frick came on the heels of a virulently anti-Semitic speech delivered by Reich Medical Leader Dr. Gerhard Wagner, the head of the party's racial-medical wing and an avowed Judeophobe.[34] Addressing a rally on September 12, Wagner promised the assembled delegates that "a law for the protection of German blood" would be forthcoming.[35] It is uncertain whether Wagner made the announcement of his own accord, or whether it was done with the connivance of Hitler. Whatever the case, the decision to proceed with anti-Semitic legislation at this time could not help but to work to the advantage of hardliners like Dr. Wagner. Already forced to work in the shadow of a forty-eight hour deadline, the officials charged with drafting the new laws would face the additional pressure generated by the hype that invariably surrounded Nazi party congresses. In such circumstances, the ability of the bureaucrats to resist interference from the NSDAP rank-and-file would be pushed to the limit.

There can be little doubt but that the ideologically charged atmosphere of the NSDAP congress favored the hardline anti-Semitic position of the party. This is borne out by an examination of the process whereby the Nuremberg Race Laws were drafted.[36] The wheels had been set in motion by Hitler's surprise announcement. Pressed for time, Frick ordered Undersecretary Wilhelm Stuckart to assemble the interior ministry's "Jewish experts" in Nuremberg. This confronted the undersecretary with two logistical problems. The first involved the actual gathering of materials and personnel. Attending the congress as a party member, Stuckart had not anticipated that he would be called upon in an official capacity. Therefore, none of the requisite ministerial files was on hand.

The second problem was more serious. Its attention often diverted to other aspects of the "Jewish Question," the interior ministry had been compelled to leave the matter of Jewish citizenship in abeyance since 1933. Other than several outdated position papers, there was little in the ministry's files that would aid the bureaucrats in the complex task of redefining the legal status of the Jews in Germany. Since this problem was beyond any immediate solution, Stuckart concentrated on matters that were within his control. Accordingly, he telephoned Lösener and ordered him to catch the first available flight to Nuremberg. His suitcase bulking with materials on the "Jewish Question," Lösener arrived in Nuremberg on the morning of September 14, and was whisked to the city's police headquarters, where Stuckart and Pfundtner had been provided with a small office. Shortly thereafter, the three officials were joined by Walter Sommer, an emissary from Dr. Wagner, whereupon they began the process of drafting segregationist and citizenship laws aimed specifically at the Jews.[37]

While conceding that the Nuremberg drafting process produced fairly harsh legislation, historians have argued that the laws would have been much more severe but for the moderating influence of the bureaucrats.[38] This view is predicated on three factors that appeared to play into the hands of the interior ministry officials. First, the privacy accorded to the drafting team suggests that its procedures were insulated from political interference.

Located in a police station, the bureaucrats ought to have been sheltered from Nazi party rallies and rowdyism. Second, notwithstanding the presence of Sommer, the hardline anti-Semitic position of Dr. Wagner was outnumbered three-to-one. Third, Wagner's representative made no attempt to press the arguments of the party's racial-medical wing. Characterizing "the entire scribbling as too stupid" to be of interest to him, Sommer passed most of his time in an adjoining room amusing himself with a toy tank that fired sparks and climbed over piles of documents.[39]

Upon closer examination of the circumstances in which the drafting team found itself, however, it appears that the bureaucrats were in fact pawns in an elaborate game of intrigue planned by the Reich medical leader. Added to the pressure of a twenty-four hour deadline was the bureaucrats' sequestration in a cramped office at the police station, a situation that must have resembled house arrest. The bureaucrats' sense of isolation surely was exacerbated by their inability to stay in touch with Frick. In order to consult with the interior minister, who was staying across town from the police station at the Villa Haberlin, a member of the drafting team would have to traverse the city on foot--demonstrations, parades, and processions had made the streets impassable to motorized traffic--conduct a hurried briefing, and then return to police headquarters, a time-consuming and probably exhausting experience.

As if their isolation was not demoralizing enough, the bureaucrats soon realized that their numerical advantage was meaningless. By Lösener's own account, he and his colleagues quickly concluded that they had been outmaneuvered by the anti-Semitic hardliners. While the working group was virtually isolated from its own minister, Wagner was a "constant companion" of Hitler, ensuring that he would have a verbal veto over any draft law that he perceived as being too mild.[40] With unlimited access to the Führer, Wagner possessed more influence over the policymaking process than Frick, who was reduced to the level of a messenger ferrying drafts back and forth between Hitler and the drafting team for comments and revisions.

Access to political leaders has long been regarded as the litmus test of influence within government. The importance of access was heightened, therefore, in the Nazi system of "charismatic rule" characterized by the capriciousness of Hitler's personal relationships and loyalties.[41] Had Dr. Wagner participated in the actual drafting process, he would have been outnumbered by the bureaucrats and unable to win them over to his hardline position. By eschewing the official drafting process in favor of an informal but decisive role in the approval process, Wagner was able to act as a kind of "kitchen cabinet" to the Führer. This suggests that Sommer's appointment as Wagner's emissary was part of a well-thought-out strategy aimed at undermining the influence of the bureaucrats. It is possible, of course, that Sommer's imbecilic behaviour was genuine.[42] More likely, however, it was calculated to avoid linking Wagner to a specific policy until Hitler had had an opportunity to comment on it, thereby investing the Reich medical leader's veto with maximum effectiveness. The argument that conditions at Nuremberg favored the bureaucrats, therefore, simply fails to stand up to close examination. Bureaucratic expertise, long considered essential for the survival of twentieth-century totalitarian dictatorships, proved to be no match for personal access in the struggle for political influence in the Third Reich.

The extent of their powerlessness was driven home to the bureaucrats during the afternoon of September 14. Frick would submit a draft to Hitler, who, after prodding by Wagner, would send it back with a number of criticisms. After several such rejections, the drafting team tried to recapture the initiative. Realizing that their separation from Frick placed them at a distinct disadvantage, the bureaucrats left Sommer at the police station and made their way to the Villa Haberlin. Proximity, the bureaucrats reasoned, would enable them to better prepare the interior minister for Wagner's obstructionist tactics.[43] Even a thoroughly-briefed Frick proved to be no match for the fanatical Wagner, however, and the strategy collapsed.

With Wagner holding out for draconian legislation, no progress was made during the evening of September 14. As his self-imposed deadline drew closer, Hitler sent the beleaguered interior minister away from their midnight meeting with the order to return with four drafts of varying severity, from which he would select one. Frick also was reminded to produce a draft citizenship law. Though exhausted, the bureaucrats completed the four drafts in under ninety minutes, and then took another hour to hammer out a provisional citizenship law. At about 2:30 A.M., the interior minister went to the Führer's quarters with the five drafts. Upon his return one hour later, Frick reported that Hitler, over the strenuous objections of Wagner, had chosen the mildest of the four draft segregationist laws--that is, the one applicable to full-Jews only. In addition, the Führer had approved the draft citizenship law, even though as written it did not distinguish between the rights of Jews and non-Jews.[44]

Hitler's selection of the mildest draft seemed to vindicate the temperate anti-Semitic position staked out by the interior ministry. The bureaucrats barely had time to savor their hard-won "victory," however, before the Führer changed his mind during an improvised Sunday morning session of the Reichstag. Though his announcement of the segregationist legislation adhered point-by-point to the mildest version submitted by the drafting team, Hitler deleted the crucial phrase "This law applies only to full-Jews."[45] In keeping with the arguments of anti-Semitic hardliners like Dr. Wagner, then, Hitler left the door open for the application of the Nuremberg Laws to persons of partial Jewish ancestry. This about-face sounded the death knell of bureaucratic attempts to moderate *Judenpolitik* by way of administrative subterfuge. The sole prerogative of officialdom during the first two years of Nazi rule, the definitional threshold of "Jewishness" had suddenly and irrevocably been opened to new (and assuredly more radical) interpretations.

Even without Hitler's deletion of its "full-Jews only" provision, the draft Law for the Protection of German Blood and German Honor wiped out decades of painstakingly constructed accommodation between the Christian and Mosaic communities of Germany. By its language alone, the segregationist legislation symbolized the radicalization of Nazi *Judenpolitik*. In a departure from the established practice of discriminating against non-"Aryans," the new law was explicitly applicable to the Jews.[46] The statute's real impact, of course, was in its codification of the most virulent Nazi prejudices. Convinced that racial hygiene, described in the draft's preamble as "the prerequisite for the continued existence of the German people," was imperilled by race mixing between "Aryans" and Jews, the racial-medical wing of the NSDAP finally had succeeded in having "Aryan"-Jewish inter-marriage and extra-marital sexual relations added to the criminal code.[47]

Short of promising imprisonment for Jewish males who committed the crime of *Rassenschande* ("race defilement"), the law did not specify how stiff the penalties might be. However, the subsequent harshness with which the Nazi regime would treat offenders against the principle of racial segregation was hinted at in one of the draft's provisions. As a concession to Nazi Gauleiter Julius Streicher's stock-in-trade characterization of the typical Jewish proprietor as a violator of female "Aryan" employees, paragraph 3 of the legislation prohibited "Aryan" women under forty-five years of age from working in Jewish households.[48] Jews who failed to comply with this clause risked penalties ranging from a fine to a prison term not exceeding one year.[49] In light of this criminalization of both sexual and ostensibly non-sexual contacts between "Aryans" and Jews, one is tempted to concur with the assessment offered by Propaganda Minister Joseph Goebbels, himself a militant anti-Semite, who confided to his diary with satisfaction that "the Jews were hit hard" by the new legislation.[50]

More damaging to the German-Jewish *modus vivendi* than racial segregation was the draft Reich Citizenship Law. As has already been noted, the Nuremberg draft did not single out Jews for diminished legal status. Rather, it distinguished between two types of "subjects" of the Third Reich. According to this new standard of citizenship, Germans were to be designated as subjects of the Reich in the sense that they were under the rule of a government that accorded them certain rights in return for unquestioning loyalty. The difference between subjects hinged on whether or not they possessed a certificate of Reich citizenship. Conferred upon subjects of "German or kindred blood," citizenship was the recognition in law that an individual's race determined whether he or she was "willing and suited to serve the German people and the Reich loyally."[51] Those subjects whose race precluded such reliability were classified as being of German "nationality." Like other subjects, German nationals were obligated to the Reich and in return could expect the "protection" of the state. Only a Reich citizen, however, was the "bearer of full political rights as provided by the laws."[52]

To be sure, political rights in the broad sense of the concept--encompassing, for example, the freedoms of speech, association, and assembly--had long since been eliminated in Nazi Germany. Short of the forfeiture of plebiscitary voting rights, then, there was little to differentiate between the disfranchisement imposed on German subjects and that already being experienced by German citizens. It was this seemingly minor distinction that prompted Lösener to refer to the draft citizenship law as "meaningless."[53] Yet the importance of the legislation went beyond mere symbolism. One practical effect of the new laws was the entrenchment of spurious racial doctrines in *Judenpolitik*. By deleting the "full-Jews only" provision from the laws drafted at Nuremberg, Hitler had extended the orbit of anti-Semitic discrimination to individuals who previously had not considered themselves to be Jews. With at least half a million persons of partial Jewish ancestry living in the Third Reich, the number of potential targets of the wrath of the Judeophobes now exceeded one million.[54]

The fate of persons of partial Jewish ancestry was not contemplated in the September draft laws. Rather, a determination of the status of part-Jews had to await the promulgation of implementing legislation in November 1935. Calling attention to the bureaucrats' creation of a "privileged" category of persons of partial Jewish descent after November, historians have tended to characterize the implementing legislation as further proof that the Nuremberg Laws represented the triumph of conservative administration over Nazi ideology.[55] This argument is plausible if the implementing legislation is compared with the bureaucracy's worst-case scenario--namely, one in which there would have been no statutory distinction between part- and full-Jews. Within the context of contemporary *Judenpolitik*, however, the November laws closely approximated that scenario. Indeed, that the denaturalization of part-Jews was considered at all in 1935 was a significant departure from the ministerial bureaucracy's previous handling of this aspect of the "Jewish Question." It also was an indication of the extent to which officialdom had been subordinated to the anti-Semitic agenda of the NSDAP.

The inclusion of part-Jews on the Nazi regime's anti-Semitic agenda was a long-sought-after objective of hardliners like Dr. Wagner. Hitler's deletion of the "full-Jews only" provision from the September draft laws fulfilled two prerequisites for the attainment of that objective. First, his September 15 speech to the NSDAP delegates assembled at Nuremberg ensured that some form of statutory discrimination against part-Jews would be forthcoming. After all, civil servants contradicted or ignored policy statements issued by the Führer at their own peril. Second, Hitler broke the bureaucracy's monopoly over the administration of *Judenpolitik*, including the all-important interpretation of what constituted "Jewishness." Prior to the 1935 Nazi party congress, the problem of defining "Jewishness" had been resolved by way of administrative regulations alone. As a result of Hitler's speech, these regulations were exposed to criticism from the party. The ensuing debate over their merits provided anti-Semitic militants with a platform whence they could voice arguments in favor of equating part- and full-Jews. This was a major contributing factor to the harshness of the implementing legislation of November 1935.

Informed by the contradictory imperatives of ideology and administration, party and state were wedded to fundamentally different conceptions of what constituted "Jewishness." The extent to which these conceptions were irreconcilable was revealed by Hitler's reluctance to get involved in post-congress disputes over the interpretation of the draft laws. Having sensed palpable disapproval for his cautious remarks on the "Jewish Question" during a September 29 address to the Nazi Gauleiters, Hitler backed out of a scheduled appearance at a second rally and ordered the NSDAP and officials of the interior ministry to work out the details of the new citizenship and segregationist laws on their own.[56] With the Führer on the sidelines, it was left to contending subordinate authorities to debate the thorny issue of the definitional threshold of "Jewishness." The harshness of the November 1935 implementing legislation was contingent on the outcome of that debate.

In the ensuing face-to-face negotiations, most of the concessions were made by the bureaucracy. Personalities alone accounted for much of the one-sidedness that characterized the talks. All of the party's spokesmen--Dr. Wagner, Dr. Friedrich Bartels, and Dr. Walter Gross--represented the radically anti-Semitic racial-medical wing of the NSDAP, whereas two of the three representatives of the state--Lösener and Hans Globke--were decidedly muted in their views on the "Jewish Question."[57] Stuckart, the senior government negotiator, had a reputation as a conceptual thinker who would readily defer to the technical expertise of his subordinates on matters of detail.[58] Since Stuckart was also a committed National Socialist, however, the possibility that he somehow undermined the negotiating position of the bureaucracy cannot be discounted.

Beyond the personalities involved, two additional factors favored the hardline position adopted by the negotiators for the Nazi party. First, contrary to recent assertions, the party's approval of the laws drafted at Nuremberg did not translate into a decline in the frequency of unauthorized anti-Jewish actions.[59] Indeed, the eight weeks between the 1935 party congress and the promulgation of the implementing legislation witnessed some of the most intense and widespread grassroots anti-Semitic activity of the year.[60] Secure in the conviction that the rank-and-file of the NSDAP was behind them, Wagner and his underlings could afford to dig in their heels. Second, the state's representatives overestimated their ability to manage events. Having succeeded in watering down anti-Jewish statutes in the past, the bureaucrats negotiated under the mistaken impression that any concession they granted could be withdrawn later by way of administrative subterfuge. A false sense of security, therefore, rendered the team of Stuckart, Lösener, and Globke more pliable to the demands of the NSDAP.

On balance, intransigence proved to be far more effective as a negotiating tactic than flexibility. A case in point was Wagner's demand that the definition of "Jewishness" be extended to persons with one Jewish great-grandparent--that is, to persons who were seven-eighths "Aryan."[61] Realizing that accession to this demand would vitiate the bureaucracy's previous efforts on behalf of quarter- and half-Jews, Lösener outlined the disadvantages of such an all-encompassing definition, including the strategically indefensible disqualification of some 45,000 men from military service.[62] Though Lösener's arguments were couched in a Nazi frame of reference (the military preparedness of the Third Reich), Wagner would not relent. Instead, the Reich medical leader tried to intimidate his adversaries by claiming that Hitler had approved of his demand and breaking off the talks. A telephone call to the Reich chancellery exposed Wagner's bluff, and he was forced to return to the negotiating table.[63] However, in order to break the impasse over the quarter-Jewish definitional threshold, the bureaucrats had to accede to Wagner's demand that membership in the Jewish religious community be considered sufficient grounds for presuming "Jewish" grandparentage.[64]

Theoretically, this trade-off ought to have favored the ministerial bureaucracy's circumscribed definition of "Jewishness." By linking grandparental descent to Jewish community membership, Wagner's demand seemed to replace rigid genealogical standards of racial investigation with flexible behavioral ones. In practice, however, accession to Wagner's demand would extend the definition of "Jewishness" well beyond the parameters established by the bureaucracy during the first two years of Nazi rule. The reason for this, ironically, was to be found in Jewish laws and customs. From the time of the first dispersions of the Jewish people, Judaism had been governed by a virtual "iron law" of maternal religious affiliation. Except in a handful of obscure circumstances, the child of a Jewish mother was considered to be a member of the Jewish religious community. Even marriage out of the faith, not deemed valid under Judaism, did not negate or diminish the binding nature of this "iron law."[65] To be sure, not every child who was the offspring of a marriage between a Jewish woman and a non-Jewish man automatically was designated as a Jew. Membership in the Jewish community required the registration of a child with the local synagogue, a non-compulsory act that some parents undoubtedly elected to forego. Prior to the twentieth century, however, the incidence of non-registration likely was quite low. Pious Jews, of course, would have registered as a matter of faith. Even among less-than-devout Jews, it was customary to join a congregation for the educational opportunities, the social life, or simply to keep up a family tradition, and most synagogues encouraged such ulterior-motivated memberships as stepping stones to a more meaningful religious commitment.[66]

German Jewry's observance of the practice of community registration could not help but work to the advantage of those in the Nazi regime who advocated a broadened definition of "Jewishness." Assuming that the incidence of marriage out of the faith was as high for Jewish women as for Jewish men, something like half of the offspring of all mixed marriages concluded in nineteenth-century Germany would have been considered Jewish under the strictures of Judaism. Included among the children of such marriages would have been the grandparents of persons who would have reached adulthood by the 1930's. Genealogical investigations conducted along the lines demanded by Dr. Wagner thus would result in the classification of those grandparents as full-Jews, and thereby would saddle their grandchildren with the burden of Jewish ancestry. This contrasts sharply with the previous bureaucratic practice of presuming "Aryan" grandparentage unless proof of Jewish great-grandparentage could be adduced.[67] By acceding to Dr. Wagner's demand, then, the bureaucrats committed themselves to the partial implementation of his one-eighth definitional threshold of "Jewishness."

Wagner's "grandfather clause" was only one of several changes in the administration of *Judenpolitik* emanating from the party-state negotiations that took place during the autumn of 1935. On balance, these changes tended to affirm the inclusive definitional criteria contained in the 1933 civil service law.[68] According to the decree implementing the Reich Citizenship Law of November 14, 1935, a full-Jew was "anyone descended from at least three grandparents who . . . (were) fully Jewish as regards race." Full-Jews, as expected, were deprived of citizenship, and, with it, "the right to vote on political matters" or to hold "public office." Part-Jews, on the other hand, no longer were designated as non-"Aryans," nor were they considered to be Jews under the new law. Instead, a separate category was created for them. Persons "descended from one or two grandparents who . . . (were) fully Jewish as regards race" were designated as Jewish *Mischlinge* in the new law and subsequently as quarter-Jewish *Mischlinge* of the second degree and half-Jewish *Mischlinge* of the first degree respectively.[69]

Under the previous definition of the term non-"Aryan," quarter- and half-Jews had been lumped together with full-Jews. In the revised citizenship law, part-Jews seemed to have been accorded a legal existence distinct from that of both "Aryans" and full-Jews. From the narrow perspective of statutory language, then, the legal status of part-Jews appears to have been improved by the new definition of "Jewishness." *De jure* analysis, of course, is not always the most reliable reflection of a *de facto* situation. Contemporary legal interpretations and applications afford the opportunity for a more accurate appraisal of the revised citizenship law than its wording alone. Any worthwhile assessment, therefore, requires a more refined analytical framework than a simple comparison of statutory language.

For the purposes of this paper, five standards of measurement will be used to compare and contrast the legal status of part-Jews before and after the promulgation of the Reich Citizenship Law of 1935. The first test is to locate the institutional focus of *Judenpolitik* in the wake of the new law. Prior to November 1935, a virtual bureaucratic monopoly over the interpretation of "Jewishness" had insulated part-Jews from the worst effects of statutory discrimination. The second test is a period-specific comparison of the citizenship rights of part-Jews. Designated as non-"Aryans" in 1933, part Jews had been susceptible to the same loss of rights experienced by their full-Jewish fellow citizens. Third, a determination of continuity or change must be made with respect to official methods of racial investigation. Between 1933 and 1935, the process of racial investigation rarely went back beyond grandparental origins. Fourth, it must be ascertained whether opportunities for the acquisition of "Aryan" status were increased or diminished in the aftermath of the implementation of the Reich Citizenship Law. Prior to 1935, effective bureaucratic control over the administration of *Judenpolitik* had enabled many quarter-Jews and some half-Jews to obtain *de facto* "Aryan" status. Finally, no analysis of the revised citizenship law would be complete without an assessment of its impact on "sideswiping." Exemption from anti-Semitic measures aimed only at full-Jews had by no means been assured during the first two and a half years of the Nazi rule, but the vigilance of the bureaucracy had kept the incidence of such "sideswiping" to a minimum.

Under the provisions of the new law, the administration of all questions pertaining to citizenship became the shared responsibility of Interior Minister Frick and Deputy-Führer Rudolf Hess, whereas exemptions were made the exclusive purview of the Führer.[70] For the quarter-Jewish *Mischlinge* of the second degree, NSDAP administrative oversight meant the end of bureaucratic leniency in the realm of racial classification. This was offset somewhat by the entrenchment of *Mischling* citizenship rights. By virtue of their "kindred blood," Jewish *Mischlinge* of the second degree were accorded the same political rights as their "Aryan" fellow citizens.[71] Owing to Dr. Wagner's "grandfather clause," of course, many persons who previously would have been considered "Aryans" without further ado henceforth were suspended between "Aryan" and full-Jewish status. Moreover, the combination of joint party-state oversight and the creation of a separate category of citizenship all but foreclosed the possibility of an upgrade from *Mischling* to "Aryan" status. Indeed, the only benefit to be derived from separate categorization was that it virtually closed the door on any future reclassification of Jewish *Mischlinge* of the second degree as Jews. "Sideswiping," in other words, had effectively been banned by statute.

Of the five comparative standards by which the legal status of

Mischlinge of the second degree can be evaluated, the revised citizenship law scored higher on two and lower on three than previous regulations. Overall, then, the status of quarter-Jews in Nazi Germany was marginally diminished by the new law. The real victims of the new law, of course, were the half-Jewish *Mischlinge* of the first degree. Like their quarter-Jewish counterparts, half-Jews suffered the negative consequences of NSDAP input into citizenship policy, Dr. Wagner's "grandfather clause," and inflexible statutory categorization, while at the same time enjoying the meagre benefits of full political rights. Unlike quarter-Jews, however, *Mischlinge* of the first degree were under constant threat of "sideswiping." According to the most important provisions of the revised citizenship law, the failure of half-Jews to adhere to strict behavioral requirements would result in their forfeit of *Mischling* status and their automatic reclassification as full-Jews.

Behavioral requirements for the retention of *Mischling* status were outlined in the so-called *Geltungsjuden* section of the new law.[72] Contained in four clauses, these requirements were strict to the point of affirming the uncompromising doctrine espoused by the Judeophobic NSDAP genealogists--namely, that half-Jews could not be integrated into the German racial community. The last two clauses were particularly harsh. In an attempt to discourage *Rassenschande*, clauses 5(2)c and 5(2)d warned that any child discovered to have been conceived after mid-November 1935 within either an illegal mixed marriage or extramarital relationship, while racially of *Mischling* stock, would be considered fully Jewish for statutory purposes.[73] If the bureaucrats' objective in promulgating these clauses was to prevent arbitrary racial classifications, then they failed miserably. A half-Jewish infant, after all, was in no way responsible for the so-called racial violations of its parents. To classify a child solely on the basis of parental conduct, then, was to defeat the purpose of the *Mischling* first-degree categorization.

Somewhat more rational, though no less oppressive, were the first two *Geltungsjuden* clauses. According to clause 5(2)b, a half-Jew "who was married to a Jew when the (revised citizenship) law was issued or has subsequently married one" forfeited his or her *Mischling* status.[74] This regulation was predicated on the assumption that the choice of a marital partner demonstrated an individual's racial tendencies. As a consequence, it represented a substantial widening of the definition of "Jewishness." Previous statutes had penalized the non-Jewish partner in mixed marriages, but the penalties never had included racial reclassification.[75] Indeed, the lone positive aspect of this clause was the regulation it did not contain.

Despite repeated demands by Dr. Wagner, sanctions were not applied to "Aryans" and quarter-Jews who were married to full-Jews.[76]

The most draconian of the behavioral requirements was that embodied by the first *Geltungsjuden* clause. According to clause 5(2)a, a half-Jew "who belonged to the Jewish religious community when the (revised citizenship) law was issued or has subsequently been admitted to it" automatically was reclassified as a full-Jew.[77] A literal reading of this clause suggests that it conformed to the behavioral standards established by the clause dealing with marriages concluded between *Mischlinge* of the first degree and full-Jews. Upon further examination, however, clause 5(2)a is revealed to have surpassed even the stringent requirements of clause 5(2)b. Whereas the choice of a marital partner arguably indicated an individual's confessional or racial preferences, the evaluative potential of membership in a religious community was far more limited. As has been observed, it was possible for a person of Jewish ancestry to register with the Jewish community without feeling any spiritual attachment to it. Unless the framers of the implementing legislation would have been prepared to argue that the failure of a non-practising Jew to have his or her name excised from a Jewish community list still constituted a deep attachment to that community, then they would have had to concede that clause 5(2)a was a wholly arbitrary and unscientific method of enforcing the law's implicit behavioral standards.

The administrative chaos that was bound to result from the enforcement of clause 5(2)a can easily be imagined. German courts, for example, would have been well within their rights to question whether an individual's inclusion on a Jewish community list was sufficient grounds for the revocation of his or her *Mischling* status, or whether proof of a demonstrable attachment--such as attendance at synagogue, the undertaking of religious instruction, or participation in fundraising activities--ought to be adduced as well. In the absence of consideration for mitigating circumstances, in other words, the behavioral standards buttressing the new racial categorizations would be undermined by the community membership clause.

Of the five comparative standards by which the legal status of half-Jews can be evaluated, the revised citizenship law scored higher on only one and lower on four than previous regulations. Circumstances for both categories of *Mischlinge*, then, can be said to have worsened as a result of the new law. Surprisingly, the negative effects of the new segregationist legislation were less evenly distributed. Issued the same day as the citizenship law, the decree implementing the Law for the Protection of German Blood and German Honor rendered permanent the provisional prohibition of both intermarriage and extramarital intercourse between "Aryans" and full-Jews.[78] Since *Mischlinge* had a choice of four potential marital or sexual partners--full-Jews, two categories of part-Jews, and "Aryans"--the regulations governing their segregation were more complicated. In the case of *Mischlinge* of the second degree, the regulations tended to favour their absorption into the German racial community. According to the new law, quarter-Jews were permitted to marry "Aryans," but were prohibited from marrying either full-Jews or one another. Special dispensation from the Reich interior ministry and the office of the Deputy-Führer was required, moreover, for the conclusion of a marriage between a *Mischling* of the second degree and a *Mischling* of the first degree.[79] Had they been implemented to the letter, then, these regulations would have had the effect of gradually eliminating the second-degree *Mischling* category by way of generational dilution. Constituting nothing less than an attempt to legislate the absorption of quarter-Jews into the "Aryan" bloodstream, these regulations were a vindication of both the longstanding bureaucratic practice of conferring *de facto* "Aryan" status on quarter-Jews and the moderate views that had informed it.

In contrast to the regulations governing the marital options of *Mischlinge* of the second degree, those applying to half-Jews seemed intended to effect their segregation from the German racial community. Marriages between *Mischlinge* of the first degree and full-Jews were permitted, of course, since they confirmed the expected behavioral patterns of persons whose "Jewish genes" were supposedly dominant. A half-Jew who wished to marry an "Aryan" or quarter-Jew, however, thereby manifesting "Aryan" inclinations, was prohibited from doing so except by special consent from the interior ministry and the office of the Deputy-Führer.[80] This effective ban on first-degree *Mischling*--"Aryan" and first-degree *Mischling*--second-degree *Mischling* marriages legitimated the views of the NSDAP genealogists who had contended that half-Jews could not be integrated into the German racial community. It also made a farce of the behavioral standards imposed on half-Jews by the revised Reich Citizenship Law. Only by marriage to one another or by self-imposed isolation could half-Jews retain the dubious benefits that accrued to them by virtue of their *Mischling* status.

Thus far, it has been demonstrated that the legal status of part-Jews in Nazi Germany was diminished by the decrees that implemented the Nuremberg Race Laws. On the basis of additional comparative analysis, it also can be adduced that Jewish *Mischlinge* were unlikely to receive any administrative relief from the harshness of the new statutes. Whereas the earlier administration of *Judenpolitik* had been characterized by temporization, after November 1935 the pendulum would swing in the other direction. The new bureaucratic radicalism was symbolized by the elevation of Deputy-Führer Hess to co-equal status with Interior Minister Frick in all matters pertaining to racial investigation and classification. Of greater significance, however, was the expanded administrative role for the NSDAP anticipated by the new legislation. Formerly entrusted to a bureaucratic monopoly, issues such as the scope of the definitional threshold of "Jewishness" henceforth were to be resolved by way of a consultative process between agencies of the Nazi party and the state. This blurring of the distinction between unofficial and official *Judenpolitik* was bound to bias the enforcement of the new laws toward more radical interpretations.

The primary administrative task associated with the enforcement of the Nuremberg Race Laws was the investigation of racial origins. The post-Nuremberg era of *Judenpolitik* witnessed two types of racial investigations. The most common were inquiries launched in conjunction with the ongoing, routine operations of the government. These inquiries were confined to the public sector, and involved investigations into the "racial suitability" of individuals employed or seeking employment in the civil service. Prior to November 1935, such investigations had been conducted by the interior ministry's expert for racial research, whose task it was to classify civil servants racially on the basis of evidence attesting to ancestry that he was able to unearth.[81] The expert's findings would then be forwarded to the ministry's personnel office for a final determination as to the employment status of the individuals under investigation. At no time during the investigative process were outside agencies--such as the NSDAP's civil service division or other party affiliates with a vested interest in the outcome--supposed to be consulted. In this way, the bureaucrats had insulated racial investigations from Nazi party pressure.

The process whereby racial origins were investigated was altered in two important respects by the implementing legislation of November 1935. First, the Office for Genealogical Research and the so-called Reich Office for Genealogical Research--the former a Nazi "think tank," the latter an ostensibly independent agency that was in fact a front for the racial-medical wing of the party--were provided with a prominent role in the investigative process.[82] This pitted the moderate racial experts of the bureaucracy against their radical counterparts in the NSDAP. The second change was inextricably linked to the first. By making Frick and Hess co-arbitrators of the intragovernmental disputes that were bound to arise from joint party-state administration of *Judenpolitik*, the November laws ensured that the ultimate investigative authority would rest with the Führer. Given Hitler's oft-articulated preference for the party's hardline views on the "Jewish Question," it was unlikely that the investigative process would favor persons of partial Jewish ancestry.[83]

Less common, but more widespread in their impact, were the racial investigations conducted by non-governmental agencies. Generally, the latter were connected either directly or indirectly with the criminal justice system. The reason for this can be traced to the criminalization of "Aryan"-Jewish sexual relations. In addition to full-Jews, a number of unfortunate persons of partial Jewish ancestry were swept up in the wave of denunciations and indictments that followed the promulgation of the Law for the Protection of German Blood and German Honor. This scenario was particularly nightmarish for *Mischlinge* of the first degree. Owing to a *lacuna* in the new segregationist legislation, half-Jews could not commit *Rassenschande*.[84] In order to convict a half-Jew, the prosecution would have to prove that the accused was in fact a full-Jew under the Nuremberg Laws. This task was facilitated by the *Geltungsjuden* section of the revised citizenship law. For anti-Semitic judges, an individual's inclusion on a Jewish community list could be cited as sufficient grounds for rendering a verdict of guilty.[85] Beyond the public humiliation and an almost guaranteed prison term, then, an inadvertent brush with the law could result in an unsolicited investigation of racial origins, the loss of *Mischling* status, and reclassification as a full-Jew.

The judiciary's brazen violations of the residual rights of part-Jews foreshadowed their future maltreatment by a regime no longer obliged to make allowances for international opinion. They also revealed the extent to which the Nuremberg Race Laws constituted a victory of the militant brand of anti-Semitism that was the stock-in-trade of the Nazi party over the moderate discriminatory posture adopted by the ministerial bureaucracy. That there had been new initiatives at all in official *Judenpolitik* was testimony to the emergence of the NSDAP in 1935 as a political force with which to be reckoned. The radical nature of the new initiatives, in turn, signalled that anti-Semitic militancy had eclipsed bureaucratic inertia and obstructionism in the administration of *Judenpolitik*.

To be sure, anti-Semitic hardliners like Dr. Wagner did not succeed in effecting the denaturalization of *all* persons of Jewish ancestry. Under the new segregationist system, quarter-Jews were considered worthy of reintegration into the "Aryan" racial community. That setback aside, however, the militants were successful in forever eliminating the possibility that second-degree Jewish *Mischlinge* would be granted "Aryan" status. As regards the situation of half-Jews, moreover, the victory of the militants was virtually complete. But for the open-endedness of the *Geltungsjuden* clauses of the Reich Citizenship Law, there would have been no practical distinction between half- and full-Jews.

By any standards of measurement, then, the promulgation of the Nuremberg Race Laws represented a two-fold triumph for the hard core of anti-Semites who comprised the Nazi party rank-and-file. In the short term, the participation of NSDAP agencies in the administration of *Judenpolitik* ensured that avowed Judeophobes would have a say in defining "Jewishness." In the long term, the criminalization of "Aryan"-Jewish sexual relations would provide anti-Semitic militants with three advantages in the formulation of future anti-Jewish policies. First, for all intents and purposes, unauthorized anti-Semitic actions carried out in the defense of racial segregation were legitimized by the new statutes. Second, whatever the state of public opinion on the "Jewish Question" in the autumn of 1935, the casting of the Jew as a sexual and social pariah was bound to promote "Aryan"-Jewish alienation in the long run. Third, the November laws opened the door to the proscription of those forms of "Aryan"-Jewish interaction (such as contractual relationships) still deemed permissible under the existing regime of legislative discrimination.

Raul Hilberg, the dean of Holocaust historians, has suggested that the Final Solution was characterized by "sure-footed planning and bureaucratic thoroughness."[86] In some respects, his conception of the Holocaust as an essentially administrative phenomenon still rings true. After all, few would deny the invaluability of bureaucratic expertise in implementing the policies of de-emancipation, segregation, and expropriation that were the prerequisites of genocide. Yet if the Holocaust was primarily administrative in execution, it was profoundly ideological in conception. Nothing in the bureaucrats' training or experience, therefore, would have prepared them for such an enterprise. As this paper has endeavored to show, there was little that was sure-footed or planned about the Nuremberg Race Laws. Despite their unquestioned mastery over technical aspects of the "Jewish Question," Reich civil servants lapsed into a predictable complacency after the initial wave of Nazi anti-Semitism had run its course in 1933. Operating in typical bureaucratic fashion, officials of the interior ministry were more concerned with consolidating existing discriminatory policies than with initiating new ones. Accordingly, it was left to Hitler to respond in plebiscitary fashion to the resurgence of anti-Semitic activism in 1935.

NOTES

1. See the NSDAP's 1920 program in Barbara Miller Lane and Leila J. Rupp, eds., *Nazi Ideology before 1933*, Austin and London, 1978, p. 41.
2. Quoted in Lucy S. Dawidowicz, *The War Against the Jews 1933-1945*, New York, 1975, p. 92.
3. Raul Hilberg, *The Destruction of the European Jews. Revised and Definitive Edition*, 3 vols., New York and London, 1985; Hans Mommsen, "The Realization of the Unthinkable. The 'Final Solution of the Jewish Question' in the Third Reich," in Gerhard Hirschfeld, eds., *The Policies of Genocide. Jews and Soviet Prisoners of War in Nazi Germany*, London, 1986; Wolfgang Scheffler, *Judenverfolgung im Dritten Reich 1933 bis 1945*, Frankfurt am Main, 1964; Karl A. Schleunes, *The Twisted Road to Auschwitz. Nazi Policy Toward German Jews 1933-1939*, Urbana, 1970.
4. For an overview of the "Jewish expert" phenomenon in the Third Reich, see Christopher R. Browning, "The Government Experts," in Henry Friedlander and Sybil Milton, eds., *The Holocaust: Ideology, Bureaucracy, and Genocide. The San Jose Papers*, New York, 1980, pp. 183-197.
5. Bernhard Lösener, "Als Rassereferent im Reichsministerium des Innnern," *Vierteljahreshefte für Zeitgeshichte* 9 (1961): 266.
6. See the Law for the Revocation of German Citizenship and Nationality, Berlin, 14 July 1933, in Joseph Walk, ed., *Das Sonderrecht für die Juden im NS-Staat. Eine Sammlung der gesetzlichen Massnahmen und Richtlinien--Inhalt und Bedeutung*, Heidelberg and Karlsruhe, 1981, Doc. 172, p. 36.
7. The law is reprinted in its entirety in Bruno Blau, ed., *Das Ausnahmerecht für die Juden in den europäischen Landern, 1933-1945*, New York, 1952, Doc. 3, pp. 13-18.
8. See the Conscription Law, Berlin, 21 May 1935, in Walk, *Sonderrecht*, Doc. 571, pp. 115-116.
9. See the Decree Implementing the Law for the Reconstitution of the Professional Civil Service, Berlin, 11 April 1933, in Blau, *Ausnahmerecht*, Doc. 6, p. 19.
10. Lösener to Frick, Berlin, 24 July 1933, in *Institut für Zeitgeschichte* (IfZ) F 71/1.
11. *Ibid.*
12. Jeremy Noakes, "The Development of Nazi Policy towards the

German-Jewish '*Mischlinge*' 1933-1945," *Leo Baeck Institute Year Book* 34 (1989): 292.
13. Walk, *Sonderrecht*, Doc. 212, p. 45.
14. See Paul Bang, state secretary in the Reich economics ministry, to Hans Lammers, state secretary in the Reich chancellery, Berlin, 6 March 1933, in *Bundesarchiv Koblenz* (BA) R 43 II/134, and Lammers to Frick, Berlin, 9 March 1933, in *ibid*.
15. Frick to the heads of the state governments, Berlin, 15 March 1933, in BA-R 43II.
16. Pfundtner's opportunistic endorsement of the "Aryan paragraph" is quoted in Browning, "Experts," p. 186. The evolution of the law can be traced through the memorandum by Pfundtner on civil service measures, Berlin, (spring 1932), in Hans Mommsen, *Beamtentum im Dritten Reich. Mit ausgewählten Quellen zur nationalsozialistischen Beamtenpolitik*, Stuttgart, 1966, Doc. I 1, pp. 127-135, the draft Law for the Reconstitution of the Professional Civil Service, Berlin, (March 1933), in *ibid*., Doc. II 1, pp. 151-155, and the conference on the draft professional civil service law between Ministerial Director Mulert of the German communal assembly and Ministerial Councillor Hans Seel of the Reich interior ministry, 27 March 1933, in *ibid*., Doc. II 2, pp. 155-156. See also Uwe D. Adam, *Judenpolitik im Dritten Reich*, Dusseldorf, 1972, pp. 59-60 n. 181.
17. Adam, *Judenpolitik*, p. 61.
18. Pfundtner to the highest authorities of the Reich, Berlin, 3 April 1935, in BA-R 43II/595.
19. See Lösener to Frick, Berlin, 30 October 1933, in Lösener, "Rassereferent," p. 269. A number of individuals retained senior positions in the ministerial bureaucracy despite their partial Jewish ancestry. The most notable examples were Erhard Milch of the aviation ministry and Leo Killy of the Reich chancellery. On Milch, see Karl D. Bracher, *The German Dictatorship. The Origins, Structure, and Effects of National Socialism*, New York and London, 1970, p. 254. On Killy, see Jane Caplan, "Civil Service Support for National Socialism: An Evaluation," in Gerhard Hirschfeld and Lothar Kettenacker, eds., *Der "Führerstaat": Mythos und Realität: Studien zur Struktur und Politik des Dritten Reiches*, Stuttgart, 1981, pp. 173-174.
20. Lösener, "Rassereferent," p. 270.
21. Reichsminister Dr. Frick, "Die Rassenfrage in der deutschen Gesetzgebung," in *Deutsche Juristen-Zeitung* 39 (1934): 5, in IfZ-F

71/1.
22. Pfundtner to Frick, 4 March 1935, in IfZ-F 71/2.
23. Schütze, Reich ministry of interior, to the Reich ministry of education, Berlin, 8 December 1934, in IfZ-F 71/1, Schütze to Lammers, Berlin, 15 April 1935, in *ibid.*, and Schütze to the state ministry in Schwerin-Mecklenburg, 16 April 1935, in IfZ-F 71/2.
24. See note 13 above.
25. Lösener, "Rassereferent," p. 278.
26. Entry for 19 June 1935, Berlin, in IfZ-F 90/3. See also Lothar Gruchmann, "'Blutschützgesetz' und Justiz. Zur Entstehung und Auswirkung des Nürnberger Gesetzes vom. 15. September 1935," *Vierteljahreshefte für Zeitgeschichte* 31 (1983): 427-428.
27. Decision of the municipal court of Wetzlar, 17 June 1935, in Ernst Noam and Wolf-Arno Kropat, eds., *Justiz vor Gericht 1933-1945. Dokumente aus hessischen Justizakten*, Wiesbaden, 1975; decision of the municipal court of Bad Sulza, 27 June 1935, in *Juristische Wochenschrift* 64 (1935): 2309; decision of the municipal court of Königsberg, (July 1935), reported in the decision of the state court in Königsberg, 26 August 1935, in *Deutsche Justiz* 97 (1935): 1387. For Frick's decision to proceed with the ban, see entry for 7 July 1935, in IfZ-F 90/4. The ban was implemented on July 26, 1935. See Frick to the Reich governors, 27 July 1935, in Kommission zur Erforschung der Geschichte der Frankfurter Juden, eds., *Dokumente zur Geschichte der Frankfurter Juden 1933-1945*, Frankfurt am Main, 1963, Doc. V 2, pp. 217-218.
28. See the reports in Martin Broszat, Elke Frolich, and Falk Wiesemann, eds., *Bayern in der NS-Zeit. Soziale Lage und politisches Verhalten der Bevölkerung im Spiegel vertraulicher Berichte*, Munich, 1977, pp. 450-453; *Deutschland-Berichte der Sopade*, vol. 2, Frankfurt am Main, 1980, pp. 800-801, 932, 1044; Thomas Klein, ed., *Die Lageberichte der Geheimen Staatspolizei uber die Provinz Hessen-Nassau*, vol. 1, Cologne and Vienna, 1986, pp. 284, 456; Robert Thevoz, Hans Branig, Cecile Lowenthal-Hensel, eds., *Pommern 1934/35 im Spiegel von Gestapo-Lageberichten und Sachakten*, vol. 12, Cologne and Berlin, 1974, p. 118.
29. Michael H. Kater, "Everyday Anti-Semitism in Prewar Nazi Germany: The Popular Bases," *Yad Vashem Studies* 16 (1984): 157.
30. Schacht to the highest authorities of the Reich, Berlin, 13 August 1935, in IfZ-F 71/2.
31. See the minutes of the interministerial conference held in the Reich

economics ministry on 20 August 1935, Berlin, 27 August 1935, in IfZ-F 71/2.
32. Frick to Schacht, 3 September 1935, in BA-R 18/5513.
33. Hilberg, *Destruction*, 1, p. 69.
34. Jeremy Noakes and Geoffrey Pridham, eds., *Nazism 1919-1945. Vol. 1. State, Economy and Society 1933-39. A Documentary Reader*, Exeter, 1984, p. 534. For Dr. Wagner's virulent anti-Semitism, see Michael H. Kater, *Doctors under Hitler*, Chapel Hill and London, 1989, ch. 6.
35. Adam, *Judenpolitik*, p. 126.
36. The following discussion is drawn from the reminiscences of one of the key participants in the drafting process, Bernhard Lösener. See Lösener, "Rassereferent," pp. 273-279. For secondary accounts of the genesis of the Nuremberg Race Laws, see Adam, *Judenpolitik*, pp. 129-142; Hilberg, *Destruction*, 1, pp. 69-70; Noakes and Pridham, *Nazism*, 2, pp. 534-535; Edward N. Peterson, *The Limits of Hitler's Power*, Princeton, 1969, pp. 137-140; Schleunes, *Twisted Road*, pp. 121-125.
37. Lösener, "Rassereferent," pp. 273-274.
38. This view informs the analyses of Hilberg, *Destruction*, 1, p. 68, and Schleunes, *Twisted Road*, p. 123.
39. Lösener, "Rassereferent," p. 274.
40. *Ibid.*
41. The importance of personal fealty in Hitler's leadership style is discussed in Joseph Nyomarky, *Charisma and Factionalism in the Nazi Party*, Minneapolis, 1967, pp. 145-150, and Robert Koehl, "Feudal Aspects of National Socialism," in Henry A. Turner Jr., ed., *Nazism and the Third Reich*, New York, 1972, pp. 158-162.
42. It is more likely that Sommer was merely playing the fool. After a long stint in the bureaucracy, Sommer was appointed president of the Reich administrative court. See Lösener, "Rassereferent," p. 274.
43. *Ibid.*
44. *Ibid.*, p. 275.
45. Lösener, "Rassereferent," p. 276.
46. See the draft Law for the Protection of German Blood and German Honor, Nuremberg, 15 September 1935, reproduced in its entirety in Kommission, *Dokumente*, Doc. V 3, pp. 218-219.
47. *Ibid.*, p. 218.
48. For this unseemly sexual caricature of the Jewish employer, see Dennis E. Showalter, *Little Man, What Now? Der Stürmer in the*

Weimar Republic, Hamden, 1982, pp. 94-99.
49. Draft Law for the Protection of German Blood and German Honor, Nuremberg, 15 September 1935, in Kommission, *Dokumente*, Doc. V 3, p. 218.
50. Entry for 17 September 1935, Berlin, in Elke Frölich, ed., *Die Tagebücher von Joseph Goebbels. Samtliche Fragmente*, vol. 2, Munich, 1987, p. 515.
51. Draft Reich Citizenship Law, Berlin, 15 September 1935, in Lucy S. Dawidowicz, *A Holocaust Reader*, New York, 1976, p. 45.
52. *Ibid.*
53. Lösener, "Rassereferent," p. 275.
54. This estimate is from Werner Cohn, "Bearers of a Common Fate? The 'Non-Aryan' Christian 'Fate Comrades' of the Paulus-Bund, 1933-1939," *Leo Baeck Institute Year Book* 33 (1988): 330, 350-353.
55. See Hilberg, *Destruction*, 1, p. 70, and Schleunes, *Twisted Road*, p. 128.
56. Lösener, "Rassereferent," p. 281.
57. *Ibid.*, p. 280.
58. For descriptions of Stuckart's hands-off approach to the management of his department, see the pre-trial interrogation of Lösener, 13 October 1947, in IfZ-ZS 1174, and the pre-trial interrogations of Lösener and Globke, 24 February 1948, in *ibid*.
59. Thus, I am taking issue with the view expressed in Ian Kershaw, *Popular Opinion and Political Dissent in the Third Reich: Bavaria 1933-1945*, Oxford, 1983, p. 239.
60. See the incidents reported in the situation report of the police commissioner in Augsburg, 1 October 1935, in Broszat et al., eds, *Bayern*, p. 454, and the situation report of the government president for Upper and Middle Franconia, in *ibid.*, p. 456; minister of education for Baden to the Reich minister of education, Mannheim, 21 September 1935, in Hans-Joachim Fliedner, ed., *Die Judenverfolgung in Mannheim 1933-1945*, vol. 2, Stuttgart, 1971, Doc. 69, pp. 136-137, and NSDAP cell leader to the Gauleiter, Mannheim, 2 October 1935, in *ibid.*, Doc. 202, p. 288; complaint filed by a Jewish businessman, a town near Trier, 30 November 1935, in Franz Josef Heyen, ed., *Nationalsozialismus im Alltag. Quellen zur Geschichte des Nationalsozialismus vornehmlich im Raum Mainz-Koblenz-Trier*, Boppard am Rhein, 1967, pp. 140-141, and report of the Gestapo in Koblenz, September 1935, in *ibid.*, pp. 142-143; report 1, in *Deutschland-Berichte der Sopade*, vol. 3, p. 30; report of the state

police office in Aachen, 7 October 1935, in Bernhard Vollmer, ed., *Volksopposition im Polizeistaat. Gestapo-und Regierungsberichte 1934-1936*, Stuttgart, 1957, p. 296; Walk, *Sonderrecht*, Doc. 45, p. 139; monthly report of the government president of Lower Franconia, 9 November 1935, in Klaus Wittstadt, ed., *Die Kirchliche Lage in Bayern nach den Regierungsprasidentenberichten 1933-1943. VI. Regierungsbezirk Unterfranken 1933-1944*, Mainz, 1981, Doc. 60, p. 76.

61. Lösener, "Rassereferent," p. 280.
62. See the position paper by Lösener, entitled "Materials on the Solution of the Part-Jewish Question," in IfZ-F 71/2.
63. Lösener, "Rassereferent," p. 281.
64. See paragraph 2, clause 2 of the decree implementing the Reich Citizenship Law of 14 November 1935, Berlin, in Blau, *Ausnahmerecht*, Doc. 78, p. 31.
65. Rabbi Hayim Halevy Donin, *To Be a Jew. A Guide to Jewish Observance in Contemporary Life*, New York, 1972, pp. 290-291.
66. *Ibid.*, pp. 189-190.
67. See note 23 above.
68. This was Stuckart's assessment. See his memorandum (to Lammers), Berlin, 6 November 1935, in IfZ-F 71/2.
69. Decree implementing the Reich Citizenship Law of 14 November 1935, Berlin, in Blau, *Ausnahmerecht*, Doc. 78, pp. 31-32.
70. Paragraphs 1, 6, and 7 of the Reich Citizenship Law of 14 November 1935, in Blau, *Ausnahmerecht*, Doc. 78, pp. 31, 33.
71. Paragraph 1, in Blau, *Ausnahmerecht*, Doc. 78, p. 31.
72. The section containing these requirements began with the phrase, "Als Jude gilt auch," meaning "also deemed a Jew." See paragraph 5, in Blau, *Ausnahmerecht*, p. 32. The phrase gave rise to the term *Geltungsjuden* as a designation for those half-Jews who failed to meet the requirements. See Hilberg, *Destruction*, 1, p. 72 n. 16.
73. See paragraph 5 of the decree implementing the Reich Citizenship Law of 14 November 1935, in Blau, *Ausnahmerecht*, Doc. 78, p. 32.
74. *Ibid.*
75. See the laws cited in Walk, *Sonderrecht*, Doc. 146-147, p. 31; Doc. 192, p. 41; Doc. 211-212, p. 45; Doc. 166, p. 61.
76. In a position paper submitted to the bureaucrats at the height of the negotiations over the implementing legislation, the Reich medical leader recommended that the "Jewish" designation ought to be extended to quarter-Jews and "Aryans" who were married to full-Jews. This was

rejected by the state's negotiating team. See Lösener, "Comments on the draft submitted by Reich Medical Leader Dr. Wagner," Berlin, 31 October 1935, in IfZ-F 71/2.
77. Paragraph 5 of the decree implementing the Reich Citizenship Law of 14 November 1935, in Blau, *Ausnahmerecht*, Doc. 78, p. 32.
78. Decree Implementing the Law for the Protection of German Blood and German Honor, Berlin, 14 November 1935, in Blau, *Ausnahmerecht*, Doc. 79, p. 33.
79. *Ibid.*
80. *Ibid.*
81. Seel, Reich interior ministry, to the state governments, Berlin, 26 October 1934, in IfZ-F 71/1. See also Walk, *Sonderrecht*, Doc. 468, p. 95.
82. Hilberg, *Destruction*, 1, p. 74.
83. For insight into the institutional and ideological biases of the Nazi regime's system of race investigation, see the case of a half-Jewish government employee, recounted in the text and documents of Hans Mommsen, "Die Geschichte des Chemnitzer Kanzleigehilfen K.B.," in Detlev Peukert and Jurgen Reulecke, eds., *Die Reihen fast geschlossen. Beitrage zur Geschichte des Alltags unterm Nationalsozialismus*, Wuppertal, 1981, pp. 337-366.
84. This is explained in Hilberg, *Destruction*, 1, pp. 160-161.
85. See the lower court rulings reported in the decision of the Reich supreme court, Leipzig, 2 September 1936, in *Deutsche Justiz* 98 (1936): 1470-1471; decision of the Reich supreme court, Leipzig, 3 November 1936, in *ibid.*, 99 (1937): 42-43; decision of the Reich supreme court, Leipzig, 7 June 1937, in *ibid.*, pp. 1085-1086; decision of the Reich supreme court, Leipzig, 21 November 1938, in *ibid.*, 101 (1939): 431; decision of the Reich supreme court, Leipzig, 23 March 1939, in *Deutsches Recht* (1939): 924-925; decision of the Prussian supreme court, Berlin, 16 January 1941, in *ibid.*, (1941): 1552-1553; decision of the Reich administrative court, Berlin, 5 June 1941, in *ibid.*, pp. 2413-2414; decision of the circuit court in Königsberg, 26 June 1942, *Judentum und Recht* (1942): 82-83, in IfZ-ED 128/18.
86. Hilberg, *Destruction*, 1, p. 62.

An Estate of Memory: Women in the Holocaust

Lillian Kremer

The most highly acclaimed works of Holocaust literary criticism focus on European and Israeli male Holocaust writers and experience. They give scant attention to significant women writers and female Holocaust history. In an effort to redress this omission, to address the study of women writers and to recognize women's historic experience, this paper examines the important neglected second novel by Ilona Karmel, *An Estate of Memory*, a novel hailed by Archibald MacLeish as "a tremendous achievement."

The narrative chronicles the experience of four women arbitrarily thrust together in the forced labor and concentration camps of Plaszow and Skarzysko. The sisterhood is composed of Tola Ohrenstein, the nineteen year-old daughter of a famous mercantile family; Barbara Grunbaum, a young country matron of generous spirit, so Aryan in appearance that she is known as the "big Pole"; Alinka, a fifteen-year-old scrubgirl who has been working for the Germans since she was thirteen, an orphan-waif, deprived of a normal childhood even before the war by a mother's death and father's political imprisonment in Siberia; and Aurelia Katz, "a professional victim,"[1] whose pregnancy provides motivation for the women to band together and nurture life in a universe of death. Deriving its contrapuntal form from the memories and dramatically articulated wartime suffering of the four women, the narrative suggests the collective Holocaust experience of Jewish women.

The focus of *An Estate of Memory*, is the forced labor and concentration camp environment and experiences of Plaszow and Skarzysko, where the novelist was imprisoned. Karmel is among the most accomplished novelists in her capacity to recreate the day to day Holocaust universe of disease, hunger, and degradation. She dramatizes policies implemented to demoralize prisoners and to so dehumanize people that Germans could perceive them a subhuman species fit for "extermination."

Bypassing the German view, Karmel presents the impact of such degradation on the victims.

Graphic description of the effects of diseases the women suffer testifies to the hellish conditions of the camp: "soon it was as if the sweetish smell of diarrhea had always filled the barracks; soon no other news but that of typhus crises was remembered...." In addition to typhus that leaves its victims with pale balding heads, purblind, and half deaf, Skarzysko is distinguished by the infamous munitions factories where the women are subjected to dangerous chemicals and acid polluted air that kills humans and the earth they inhabit.

> This was the yellow place. The air declared it so bitter that each breath hurt, the earth glittering with a phosphorescent sheen, and the trees, a yellow-green lichen eating their trunks so that they cracked and split in half, the branches denuded but for a scorched fringe trailing through the mud. Behind the trees sprawled puddles of color of phlegm; in the brown canvas spread over squarish piles, holes gaped, their green edges jagged as though gnawed by sharp teeth; farther off stood a brick building, the windows coated so thick by the mosslike film that no light came.... "Picrine" was the name of this place... from the picric acid (115).

For the typhus survivors who could get some decent food there was hope. For the Picrine people, considered expendable by the Reich, the situation was hopeless; "their disease pursued them in the yellow dust, poisoning their breath, poisoning whatever came near them..." (120).

Karmel's characters are preoccupied by hunger. Prisoners' lives focus on the distribution and supplementation of inadequate rations; their conversations and relationships are food centered. The women think about food, talk about it, imagine it, dream about it. Occasionally daydreams of food comfort the victims as when they plan to eat in each other's houses after the war. More often, they measure their value to the Germans by food distribution. The German policy of withholding or distributing food as punishment and reward permits the prisoners to understand that they are meant to survive when they are given food for the journey from Plaszow to Skarzysko. It is most often in conjunction with hunger and illness that the women's dedication to each other's survival evidences itself most profoundly.

In addition to hunger and illness, a staple of the concentrationary experience is periodic selections. Never evident whether a selection is to be for a work transport or for death, each is cause for panic. Combining stream of consciousness and third person description, Karmel faithfully captures the terror that overtakes the women as they become aware that a selection is to occur. The sudden and capricious nature of the selection is telegraphed to readers by Karmel's juxtaposition of the announcement with a relatively calm scene where the women are enjoying a brief respite from work, preparing food and sharing comradery in the absence of O.D. men. From Tola's perspective, we watch the women scurry, some concealing their money in their clothing, some trying to find suitable hiding places, some muttering about the selfishness of the escapee who knew that those left behind would be punished for his escape, the older ones rouging their pallid faces, the young deluding themselves that only the old, less productive workers would be taken and finally admitting that anyone is subject to selection.

Skarzysko selections are presented dramatically from the initial selection for transfer to the camp to its liquidation. To the women it is a night like any other when O.D. men suddenly burst into their work barracks, tear the women from their seats, kicking and pushing them outside, driving them to the quarantine barracks where those destined to be shot are kept. They seem doomed when O.D. men excuse relatives, friends, and mistresses whose names they read from prepared lists. Finally, an O.D. man vainly tries to calm their fears by swearing that they are simply going to another camp. But, not until the women are given bread and cheese, a sign that the Germans still consider them worthy of work, do they accept the O.D. man's word. At Skarzysko, the women are again subject to selections to determine their work assignments marking them either for picrine work and a relatively quick and painful death; for the trotyl plant, where they will fill shells with trotyl powder that tinges the hair red; or for Werke C where they will be more likely to die from starvation or conventional camp illnesses like typhus.

Because Karmel sets her work in camps that subjected men and women to similar hardships she notes no gender distinction in their suffering aside from one character's efforts to sustain an "illegal" pregnancy. Her manner of delineating camp coping strategies does, however, draw on virtues often associated with female attitudes and behavior, principally bonding and creating substitute families.

Holocaust novels written by men rarely reflect the intensity of male bonding described by Primo Levi in *Survival in Auschwitz*. Female bonding, however, is a major theme in women's Holocaust literature. In private conversation and in fictional voice, Karmel testifies to the decency and generosity which the women she knew extended to one another while living in deprivation, humiliation, and terror. Repeatedly Karmel's women call upon gender-related nurturing faculties to sustain hope and life. Like the female survivors whose testimony constitutes the *Proceedings of the Conference on Women Surviving the Holocaust* (Ringelheim & Katz), Karmel's characters huddle together to bring a small measure of warmth to their frozen bodies, share precious food, nurse each other through typhus and dysentery, tend to each other's wounds after punishments and beatings, assist each other or replace each other at work, comfort and encourage each other through depression and fear, and share memories and hope for the future. Those who have survival strategies coach newcomers. The oldtimers who survived Majdanek before coming to Skarzysko, advise the novices to get a "cousin," a male who will take care of them and without whom it will be difficult to survive. The women form small "makeshift camp families" who share food, work, and nursing duties to enhance their chances for survival. This practice speaks eloquently to their dignity in the midst of barbarism, demonstrating that no matter how beleaguered these women are, they wage a constant battle to retain the very humanity the Nazis seek to demean.

Representative of the bonding theme are scenes of nursing the ill during a typhus epidemic. Starved and sick women, who are themselves exhausted from slave labor, nurse those who are even closer to death.[2] To help one another through dysentery, typhus, and starvation, the women engage in buying and selling to get bits of food, a cup of soup, or medicine. Tola scurries from one barracks to another bartering whatever she can, cornmeal, beet-marmalade, bread, even clothing from the dead. Tola even undergoes primitive dental surgery, selling her gold tooth to buy extra food for the women. Barbara tries to arrange sale of her estate property to provide for the women of her barracks and Picrine. When she has nothing to sell, Barbara helps Aurelia through her labor, doing laundry, washing floors, managing thereby to buy a few potatoes or a piece of bread.

Group solidarity is a survival mechanism in the concentrationary universe. Individual strength to endure the unbearable comes from the common need to keep self and group alive. The importance of the bonding theme may be judged not only from its dramatic and conceptual development, but from Karmel's own statement of its importance to her psyche. She believes "one needed to love someone because you couldn't love yourself. If you could love someone, you could come back to yourself. . . . One had to have an image of a person to save oneself from seeing everyone like so much eating, defecating flesh."[3] Without labeling it as a bonding relationship, in his book *Survivors*, Terrence Des Pres characterizes the bonding experience as evidence that "the need *to* help is as basic as the need *for* help"[4] and associates those needs with the social nature of life in the camps and the tendency for "gift giving" among inmates, acts which "were enormously valuable both as morale boosters and often as real aids in the struggle for life." [5] The gifts, which were usually food, became a means of sharing vital wealth, "based on the elementary social act of reciprocity or mutual exchange."[6] This form of assistance created bonds that were at once social and economic, spiritual and physical. Thus, in a system designed to dehumanize the victims, the victims themselves found ways to defeat the Nazi goals and sustain their humanity.

Beyond her powerful rendering of the physical deprivation in concentration camps, Karmel's achievement lies in dramatizing the victims' moral dilemmas, mental anguish, and psychological survival strategies. Her characters confront the pervasive ethical quandries of the Holocaust universe that are routinely short shrifted in Holocaust fiction. In *Estate of Memory* characters question whether one should save oneself or forego escape knowing it will result in massive retaliation against those prisoners who remain. They ask how one may control her tongue rather than lash out against a tormentor, an indifferent witness to one's public humiliation, an informer, or a denouncer. They ask whether one should protect oneself during a "selection" knowing that the quota will be filled by another, whether one must allow a needy friend to hide where one had intended to conceal oneself? At what point, a character asks, may generosity be extended to self-preservation: "Anything done for someone else is a sacrifice, a noble deed: but try to do the same thing for yourself and the sacrifice becomes a disgrace. Why? I too am someone: I've no contract for survival. I too am afraid" (342).

Moral and ethical dilemmas of the Jewish characters are at the heart of *An Estate of Memory*. Camp conditions were designed to make life for the inmates unbearable, to intensively exploit their labor and to consign them to death through disease, starvation, exposure, or machine gun squad. Survival depended on illegal activities by the prisoners, activities that came to be known as "organization." "To organize" was to obtain food, clothing, medicine, anything one needed to prolong life, without harming another prisoner. When life itself is a crime, the women's activities to acquire food, to maintain their health through illegal purchases of medicine, to assist a pregnant woman to survive and deliver her child and then smuggle it from the camp are heroic acts of resistance. Karmel's women engage in the characteristic Cracow Ghetto and Plaszow camp practices of selling contraband to Poles to supplement the starvation rations. To survive, one somehow had to supplement, whether buying some extra food that had been smuggled into the camp or getting that which was still protected outside the camp. Thus one woman dons layers of clothing and sells the items to Poles at work and another tries to get a message to her estate manager to sell some of her property. When the work unit returns to camp, money is "hidden in handkerchiefs or rolled-up gloves; food in pockets of coats slung across the arm, so that in case of a search they could be thrown aside at once" (15).[7]

The camp careers of Tola Ohrenstein and Barbara Grunbaum constitute the central morality drama of *An Estate of Memory*. Tola's story exemplifies accommodation to the Nazi universe. Barbara's tale is one of Jewish ethical defiance. In Barbara's portrait the dignity of the victim is preeminent; her moral decisions are testimony to the decency of thousands who daily faced ethical dilemmas. Entering Plaszow with the advantage of an assumed Polish identity, Barbara later voluntarily abandons the ruse. She walks away from the Polish prisoners destined for labor in Germany to join her Jewish sisters whose fate she knows is far worse. Despite the danger, she is relieved to return to her Jewish identity because "she hungered for the sound of her name, longed to hear it spoken and to speak of herself, . . . she would not spend this war like a parasite, helping no one, thinking of nothing but saving her own skin" (84). Ever vigilant against moral lapses, Barbara guards against succumbing to the

> Two kinds of evil, she felt were at work here. The first came from outside: once localized, once enclosed within huge helmeted figures, it grew ubiquitous here, lurking in hunger, in typhus and the bitter dust. The other evil was new. It came from within. It had a shape--of the "leeches," the vendors whom she loathed . . . they would invade the barracks . . . with delicacies obscene in this place, white bread, butter, eggs tempting everyone: the rich to spend their wealth on themselves rather than to share it as they should, the poor to barter away their very last" (121).

Although Barbara's moral decline is much less devastating than is Tola's, there is nevertheless a significant metamorphosis from Plaszow saint to Skarzysko benevolent despot. Barbara's motive is not self-interest as is Tola's, but she too becomes a fierce disciplinarian of all in her charge. Nursing sixty women, soft words yield to a commanding tone. No longer tender and solicitous, she becomes a fiend for cleanliness. High fever cannot excuse allowing something to drop on the floor. Even the sick must air and sweep the barracks and wash although they feel too weak to move. Barbara howls at hoarders, calling them "Rodents, scavengers!" She beats the women without remorse and insults them without apology, determined to get them to fight their illness. According to Karmel, Barbara needed to learn that speaking sweetly in conditions of extremity was not always effective.[8] In the concentrationary universe discipline had its place.

Of the four women, Tola's concentrationary metamorphosis is most extreme, her moral decline most dangerous. Exhausted by her efforts to feed the group and keep its members alive, Tola transforms herself from civilized aristocrat to peddler-survivor and finally to guard-survivor. Obsession with personal survival apart from group survival emerges only after years of accommodation to the concentrationary world, during which the hieress to a mercantile fortune delivers scraps, old clothes, "coats from which the lining had been ripped out to make a dress, dresses reeking of sweat; and crooked shoes" (171) to women who sell them to the Poles in exchange for two cups of soup for the four women to share. Although honesty and fair prices were consistent in her business operations for years, near war's end with desperation at its height, she is more cynical recognizing that "with the market so glutted by typhus that lockets and gold teeth went for a crust of bread, she earned hardly a pittance, cheat though she did" (329).

When Tola privatizes her survival strategy, she undertakes a course of action which she knows demands separation from the group. She applies, near war's end, for the *Anweiserin* position, a job which demands that she assure work quotas, oversee the work of others, accept responsibility for the production and behavior of her group. Barbara rebukes Tola, assuming that she accepted the burden to help the foursome, and tells her one must draw the line there, that she cannot accept that role to help them. But Tola acknowledges that her motive is self interest. "She wanted safety and the bread that would come later at night" (381). To the charge that she will be a slave driver, that she will be ordered to do something terrible, Tola's response demonstrates the cynical reality of the concentrationary world: "Someone else will do it if I don't" (343). She admits taking the job to save herself, to avoid having the others drag her down. As she becomes tainted, memories invoking the moral norms of her former life, memories which might have served as a foothold to the future, become reproaches.

To judge the conduct of the victims one must recognize the status structure of the camps which included an SS aristocracy and a secondary supervisory staff drawn from German Ukrainian allies, privileged prisoners chosen either for their known criminal brutality, because of their friends, or their German language skills which permitted them to translate German orders to the non-German speaking prison populace. Although German criminals and other nationals were likely to be in privileged positions, in some camps, like Plaszow and Skarzysko, Jews were among the lower ranks of work and barracks supervisors who were in positions to garner better treatment than their underlings. The SS policy of using prisoners to fill key positions as block elders, kapos, and work supervisors was effective because they felt obliged to follow German orders as life insurance for themselves and their families. Failure to discipline or make the crews productive meant death for the supervisors. Success meant extra food and better living conditions. Their survival at stake, many performed their duties brutally, beating the inmates for slight, and imagined, infractions of the rules in order to impress the SS. The system frequently provoked arbitrary and unequal harassment, bribery, and unrelenting cruelty. There were decent kapos and block elders who tried to alleviate the suffering of their charges, but they were a distinct minority.

Tola's transformation is charted from her initial hesitant acceptance of the privileged role, accompanied by painful accommodation to harsh supervision of underlings and denial of work exemptions under any circumstances, to her hardened acquiescence to a hierarchy of evil and absurdity. Toward the end, she simply rationalizes her behavior and ignores peer disapproval, driving the women in her charge to secure her own bread and survival. Tola rejects Barbara's advice that she motivate the women through self-preservation, beating them and yelling at them if necessary as long as she convinces them that they must work for themselves, "each for herself, because if they don't something terrible might be done to them" (367). Tola asks: "Why should I tell them that they want to live, when it's easier for me to threaten with Rost? Much easier!" (367) Tola rejects Barbara's advice, insisting "there's no glory to be got out of me, not a shred. I'm not like you, I must be an *Anweiserin* in my own way" (367). As *Anweiserin*, Tola leads a double life, constantly plotting how she will manipulate the women to satisfy the Germans to whom she is responsible. She grows hostile toward her charges, ever fearful that they are sabotaging her efforts, trying to get away with less labor, standing watch against her barracks arrival as she had earlier done against other supervisors.

Although Tola has certainly undergone a metamorphosis, accelerated by the *Anweiserin* position, she has not been entirely corrupted. If she can help her fellow victims, she does; as when she strives to protect the most debilitated women during a selection for extra shell loading by asking the stronger women to volunteer and spare the feeble in their ranks. In the final days of Skarzysko, Tola realizes that the price of survival is too dear. As the women dig a mass grave, she decides to try to save them or die with them rather than continue in collaborative isolation. She weeps purgative tears "for what has been done to her and for what she has done to those ... with whom she would soon be together" (433). In the Epilogue we learn that Tola died in a death march while trying to shield a starving girl running from the line into a field of oats. She saw a guard taking aim at the girl, ran to warn her and took the bullet meant for the girl.

In an environment where active resistance is severely limited, the women wage psychological resistance daily. Whether smuggling news of Allied progress against the Axis forces or praying, the women fight to remain true to their own values. Illustrative of this dignity is a barracks Sabbath scene when an old Rebbetzyn follows her day of labor by sweeping the last crumb from the barracks floor and "lighting two tallow butts stuck into scooped-out potatoes" (141). The old woman blessed the candles and honored the commandment to light the Sabbath candles as Jewish women have done through the centuries. During this short scene the mood shifts from Holocaust darkness to Sabbath light as other women enter the barracks for Sabbath visits, "when to greet them the women leaned out of their bunks, the barracks came to resemble a quiet street, where neighbors lean out of their windows to chat with those passing by" (141). Some sing. Some rest. Some delouse and repair their clothes. There are no quarrels, no arguments, no shouting to marr the rare Sabbath peace.

Memory of prewar normality is another means of psychological resistance to the daily rounds of humiliation the women suffer. "The effect of memory on Barbara and on the others to the extent that they adopt her method of coping, is to relativize the present reality and provide an avenue of mental escape."[9] Historic testimonies often allude to women sharing stories of their family histories, the households, and food preparation. Karmel too attests to the importance of these exchanges of prewar experience as distraction from concentrationary brutality, of briefly and temporarily transcending the present, and as means of maintaining hope for the eventual return to normality. The novel takes its title from such sustaining memories and from the listener's recognition that most of the people recollected were probably no longer among the living, hence "After the names of husband and child came 'of blessed memory'--the inevitable epithet ... and memory seemed an estate where those remembered had chosen to dwell" (397). The psychiatrist-survivor Viktor Frankl attests to the salutary effects of memory, arguing:

This intensification of inner life helped the prisoner find a refuge from the emptiness, desolation, and spiritual poverty of his existence, by letting him escape into the past. When given free rein, his imagination played with past events.[10]

For Barbara the future is "the past transplanted" (p. 120). Barbara's dream of return to her husband's embrace, to the welcome reception of the household servants, and even to the furnishings in her manor, is gradually adopted as a survival dream by the others. The lone woman among the group who has--or at least can believe she has--someone and some place to return to, Barbara serves as guide to the future. Diaries and testimonies, especially those of women, often make reference to female prisoners sharing family stories. The conviction that there was someone to return to contributed mightily to the weakened prisoner's determination to survive.

Active resistance occurs as the women sabotage the ammunition they work on and "stand six," watching for the arrival of the Germans and their flunkies, while the women stop work to rest or warm food scraps on the stove. A rare overt act of resistance is taken by Barbara on Alinka's behalf. Soldiers come in to clear the hospital barracks during the Skarzysko liquidation, but Barbara refuses to allow Alinka to join the other victims. She commands the girl to stay put and pushes the soldier away. Perhaps the act of frustrating the guard's interest in taking Alinka seals Barbara's fate. As she pushes Alinka away once more, this time as she is lifting other victims onto the truck, the guard sweeps Barbara up with those destined for murder. So intense is Barbara's determination to save Alinka, that she hardly knew it "when she herself was pulled by gloved hands back and up onto the truck" (437). The last concerted effort by Barbara and Tola is to save Alinka. As the truck pulls away and Alinka runs toward it, Barbara at first hurls things at her, and then encourages the doctor and O.D. men to hold her, but finally, it is Tola who clasps the child in a protective embrace.

The shared determination to bring Aurelia's pregnancy to successful term and to smuggle her infant to safety constitutes a major act of resistance to the Nazi ban on Jewish pregnancies. For Aurelia, sustaining a fetus in the concentrationary universe is an exercise in concealment. For the other women, Aurelia's pregnancy intensifies efforts to secure extra food and leads them to organize a safe delivery and escape for the infant knowing they would lose their own lives if caught in this offense against the Reich. News of Aurelia's child's survival sustains the spiritual resistance of many women in the camp. If they can believe, as some do, that an underground organization rescued the child or that a partisan fighter actually entered the camp to smuggle the child out, then perhaps they too can be rescued. The tale of the delivery of Aurelia's baby from Skarzysko "was big enough to take upon itself the burden of their longing for proof, for the least sign that out 'in the Freedom' they still mattered" (277).

Karmel celebrates the success of conspiratorial efforts by these concentration camp sisters who help each other survive and sustain the birth, and escape, of a child in the charnel house of death. Only the baby and Alinka live, yet all the women will live on in the estate of reader memory, in part because they appear in roles most often attributed to male Holocaust characters--they are questers and actors struggling to control their own destinies in an environment designed first to debase and then to destroy them. Rather than dismissing the female perspective as marginal, as much male-written Holocaust fiction does, Ilona Karmel creates fully defined female protagonists and thereby contributes to the recovery and remembrance of Jewish women's Holocaust history. In this way Karmel is worthy of the praise Ellen Morgan offers writers who enable "living women to view women's past in their own terms, thus clearing away that part of women's conditioning which has resulted from the focus of history on exclusively male pursuits and the concomitant diminishing of women as ancillary to the process of civilization."[11]

NOTES

1. Ilona Karmel, *An Estate of Memory*. (Boston: Houghton Mifflin Company, 1969), 138.
2. Karmel, her mother, and sister "adopted" a young typhus patient. The author's mother nursed her as she did her own children. (Lillian Kremer Interview with Ilona Karmel, 24 May 1988).
3. Kremer/Karmel Interview.
4. Terrence Des Pres, *The Survivor: An Anatomy of Life in the Death Camps*. (New York: Oxford University Press, 1976), 136.
5. Des Pres, 136.
6. Des Pres, 138.
7. The source of this scene is probably the practice Karmel describes of a guard she knew who allowed prisoners to smuggle what they could into Plaszow. (Kremer/Karmel Interview).
8. Kremer/Karmel Interview.
9. Sidra DeKoven Ezrahi, *By Words Alone: The Holocaust in Literature*. (Chicago and London: The University of Chicago Press, 1980) 83.
10. Viktor Frankl, *From Death Camp to Existentialism: A Psychiatrist's Path to New Therapy*, p. 38.
11. Ellen Morgan, "Humanbecoming: Form and Focus in the Neo-Feminist Novel," *Images of Women in Fiction: FeministPerspectives* ed. Susan Koppelman Cornillon (Bowling Green: Bowling Green University Popular Press, 1972) 187.

Sylvia Plath and the Reporting of the Holocaust in the Popular Press

Gary M. Leonard

Ariel was Sylvia Plath's final collection of poems, published posthumously in 1965, three years after she took her own life. This collection was the first evidence of Sylvia Plath's overt use of the Holocaust as a metaphor in her poetry. Four years after the publication of *Ariel*, George Steiner posed the unsettling question that has since become part of the Sylvia Plath myth: "Does any writer . . . other than an actual survivor have the right to put on this death-rig? . . . what extraterritorial right had Sylvia Plath . . . to draw on the animate horror in the ash and the children's shoes? . . . Do any of us have license to locate our personal disaster, raw as these may be, in Auschwitz?" (Steiner 1970, 305). Is Plath's use of the reality of the Nazi concentration camps a personal self-indulgence that trivializes the historical event? Steiner suggests the complexity of this issue by the fact that he defines the question clearly, but attempts no answer.

Five years after Steiner's question, Brian Murdoch offers this response: "There is no reason . . . why the assumption of the 'death-rig' should not be honorable, even when there is no memorial intended. Sylvia Plath uses the imagery to underline her own suffering, but a symbol must always carry a concrete meaning of its own. The initial cognitive response of Sylvia Plath's use of Auschwitz imagery serves as a memorial in its own right" (Murdoch, 146). I might highlight Murdoch's point about Plath's response being a memorial of sorts by mentioning that of the over three hundred poems by Plath that we know of, only four contain overt allusions to the Holocaust. Yet these four poems have kept the horror of the camps as a vivid and disturbing image in the minds of students and scholars for nearly thirty years. In his conclusion, Murdoch comments that "in some ways, Sylvia Plath comes closer to the horror, even though not directly caught up in it historically, than many of the more involved poets."

Steiner, despite what I have quoted above, comes to a similar conclusion in a later essay and then speculates further about why this may be so:

> Sylvia Plath is only one of a number of young contemporary poets, novelists and playwrights, themselves in no way implicated in the actual Holocaust, who have done most to counter the general inclination to forget the death camps. Perhaps it is only those who had no part in the events who *can* focus on them rationally and imaginatively; to those who experienced the thing it has stepped outside the real (Steiner 1970a, 217).

This assessment is instructive on two points, at least. First, it acknowledges the imaginative power of Plath's poetry, and secondly it reminds us she is only one of many writers who, even though they were not a part of the historical event, use imagery derived from the fact of the Holocaust. Plath, of course, was a poet, not a historian, and one dimension of this issue that has been overlooked is that nearly all of her information about the Holocaust has been presented in the ahistorical format of popular American magazines (primarily *Life* and *Time*). These highly commercial and intensely competitive magazines surrounded the text and photographs of the Holocaust reports with garish, technicolor advertisements for the innumerable commodities soon to be available in the prosperous economy of a victorious post-World War II America. Ironically, because Plath has been one of the most effective artists to give permanence to the horror of the Holocaust, she has also been the one censured most often. "Images deriving from the horrors of the Nazi concentration camps have become commonplace in much modern lyric poetry," Murdoch says "in a manner that does not hold true for other large scale crimes against humanity" (123). Murdoch does not speculate why this is so, but I would like to try. Nazi atrocities compel in their own right, but the way they were revealed to the American public must also be taken into account when commenting upon Plath's use of this imagery.

There was a steady, measured progression to these revelations in the press, a progression which matched the methodical approach of the American Army into Berlin. Unconfirmed and unbelievable rumors were gradually shown, via shocking photographic evidence, to be true. The stories and photographs of the camps came to an American people eager for news about the villainy of their enemy. Typically, the focus of the articles is on the atrocity of the Nazi regime and not on the plight of the victims and survivors of the camps. Those who continued to remember what the magazines depicted, remembered the photographs. Susan Sontag, in her book *On Photography*, describes the effect of seeing the photographs, both at the time she viewed them and thirty years later:

> One's first encounter with the photographic inventory of ultimate horror is a kind of revelation, the prototypically modern refelation: a negative epiphany. For me it was photographs of Bergen-Belsen and Dachau which I came across by chance in a bookstore in Santa Monica in July 1945. Nothing I have seen--in photographs or in real life--ever cut me as sharply, deeply, instantaneously.... When I looked at those photographs, something broke. Some limit had been reached, and not only that of horror I felt irrevocably grieved, wounded, but a part of my feelings started to tighten; something went dead; something is still crying (Sontag, 19-20).

There is no comparing Sontag's suffering with that of a concentration camp survivor, but it would be wrong, I think, and even a step towards allowing the Holocaust to be forgotten, to dismiss her reaction--as too removed from the heart of the darkness to be valid. Unlike traditional historical accounts of world events, the massive and appalling documentation of the Holocaust was made "public" by commercial "popular" magazines *immediately* upon there being found.

In other words, what we might call Holocaust "scholarship" did not exist until virtually everyone had seen the raw and unprocessed data that scholars now study. In an unprecedented way, the first interpreters of the Holocaust were harried feature editors, journalists on deadline, and managing editors with one eye on the profitable "scoops" being made either by their magazine or by a competing magazine. Eyewitness stories and grainy photographs, virtually without scholarly commentary or historical and geographical context, is what any viewer with the price of a magazine might see. If the virtually unmediated, sudden, and massive dissemination of atrocity disclosures is taken into account, we may understand better why "[i]mages deriving from the horrors of the Nazi concentration camps have become commonplace in much modern lyric poetry in a manner that does not hold true for other large scale crimes against humanity." As I hope to show, it was not only the "popular" format of the disclosures to a mass audience, but also the commercial format of the magazines. The Holocaust stories were surrounded by advertisements and other aggressively cheerful features designed to sell both commodities and a post-World War II American ideology that the "good life" was now available for one and all (in direct contrast to the Holocaust images of devastation, despair, and death). The American mass audience looked directly at mass murder in a context that insisted every atrocity being uncovered (blurry, anonymous, barren) could be understood as a foil for the increasingly bright ("technicolor") future of America.

James E. Young, in his 1988 book *Writing and Rewriting the Holocaust*, indicates that, as with the execution of the Rosenbergs, Plath, when employing imagery of the Holocaust, is reacting to the explosion of mass-media coverage and not purely to the historical events depicted and described:

> The choice of the Holocaust Jew as a trope ... by Plath has less to do with its intrinsic appropriateness than it does with its visibility as a public figure for suffering. As was the case to some extent with the Rosenberg's execution, the salient aspect of the Holocaust was its wide public knowledge, its place as a figure in the public mind. Where figures of destruction had traditionally taken generations to enter the literary imagination being passed down an epoch and a book at a time, in America's mass media of the fifties and England's of the sixties, generations of inherited memory were compressed within the space of months. Image selected by the media for their spectacular and often horrifying qualities became the most common figures of all (120).

What I wish to add to Young's insightful reading is that the mass media was much more of a commercial enterprise than an historical one, and thus Plath's so-called "Holocaust poems" can be read as an angry indictment of an American popular press that exposed Nazi atrocities in an atmosphere of relentless consumerism. By surrounding the text with advertisements for shoes, frozen TV Dinners, shampoos and so on, the documentation of the Holocaust became, primarily, a vehicle for selling commodities and only secondarily a historical account or a truly sympathetic commentary.

Plath may have adopted the figure of a Holocaust Jew as a trope for her own suffering because every depiction of the Holocaust in the popular press confidently presented the atrocities as something shockingly antithetical to the post-war prosperity of what was triumphantly labelled "the American way of life." In her novel *The Bell Jar*, Plath exposes the manipulative photographic optimism of the magazine *Ladies' Day* (*Mademoiselle*, in actuality) by showing that even the cheerful photographs of the narrator bear a false relationship to her actual emotional state: "[W]hen my picture came out in the magazine ... drinking martinis in a skimpy, imitation silver-lame bodice stuck on to a big, fat cloud of white tulle, on some Starlight Roof, in the company of several anonymous young men with all-American bone structures hired or loaned for the occasion--everybody would think I must be having a real whirl" (2). As the narrator slowly descends into a suicidal depression, she is constantly required to radiate optimism for the insatiable lens of the *Ladies' Day* camera: "When they asked me what I wanted to be I said I didn't know. 'Oh, sure you know,' the photographer said. . . . I said I wanted to be a poet. . . . The photographer fiddled with his hot white lights. 'Show us how happy it makes you to write a poem'" (83). Everything about American culture must radiate happiness, and the irredeemable black and white grimness of the *European* Holocaust becomes just another way to celebrate the triumphant, technicolor excess of American commodity culture.

In *Life* magazine, September 18, 1944, for example, an eye-witness account of a young girl being thrust alive into an oven shares the page with an advertisement for a dandruff shampoo. The first account reads "[t]hey grabbed the girl and bound her hands and legs. She was carried to the crematorium, where they put her on one of the iron stretchers and slid her into an oven. . . . 'There was one loud scream. Her hair flared up in the flames momentarily. Then I could see no more'" (18). The advertisement in the column to the left of this story features a mother scolding her grown son and insisting that he will not succeed if he does not take better care of his hair: "This time you'll listen to me, Sonny Boy! I'm getting plenty sick of you looking like Flaky Joe, Hair's Horrible Example! . . . Every morning and night she herded me into the bathroom and doused on Listerine Antiseptic. . . . Boy! Did my scalp feel like a million." Verbs like "herded" and "doused," as well as epitaphs like "Hair's Horrible Example!" take on a macabre and hysterical tone once they are *consciously* juxtaposed with the eyewitness account. My point, however, is not that the editors of *Life* were cynical or heartless in allowing this juxtaposition; quite the opposite, what is most startling (and instructive) is that they obviously thought nothing of it at all.

Still, consciously or not, it is an unavoidable fact that long before Plath's appropriation of Holocaust imagery became the subject of heated debate, the very first presentations of the Holocaust to the American public were done in a format where the information helped to sell shampoo, soda--even soap and shoes. In a *Life* article dated October 30, 1944, John Hersey recounts the story he has been told of the wooden pyres built for the purpose of mass execution: "SS men with revolvers stepped onto the platforms and shot those who were lying there, one by one, in the back of the head." On the left hand column, in splashy type, one reads "A Tomato Juice cocktail with plenty of zip--it's a WOW!" On the right hand column is a shoe advertisement: "You can't be at your best unless your feet are. Avoid that tired-all-over feeling with the double comfort of Porto-Ped Shoes. You'll enjoy the pillowing effect of the patented, resilient air cushion. . . ." Again, the absurd over-emphasis on comfort and sensation seems bizarre at best, but what it most profoundly demonstrates is the extent to which the American economy--as well as American advertising and popular culture--seemed to be headed away from any historical involvement with the war toward a blissful technicolor future of unambivalent comfort and joy. In other words, the first accounts of the Holocaust are already framed in a way that allows them to horrify, while at the same time assuring the reader that such stories have no relevance to the future of America, except to make us that much prouder of the monstrous enemy we have defeated.

From an early age, Plath was very familiar with the world of popular magazines. While still in high school, she submitted forty-five stories to the magazine *Seventeen* before one was accepted. Later, she won first prize in fiction for her short story "Sunday at the Mintons" which appeared in the August 1952 issue of *Mademoiselle*. As one of her biographers remarks, "[t]hroughout her life, Sylvia was infatuated with the idea of becoming a professional writer of short stories for the 'slick' magazines . . ." (Butscher 248). As we shall see, however, this "infatuation" was extremely ambivalent, and Plath alternated between her ambition to write upbeat "women's stories" and her rage against the mindlessly optimistic fluff and fashion of "women's" magazines. Finally, while a sophomore at Smith college, she was one of twenty women (picked from nearly a thousand applicants) to serve on the guest editorial board for the August 1953 College Issue of *Mademoiselle*. Nothing about the Holocaust ever appeared in any issue of these magazines, a point that was not lost on Plath.

In *The Bell Jar*, the first person narrator cannot get over the gap between the antiseptic magazine *Ladies' Day* and the brutal fact of the Rosenbergs' impending electrocution: "I knew something was wrong with me that summer, because all I could think about was the Rosenbergs and how stupid I'd been to buy all those uncomfortable, expensive clothes, hanging limp as fish in my closet, and how all the little successes I'd totted up so happily at college fizzled to nothing outside the slick marble and plate-glass fronts along Madison Avenue" (1-2). The advertising and popular culture represented by Madison Avenue is hermetically sealed against events such as the execution of the Rosenbergs, and the narrator is frightened by her own frenetic complicity in this censorship. It is a complicity that Plath herself was not able to abandon until the last few years of her life. In the early sixties, at the time she was writing what would be her final poems, she harshly rejects her mother's advice to try and write cheerful stories for magazines such as *Mademoiselle* and *Ladies' Home Journal* (advice she had diligently followed in the past): "Don't talk to me about the world needing cheerful stuff," she wrote her mother in October 1962. "What the person out of Belsen, physical or psychological, wants is nobody saying the birdies go tweet-tweet, but the full knowledge that somebody else has been there and knows the worst, just what it is like. It is much more help for me, for example, to know that people are divorced and go through hell, than to hear about happy marriages. Let the *Ladies' Home Journal* blither about *those*" (*Letters Home*, 473). I would suggest that when Plath's later poetic voice says "I may be a Jew" she is speaking as someone who has been invited behind the implacable plate-glass fronts of Madison Avenue; that is to say, she intends her announcement, delivered from *inside* the plate glass walls, as a deliberate subversion of the false yet profitable image of the world of happy consumption that is formulated by the magazine.

Judith Doneson, in her recent essay "The American History of Anne Frank's Diary," reports that "[i]n 1947, a journalist visiting displaced persons' camps could not help but compare the continuing presence and influence of the war and destruction in Europe with the existing atmosphere in the United States: 'America has already come out of the war, has almost forgotten it. Even the post-World War II mood is in back of us'" (149). Doneson goes on to make the case that Anne Frank's famous ending--"In spite of all, I still believe men are good"--soon came to be interpreted by mass audiences as "the forgiving of a Christian lapse of goodness" (156). Such a popular interpretation insisted on seeing Frank's statement of forgiveness as her final word on the subject of the Holocaust, even though it was necessarily written before her fatal deportation. Anne Frank's view of the "final solution" at the time she completed her diary, though horrible enough, was still quite limited; ironically, her penultimate statement was increasingly accepted and popularized by the popular press as details of other Nazi atrocities--about which she knew nothing--continued to find their way into the mass media. Her phrase, or rather its translation--"in spite of all"--allows for a moment of sober recollection that in no way hinders the pressing business of celebrating what Doneson characterizes as a specifically American "postwar period . . . of unparalleled prosperity" (149). There is much gasping and wringing of hands by the editors, journalists and writers who introduce Holocaust stories into the popular press, but equally strong is the implication--conveyed by advertisements as well as the other feature articles in the magazines--that all is safe now for a full indulgence in the commodity fetishism of "the American way."

As I hope to show, it is this self-satisfied packaging of the Holocaust that Plath found frightening, and which she sought to subvert with her use of Holocaust imagery. While she may have used Holocaust imagery to figure her own pain, she was also making the larger point that the Holocaust figures a tragedy at the heart of the human condition, and to present one's self or one's culture as being somehow above it is to sow the seeds of ignorance necessary for its eventual reoccurrence. Indeed, Plath most likely did not arrive at this point of view entirely on her own. Alfred Kazin, a scholar who taught Plath for two semesters at Smith College and who then contributed a recommendation for her successful Fulbright application, wrote an essay in 1944 in *The New Republic* that deplored "the desperate and unreal optimism, with which we try to cover up the void in ourselves." He went on to warn that "fascism remains, even though fascists, too, can die." His final indictment is of "the materialism" of people "who want only to live and let live, to have the good life back--and who think that you can dump three million helpless Jews into your furnace, and sigh in the genuine impotence of your undeniable regret . . . where so great a murder has been allowed, no one is safe . . . men are not ashamed of what they have been in this time, and are therefore not prepared for the further outbreaks of fascism which are so deep in all of us."

The occasion for Kazin's essay was a suicide letter left by Shmuel Ziegelboim, a Polish survivor of a concentration camp and then published "in a negligible corner of *The New York Times*." At the conclusion of the text of the letter, *The Times* added a bit of what Kazin calls "mechanical emotion," stating that "Shmuel Ziegelboim will have accomplished as much in dying as he did in living." Kazin remarks "[o]f course the newspaper writer did not believe that he had accomplished anything; nor did the Polish National Council, which released it to the world; nor do I." Kazin's anger is not directed at the letter, but at the way the letter is carelessly depicted, against all logic, as something hopeful. Ziegelboim's letter states, in part: "The responsibility for this crime of murdering the entire Jewish population of Poland falls in the first instance on the perpetrators, but indirectly it is also a burden on the whole of humanity. . . ." Kazin conjectures "he was thinking not only of his own people at the end, but of the hollowness of a world in which such a massacre could have so little meaning." Plath not only took courses with Kazin, she requested extra time to talk with him outside of class, and wrote an article about him for the *Smith Alumnae Quarterly*; it is unlikely that the obsessively thorough Plath knew nothing of this essay.

It is crucial to consider the effect of such an essay on Plath, because then, to choose just one example, her stark statement "[e]very woman adores a Fascist"--a famous line from her poem "Daddy"--may be seen as a considered reaction to the phenomenon of the Holocaust. Her observation contains an insistence that the world is not safe--can never be safe--in a world of nuclear capability that continues to figure absolute power as a force that is viewed as attractive--and even erotic--precisely because it presents itself as beyond morality. Kazin's speculation that Ziegelboim's final despair was not a result of the Holocaust itself, but of "the hollowness of a world in which such a massacre could have so little meaning," is similar to the despair the narrator of *The Bell Jar* feels when one of her fellow editors comments on the upcoming execution of the Rosenbergs:

"I'm so glad they're going to die."
Hilda arched her cat-limbs in a yawn, buried her head in her arms on the conference table and went back to sleep. A wisp of bilious green straw perched on her brow like a tropical bird.
Bile green. They were promoting it for fall. . . . Fashion blurbs, silver and full of nothing, sent up their fishy bubbles in my brain. They surfaced with a hollow pop (81).

The "hollow pop" of the fashion and advertising world is as uncomfortable for the narrator as "those . . . expensive clothes, hanging limp as fish in my closet." But what really frightens her about Hilda is the way she speaks like one in a trance, an unthinking and uninformed fashion plate perfectly brainwashed by anti-Rosenberg cold war propaganda: "Hilda moved like a mannequin. . . . The night before I'd seen a play where the heroine was possessed by a dybbuk. . . . Well, Hilda's voice sounded just like the voice of that dybbuk" (81).

In this analogy, the mass-media possesses the individual and substitutes prefabricated opinion--"fashion blurbs," if you will--for more substantive thought. Certainly Plath knew about the "hollow" content of popular magazines first hand. The application for a *Mademoiselle* guest editorship defined the job as follows: "You'll work on the College issue, go to parties, the theatre, and interview celebrities in your field of interest." *Mademoiselle* subtitles itself "For Smart Young Women," but the best and brightest of this set are not expected to do anything more than endlessly certify that everything about America guarantees, sanctions--and even

They are always with us, the thin people
Meager of dimension as the gray people
On a movie-screen. They
Are unreal, we say:
It was only in a movie, it was only
In a war making evil headlines when we
Were small that they famished and
Grew so lean and would not round
Out their stalky limbs again though peace
Plumped the bellies of the mice
Under the meanest table.
It was during the long hunger-battle
They found their talent to persevere
In thinness, to come, later,
Into our bad dreams, their menace
Not guns, not abuses,
But a thin silence.
Wrapped in flea-ridden donkey skins,
Empty of complaint, forever
Drinking vinegar from tin cups: they wore
The insufferable nimbus of the lot-drawn
Scapegoat. But so thin,
So weedy a race could not remain in dreams,
Could not remain outlandish victims
In the contracted country of the head
Any more than the old woman in her mud hut could
Keep from cutting fat meat
Out of the side of the generous moon when it
Set foot nightly in her yard
Until her knife had pared
The moon to a rind of little light.
Now the thin people do not obliterate
Themselves as the dawn
Grayness blues, reddens, and the outline
Of the world comes clear and fills with color.
They persist in the sunlit room: the wallpaper
Frieze of cabbage-roses and cornflowers pales
Under their thin-lipped smiles,
Their withering kingship.
How they prop each other up!

mandates--the permanent establishment of "the good life" based on a consumer culture. Plath herself is given the byline for a "fashion blurb" she wrote for the August 1953 issue: "We're stargazers this season. . . . Focusing our telescope on college news around the globe, we debate and deliberate." In keeping with the "hollow pop" motif, however, such "news" items include essays entitled "Sororities: I'm glad I joined/I'm glad I didn't."

Another guest editor recalls the "proudest moment for all of us sight-seers--the UN, with its buildings and galaxy of delegates. We lunched in the delegates' own dining room where the view of the East River was as exciting as the international menu." As it stands, the statement is innocuous enough, but there is something "desperately optimistic," to borrow Kazin's phrase, about bright young college students gaining access to the diplomatic dining room of the United Nations, only to gush over the menu and the view. The resolute superficiality of this visit to the center of the post-World War II peace effort is underlined by the nearly identical description of the ladies' trip to Macy's. This equally big and famous building--devoted to a historical consumerism rather than quotidian diplomacy--is also described as a special tour beginning with a privileged meal: "Behind the scenes at Macy's, we breakfasted in the executives' dining room and explored the working of the world's largest department store." The young women are taken "behind the scenes" at Macy's and the United Nations, but only in order that they might perform the role of attesting that unambivalent goodness resides everywhere in the form of various commodities and amenities. In *The Bell Jar*, the fancy lunch of crabmeat offered by the chefs of *Ladies' Day* turns out to be "chock full of ptomaine," and the narrator extends the idea of hidden poison to include the photographs of the crabmeat dish that will eventually appear as "perfect" in the slick pages of the magazine: "I had a vision of the celestially white kitchens of *Ladies' Day* stretching into infinity. I saw avocado pear after avocado pear being stuffed with crabmeat and mayonnaise and photographed under brilliant lights. . . . Poison" (39).

In 1957, five years before writing her famous poems "Daddy" and "Lady Lazarus," Sylvia Plath writes a poem called "The Thin People." She would have been fifteen upon first viewing the photographs that so affected Sontag. In this poem, Plath goes further than Sontag in describing the affect of the photographs on her; she goes further because she insists that they have changed not only her, but also the world, forever. But even this does not bother the narrator as much as her realization that America is already refusing anything but a superficial--that is to say commercial--relationship to the images of the Holocaust:

We own no wilderness rich and deep enough
For stronghold against their stiff
Battalions. See, how the tree boles flatten
And lose their good browns
If the thin people simply stand in the forest,
Making the world go thin as a wasp's nest
And grayer; not even moving their bones.
(*The Collected Works*, 64-65.)

I have not seen this poem discussed as part of Plath's use of the Holocaust, perhaps because it was uncollected and unpublished until the complete poems were published in 1982. Certainly this poem contradicts Murdoch's generalization (written before he could have seen this poem) that "for Sylvia Plath the imagery exists for itself alone."

"They are always with *us*" Plath tells the reader. "They are unreal, *we* say," she continues, "It was only in a movie, it was only/In a war making evil headlines when we/Were small that they famished...." There is, in my reading of these lines, clear social protest, and even a political warning that the world cannot go on as before, that America cannot bury what happened underneath the plenitude of post-war prosperity. Yet in *Life* magazine, where Plath most likely first saw the photographs, black and white images of "thin people" often appear adjacent to brightly colored advertisements for makeup, kitchen appliances, and bath towels. The insensitivity of this sort of layout seems to be underlined by Plath's unsettling reminder that the thin people "would not round/Out their stalky limbs again though peace/Plumped the bellies of the mice/Under the meanest table." As post-war prosperity warms the country and further brightens the pages of the magazines, the gray thin people are still gray, and still thin, even though one might have expected them to fade: "Now the thin people do not obliterate/Themselves as the dawn/Grayness blues, reddens, and the outline/Of the world comes clear and fills with color." In "The Thin People," Plath makes the point that the victims of the Holocaust, though depicted as starved and helpless, nonetheless convey a *moral* message that is much more powerful than the physical might of any army: "We own no wilderness/rich and deep enough/For stronghold against their stiff/Battalions. See, how the tree boles flatten/And lose their good browns...." Plath's use of the word wilderness brings to mind America's vast resources which will further promote prosperity in America, but this, like the colorful, plump world, is no stronghold against the fact of the Holocaust; in short, its victims cannot be fattened no matter how much we gorge ourselves.

In "The Disquieting Muses," a poem written in the same year as "The Thin People" (1957), there is no use of Holocaust imagery, but the theme of intractable evil being forcefully denied by energetic, colorful fantasies is still pervasive. This poem is set in the personal and domestic realm--not the political--but both this poem and "The Thin People" represent the political and domestic metaphors that Plath will later blend in her most powerful poems "Daddy" and "Lady Lazarus." The poem opens by recalling the fairy tale of Snow White: "Mother, mother, what ill bred aunt/Or what disfigured and unsightly/Cousin did you so unwisely keep/Unasked to my Christening, that she/sent these ladies in her stead . . ." (*The Collected Works*, 74). Like the thin people who are ignored but will not fade, "these ladies" turn out to be silent, ominous figures who represent the disquieting evil that her mother's perfectly resolved fairy tales deny. She describes them as "nodding by night around my bed,/Mouthless, eyeless, with stitched bald head." They have the look and function of "the thin people," of whom Plath said: "They found their talent to persevere/In thinness, to come, later,/Into our bad dreams, their menace/Not guns, not abuses,/But a thin silence." The persona of "The Disquieting Muses" feels betrayed upon learning that the fantastically safe, sanitized world that has been presented to her since childhood, is a fairy tale. Later, she recalls a second fairy tale when she speaks, with a mixture of wonder and despair, of "Mother, whose witches always, always/Got baked into gingerbread. . . ." The story "Hansel and Gretel" contains, as its centerpiece, the most famous oven in folklore known to Americans. It is an extremely subtle allusion to the Holocaust, where *the witches* manned the oven night and day, where Hansel starved in earnest; the result was not a gingerbread house but mass graves.

The Holocaust imagery of technological murder and the theme of innocence betrayed may have come together for Plath in 1953, at the point where she was institutionalized after her first suicide attempt at the age of twenty-two. While there she was given a regimen of shock treatments and insulin therapy, and this treatment constituted her introduction to the underside of a technological world. About this time she wrote a poem entitled "The Trial of Man." The scope of the title makes it clear immediately that she has enlarged the personal experience of shock therapy to include the technological murder employed in the Holocaust:

> The ordinary milkman brought that dawn
> Of destiny, delivered to the door
> In square hermetic bottles, while the sun
> Ruled decree of doomsday on the floor.

> The morning paper clocked the headline hour
> You drank your coffee like original sin,
> And at the jet-plane anger of God's roar
> Got up to let the suave blue policeman in.
>
> Impaled upon a stern angelic stare
> You were condemned to serve the legal limit
> And burn to death within your neon hell.
>
> Now, disciplined in the strict ancestral chair,
> You sit, solemn-eyed, about to vomit,
> The future an electrode in your skull.
> (*The Collected Poems*, 312.)

This recalls, of course, the opening of *The Bell Jar*, already mentioned above, where there is another account of technological execution; this one is applauded--via "goggle-eyed headlines"--by the same press that piously deplored the Holocaust: "It was a queer, sultry summer, the summer they electrocuted the Rosenbergs . . . that's all there was to read about in the papers--goggle-eyed headlines staring up at me on every street corner . . ." (1). The narrator of "The Trial of Man" makes the frightening connection that "the ordinary milkman" and the "square hermetic bottles" embody a sort of prosaic perfection that depend on conformity. In this case, a girl who finds herself unable to whole heartedly accept "the American way of life" waits to be partially electrocuted, or, in a favorite Fascist euphemism, "disciplined."

The "jet plane anger of God's roar" posits a moral system devoted to the preservation of a booming, technological economy, one where "suave policeman," rather than arrogant stormtroopers, "impale" the victim with an "angelic stare" and "condemn" them to "serve the legal limit." Plath takes an apparently idyllic scene of American suburbia and laces it with genteel menace and the false calm of impending violence. Like some of the first hand observers of the Holocaust, everyone feigns ignorance about the horror soon to be enacted--everyone except the subject who has been singled out as dangerously different. The placid indifference of the authority figures in the poem might well remind us of Kazin's warning that "men are not ashamed of what they have been in this time, and are therefore not prepared for the further outbreaks of fascism which are so deep in all of us" (46). Plath's concept of the "legal-limit" is likewise chilling because it reminds us that most of what was done to the Jews was "legal." "Laws" and methods of "discipline" can be rewritten in a manner that legitimizes and institutionalizes fear, hatred, and greed. Once such laws are in place, the executions they allow can be delivered as regularly and efficiently as the morning milk.

In most of the articles accompanying the photographs of the death camps, the emphasis is primarily on how the existence of the camps confirms the "inherent" goodness of the American way of life. Germany is the disease; America the cure. A sampling of titles from 1945-1946 may make my point: "Is Hitler Youth Curable?" in *The New Republic*, "Can the Germans Cure Themselves?" in *The New York Times Magazine*, "Will Shock Treatment Cure Germany's Ills?" In *The Saturday Evening Post*, and "Are Germans Human?" in *Woman's Home Companion*. Almost uniformly, Germany was presented as mentally ill, and America was its psychiatrist who must correct the patient operating from a position of dominance without considering any possible relationship, any more than Plath's Hilda considers the Rosenbergs human. Like the Rosenbergs trapped within the American myth of moral supremacy, or the Jewish population trapped within the German myth of genetic perfection, Plath begins to see herself as designated insane so that those around her can further bolster their own beliefs. When the narrator of *The Bell Jar* visits a psychiatrist for the first time, she is immediately driven into an angry and alienated silence by the insufferable air of uniform and complacent superiority that the office decor conveys: "The walls were beige, and the carpets were beige, and the upholstered chairs and sofas were beige" (104). There is also a photograph of the Doctor with his happy family--half turned toward the patient--and the narrator sees this, too, as an immediate trivialization of her growing despair: "Then I thought, how could this Doctor Gordon help me anyway, with a beautiful wife and beautiful children and a beautiful dog haloing him like the angels on a Christmas card?" (106). When a highly defined version of "normalcy" is upheld by the psychiatric establishment, then "therapy" becomes just a slightly more subtle system for teaching the patient how to conform. Early on, Plath was questioning the "inherent" goodness of an American culture that shocked the mental ill, electrocuted the "unAmerican," and sought, through the McCarthy hearings, to disgrace anyone who appeared to doubt the American myth of moral superiority.

In his book *Writing and Rewriting the Holocaust*, Young has made a point that is relevant to my thesis. He points out that the capture, trial, and execution of Adolph Eichmann in Israel--a prolonged event which generated another mass-media explosion about the Holocaust--took place between April and December of 1961. He adds, "[b]etween September and December 1962 . . . Plath wrote "Mary's Song," "Lady Lazarus," and "Daddy," her so-called Holocaust poems" (118). The point the popular press makes again and again about Eichmann is how distressingly mediocre and forgettable he seems; quite simply, his genius was disconcertingly bureaucratic rather than conveniently psychotic. *Life* magazine of December 5, 1960 defends its editorial decision to publish Eichmann's own account of his role in "the final solution," but in doing so, the editors cannot help lamenting "the depressing fact . . . that Eichmann is basically a rather unextraordinary man. . . . What he did with himself could have been done by anyone with an equal talent for keeping his place, 'doing his duty,' taking his orders, and turning his conscience over to the care of the State." Even the Israeli secret commando force telegraphed their successful abduction of Eichmann with the phrase "the Beast is in chains." But despite all this, the man who eventually sat in the glass booth appeared too ordinary--both in his appearance and within his own narrative--to be credibly described as a monstrous aberration of human nature. This tension between Eichmann's unexceptional appearance and the appalling mass murder he promoted and expedited, almost certainly strengthened Plath's sense that the Holocaust depicts a condition of the human mind and not solely the supposedly unique perversity of Nazi culture.

In her poem "Mary's Song," Plath begins with a strong image of American domestic security ("The Sunday lamb cracks in its fat") but then subverts this myth with a succession of images which reveal--beneath the facade of mere contentment--a world of dominance and aggression stripped of all comforting ideologies. In a sense, Plath's juxtaposition of the domestic with the horrific can be seen as a deliberate reproduction of what *Life* magazine had already presented, presumably without malice of forethought. On the page opposite *Life's* explanation of why they chose to print Eichmann's version of the Holocaust, there is a brightly colored advertisement for Swanson's TV Dinner: "Trust Swanson . . . choice slices of tender turkey, carved exclusively from meaty breasts and thighs." The whole appeal of this product, of course, is that you "just put it in the oven," and once again I would suggest Plath's sense of unacknowledged menace lurking in scenes of contentment is a tension that she found originally in the magazine format which reported Nazi atrocities to a mass audience. "*Trust* Swanson" is also an odd command when set side by side with *Life's* editorial plea to think independently in order to avoid fascism. A culture that urges citizens to pledge allegiance to a frozen dinner may not be completely immune from the manipulation of a fascist revival after all.

The persona and central action of Mary's involves the Virgin Mary sending her son into the world and to his death. Thus, in this poem it is not only the Jews who are killed, but Christ who is killed as well; both are destroyed by similar forces of greed and appropriation. Judaism and Christianity are portrayed in this poem as merely two different examples of elaborate systems that disguise the indifferent destructiveness of the potentially carnivorous human spirit. Such a spirit will wreak murderous havoc on true believers once licensed to do so by any self-righteous culture that pursues its interests and prosecutes its values with single-minded ruthlessness. This effectively explodes another ready explanation for the Holocaust--that it was the vengeance of a Christian god on the people who are blamed for his son's death:

> The Sunday lamb cracks in its fat.
> The fat
> Sacrifices its opacity. . . .
> A window, holy gold.
> The fire makes it precious,
> The same fire
> Melting the tallow heretics,
> Ousting the Jews.
> Their thick palls float
> Over the cicatrix of Poland, burnt-out
> Germany.
> They do not die.
> Gray birds obsess my heart,
> Mouth-ash, ash of eye.
> They settle. On the high
> Precipice
> That emptied one man into space
> The ovens glowed like heavens, incandescent.
> It is a heart.
> This Holocaust I walk in.
> O golden child the world will kill and eat.
> (*The Collected Works*, 257.)

"The Sunday lamb cracks in its fat" seems a deliberate and grotesque parody of Blake's *Songs of Innocence*. "The Sunday lamb" is an image, derived from American culture, that normally connotes domestic security, financial comfort and nourishment. But here the lamb is in an oven, the glow of the fat is associated with the "holy gold" that has caused a people to be melted down into tallow as part of an economic and technological nightmare which converts even people into domestic products such as candles and soap.

As with her poem "The Thin People," Plath emphasizes that the victims continue to observe the world with a "thin silence" that is easily ignored in the colorful bustle of a consumer culture--and yet impossible to eradicate. What she really means, of course, is that in the midst of all hyperbolic advertising for an excessive amount of trivial items, she imagines the accusatory gaze of people who lost everything in a war that has since proved enormously profitable to a jubilant American culture. The Christian rationalization that the Holocaust was the result of divine justice is rendered meaningless in"Mary's Song," since the entire poem is Mary's song to her doomed son as she sends him out into "the Holocaust I walk in" and announces his fate in her farewell: "O golden child the world will kill and eat." The point is that no mythology is believable to Plath after the Holocaust--not the gingerbread her mother bakes, nor various religious faiths. A Lamb, the creative symbol of the Christian faith, is put into the oven along with the "heretics" who defy this symbol. Symbols of horror and spiritual hope are interchangeable: "The ovens glowed like heavens" we are told; "Herr God, Herr Lucifer" Plath writes in one line of "Lady Lazarus," observing no distinction between the two. In Plath's poetic vision there is innocence unaware and innocence betrayed; nothing lives happily ever after except in cultural myths.

Four years earlier, in a poem called "The Death of Myth-Making" (1958), Plath made this same point, that myth is an elaborate illusion that makes all issues appear morally clear while actually interpreting nothing:

> Two virtues ride, by stallion, by nag,
> To grind our knives and scissors:
> Lantern-jawed Reason, squat Common Sense,
> One courting doctors of all sorts,
> One, housewives and shopkeepers.
> The trees are lopped, the poodles trim,
> The laborer's nails pared level. . . .
> (*The Collected Poems*, 104.)

The obsessive division and maintenance of suburban property is as false a solution to human evil as the division of Germany after the war. The implied cruelty of lopping the trees and trimming the poodles announces the very dominant tendency that these actions are intended to hide. Reason and Common Sense sharpen our scissors and knives. They are the cookie cutters by which all our witches get baked into gingerbread.

In "Daddy" Plath is dismantling the most central myth of her life: the infallibility of her father. On the one hand she is amazed that the myth she thought was protecting her was in fact imprisoning her. On another level, she is devastated that the myth has been exposed, and that she can no longer believe in it. She would like to remain in the world of pared lawns and trimmed poodles, but this is to walk into the oven of a world that will kill and eat even the god sent to save it. The daddy of Plath's poem is explicitly made a Nazi, but he is also explicitly made Satan and a Vampire--all symbols of life-denying forces that destroy those they seduce. For Plath, Nazism is a manifestation of an archetypal evil, and ideologies which seek to conceal this actually pave the way for its reappearance. What Nazism, Satanism and Vampirism all have in common is that they seduce with charm in order to destroy later with an even more efficient use of force. Those who saw Hitler as the savior of Germany were not anxious to see him as the anti-Christ or the dybbuk of Jewish lore. There is, Plath's poetry seems to insist, something in us that craves the simplicity of evil because it allows for a progress towards profit and power that is unimpeded by ethics; it is equally uninhibited by any doubts that a self-affirming doctrine of truth might be a delusional myth that makes the murderous power of complete dominance palatable and even "one's duty."

But "Daddy" makes a subtler point--and perhaps a more controversial one as well--which is that the victim, the dominated one, comes to believe the doctrine and succumbs to its rigid doctrine which is then experienced as the hopeless consequence of incontrovertible fate. In this situation, the victim has as much need of protective ideologies as the persecutor: "Every woman adores a Fascist,/The boot in the face, the brute/Brute heart of a brute like you" (*The Collected Works*, 223). So used to being a part of an accepted order, however repressive or even murderous, the persona of Plath's poem resurrects her dead father by marrying his image:

> I made a model of you,
> A man in black with a Meinkampf look
> And a love of the rack and the screw
> and I said I do, I do.
> (*The Collected Works*, 224.)

The way Plath deliberately mixes up her symbols of dominance in this and other passages has been insufficiently noted by those readers who isolate the Holocaust imagery and fail to see that the poem is about the evil of dominance in general. The rack and the screw recall the Spanish Inquisition, an order of Christians who tortured and murdered those who did not believe as they do. Further, in the context of marriage, a man who loves "the rack and the screw" suggests a man who will rule a woman by sexual dominance, operating somewhere between the two poles of seduction and rape. In what we now may be able to see as a deliberate transition on Plath's part, the final metamorphosis of "Daddy" is into the form of a vampire. Now that the personal claims to have killed both the father and the model that was her husband, the image converts into something that knows how to survive even death by *secretly* living off a victim. Of course she tells him "there's a stake in your fat black heart," but the stock opening of most horror films is an explanation of why the monster, though apparently annihilated before, has somehow survived. The monster and the victim perish together in the conclusion of this poem, but the implication is that both will return; the circle is unbroken.

A. Alvarez, a writer and editor who published and praised Plath's poetry, and who knew her personally as well, wrote an essay entitled "The Concentration Camps" in *The Atlantic Monthly* (December 1962), a magazine that also published Plath's poetry. Added to this, a recent Plath biographer has noted that Plath invited Alvarez to her apartment for a drink on Christmas Eve, 1962 (which would have been shortly after the essay appeared). There is every reason to believe, therefore, that Plath knew of the essay, and that she may have talked with Alvarez in more detail about his views (the editor of the piece notes that Alvarez has visited Auschwitz twice in 1962 before writing the piece). In this essay, Alvarez deplores the superficial popularity that the concentration camp memorials have attained in the wake of the Eichmann trial--as if the evil they called to mind had been safely dispatched:

> Behind vast plate-glass windows are mountains of human hair, suitcases, spectacles, artificial limbs. . . . It has made descriptions of Nazi atrocities best sellers in the shady bookshops of Soho. It also makes the camps unimportant; if they were simply playgrounds for sadists who in another society would have been locked away, then they are an aberration best forgotten, for they prove only that our sickest fantasies can be acted out. The Eichmann affair has shown that they were not (69).

Three times in his essay, Alvarez quotes what he calls "a curious generalization" from Primo Levi's *If This Is a Man*. Levi wrote "[i]f from the inside of the Lager, a message could have seeped out to free men, it would have been this: Take care not to suffer in your own homes what is inflicted here." To me, this seems the very essence of what Plath tries to do in her use of Holocaust imagery: sound the alarm, just as Levi imagined doing, in order to announce--with the urgency of a trumpet blast--that suffering and despair may take place "in your own home," and that is why the memorials to the Holocaust should be understood as a contemporary warning to the living rather than a mausoleum for the dead.

In a connection that could not have failed to fascinate Plath, Alvarez draws a disconcerting connection between the way Jews were managed in the camps and the way the modern consumer is directed by contemporary mass media: "At the extermination camp Treblinka, the victims were cajoled into walking quietly by the thousands to the gas chambers by a kind of super advertising campaign. . . . The techniques are those of our own industrialized mass society. Only the moral framework is different" (72). The point I wish to make relative to Plath is that Alvarez, too, sorts through Holocaust imagery looking for a way to draw out what it has to say about contemporary life. As Young argues in *Writing and Rewriting the Holocaust*, countless journalists were doing this in the mass media of the early sixties, and thus it is surprising that Plath was virtually singled out, *de facto*, as a voice of doubtful authenticity: "In Plath's case, rather than disputing the authenticity of her figures, we might look to her poetry for the ways the Holocaust has entered public consciousness as a trope. . . . Entered as it was onto the 'public record' during the Eichmann trial in Jerusalem, a time when images of the camps flooded the media and commanded world attention as they had not since the war, the Holocaust necessarily began to inform all writers' literary imagination as a prospective trope. . . . It is therefore surprising that its figurative use should then be critically sanctioned and made unavailable to all those for whom the Holocaust was not 'authentic' experience" (132).

Indeed, a contemporary account of the trial in *Time* magazine (April 14, 1961), states unequivocally that the purpose of the trial is to transcribe the horror of the Holocaust onto the "public record" of mass media: "In the amphitheater at his right will be the world's press, TV and radio correspondents. The latter clearly were the more important audience, for Eichmann's guilt already was clear; the real purpose of the trial was to fix forever in the mind of the world the monstrous wartime crimes of the Nazis" (34). Typical of many accounts of the trial in the popular press, this *Time* account exudes confidence that however horrifying the revelations of the trial, the atrocities should be understood as a unique, unreproducible manifestation of Nazi culture. What Alvarez and Plath emphasize (and what Kazin brought up even earlier) is that too immediate and pronounced a reaction of horror becomes an indulgence and an escape: "The more we know of the camps, the more they seem like a mirror thrust into our faces. But it is a distorting mirror in which the image is warped by all the pain and horror. And this is a consolation; it helps us not to recognize our own features" (72). Plath makes her features "Jewish" in an effort to correct this consoling distortion and to shock her audience into seeing the events of the Holocaust as a possible type of their own future, and not merely an infinitely regrettable memorial to someone else's past.

In "Lady Lazarus," Plath makes her most direct connection between the way a doctor observes a mental patient with a sort of cool fascination, and the way America, primarily through the popular press, interpreted and presented the fact of the Holocaust. In both cases, Plath would have it, the observer sifts through another's ashes in order to be assured that their own way of life is the correct and dominant one. In the logic of this equation, ironically, the more heinous the suffering, the more reassured the observer feels. Plath's poetic persona attacks this inhuman complacency:

> There is a charge
> For the eyeing of my scars, there is a charge
> For the hearing of my heart--
> It really goes.
>
> And there is a charge, a very large charge
> For a word or a touch
> Or a bit of blood
> Or a piece of my hair or my clothes.
> (*The Collected Works*, 246.)

Certainly this is an injunction against the discompassionate fascination with the Holocaust exhibited by the media. It is also an allusion to the practice in the middle ages of securing a bit of cloth or hair from Christian martyrs about to be burned at the stake. In this image, as in the images of "Mary's Song," Judaism and Christianity are again collapsed, one into the other, as are hundreds of years of history, to make the single point that gaining solace by observing suffering is a way to condone domination, to revel in the secret love for the boot in the face, and, ultimately, to guarantee that the monster will resurrect itself no matter how often the villagers pound a stake into its "fat black heart."

The myths that make us feel holy can be the same ones that license us to kill. During the time Plath was writing the poems of *Ariel*, she was living in a house in London once occupied by Yeats. She considered this fortuitous as he was one of her favorite poets. Perhaps it was from him that she learned her technique of inverting symbols of hope into harbingers of destruction. Certainly she knew the concluding lines of his most famous poem "The Second Coming." In this poem, Yeats inverted the central myth of Christianity to describe the evil he felt was approaching in Europe: "And what rough beast/Its hour come round at last,/Slouches towards Bethlehem to be born." In "Lady Lazarus" the anti-mythical beast is born out of all the Holocaust remnants that were made into "household words" by the mass media. This is the terrifying beast that Eichmann never could be, and Plath gives it a voice--a voice that shatters the enforced serenity and desperate optimism of forgetfulness:

> A sort of walking miracle, my skin
> Bright as a nazi lamp shade,
> My right foot
> A paperweight,
> My face a featureless, fine
> Jew linen.
> Peel off the napkin
> O my enemy.
> Do I terrify?
> (*The Collected Works*, 244.)

WORKS CITED

A. Alvarez. "The Concentration Camps." *The Atlantic Monthly.* December, 1962: 69-72.

Edward Butscher. *Sylvia Plath: Method and Madness* (New York: Simon & Schuster), 1981.

Judith E. Doneson. "The American History of Anne Frank's Diary." *Holocaust and Genocide Studies* 1987 2.1: 149-60.

Alfred Kazin. *The New Republic.* "In Every Voice, in Every Ban: Effect of our Silent Complicity in the Massacre of the Jews." 110. January 10, 1944: 44-46.

Life Magazine. "Sunday in Poland." 17. September 18, 1944: 17-18.

Life Magazine. "Prisoner 339, Klooga." 17. October 30, 1944: 73-81.

Life Magazine. "Eichmann and the Duty of Man." 49. December 5, 1960: 46.

Mademoiselle. August, 1953.

Brian Murdoch. "Transformation of the Holocaust: Auschwitz in Modern Lyric Poetry." *Comparative Literature Studies* XI. 1 March 1974: 123-50.

Sylvia Plath. *The Bell Jar* (New York: Harper and Row) 1971.

Sylvia Plath. *The Collected Poems*, ed. Ted Hughes (New York: Harper & Row) 1981.

Sylvia Plath. *Letters Home*, ed. Aurelia Schober Plath (New York: Harper & Row), 1975.

Susan Sontag. *On Photography.* (New York: Delta), 1973.

George Steiner, 1970. "In Extremis" (originally in *The Cambridge Review*, 7, February 1969). *The Cambridge Mind*, ed. Eric Homberger, William Janeway, and Simon Schama (London, 1970) 305.

George Steiner, 1970a. "Dying is an Art" in *The Art of Sylvia Plath: A Symposium*, ed. Charles Newman (Bloomington: Indiana U P, 1970) 211-218.

Time Magazine "In the Dock." 77. April 14, 1961: 33-4.

James E. Young. *Writing and Rewriting the Holocaust: Narrative and the Consequences of Interpretation* (Bloomington: Indiana U P), 1988.

The Holocaust and the Shaping of the New Germany

Frank Buscher

1990 was a watershed in postwar European history. With breathtaking speed, the old and familiar Cold War order, which had been in place since the 1940s, was replaced with a new one. In less than a year, between November 1989 and October 1990, the division of Europe into two hostile and heavily armed camps came to a surprisingly abrupt end. This process gave rise to feelings of hope and optimism about the continent's future which appeared bright now that Stalinism had quickly withered away in Eastern Europe and the former Soviet satellites were fast subscribing to Western values such as democracy and capitalism.[1]

By all accounts, 1990 was also the year of the Germans. After more than 40 years of division, the two Germanies were reunited in October 1990 when the former German Democratic Republic was absorbed by the Federal Republic. The new German state has less territory than its pre-1945 predecessors. Yet, with a population of 80 million and the strongest economy in Europe, the Federal Republic is clearly an enormously powerful country. Its stature is further enhanced by its geographic location as the connecting link between West and East.

German reunification would not have been possible without the consent of the World War II Allies. At first, the leaders of the major Allied countries seemed apprehensive, but in the end their doubts were not strong enough to prevent the Allies and the Germans from finally settling their affairs, thus giving the two Germanies full sovereignty and permitting them to reunite. Above all, the signing of the Allied-German treaty was an expression of Allied confidence that the Federal Republic had developed into a viable and stable democratic state during the past forty years.[2]

Somewhat lost in last fall's headlines was another endorsement for the new Germany, but one that also served as a reminder of that country's terrible past. Tens of thousands of Soviet Jews, it was reported, were applying for permission to immigrate into Germany. Clearly, these Jews first and foremost wanted to escape the rapidly deteriorating conditions at home, even at the cost of imigrating to the country which had systematically murdered their ancestors from 1941 to 1945. Yet, while economic reasons provided the impetus for the Soviet Jewish immigration, many of the new arrivals were also convinced that Germany was now a stable democracy where Jews no longer had anything to fear.[3]

The above episode demonstrates anew the peculiarity of the relationship between Jews and Germans after the Holocaust. Despite demands on the part of many Germans to draw a *Schlubstrich* (final line) under the Nazi past, the Holocaust has been inextricably connected with the evolution of the Federal Republic. Several recent studies propose a largely negative view of this development, arguing that many of West Germany's advances such as regaining almost complete sovereignty in the 1950s and becoming a reliable and increasingly respected partner of the West came at the expense of the Jews.[4] There were numerous incidents during the 1980s alone--Bitburg, the *Historikerstreit*, Chancellor Helmut Kohl's embarrassing insistence on the "*Gnade der späten Geburt*" (grace of his late birth)--to underscore this argument. Yet, at the same time, this interpretation appears too narrow, and it ignores the role played by the Holocaust in the democratization of the Federal Republic and thus in the shaping of the new Europe.

I believe that the Nazi crime against the Jews was crucial in three respects for West Germany's postwar development as a democracy. For one, it contributed to the Allied, and particularly American, goal to use the occupation for the purpose of democratizing the Germans. Second, it was the memory of the Holocaust which caused the international community to scrutinize the Federal Republic more than any other country in recent history. Such scrutiny ranged from frequent reports in the Western press during the early 1950s warning against a recrudescence of right-wing extremism to worldwide outrage over the conduct of some German war crimes trials and the ill-considered writings of several conservative German historians during the 1980s. Confronted with the highly negative foreign publicity following these incidents, the West Germans at all cost wanted to reassure the world, and particularly their allies, that their state had become a stable democracy and reliable partner. In short, when faced with foreign criticism, the West Germans reacted by posing as the world's model democrats, or as the German-Jewish historian Michael Wolffsohn pointed out recently in more amusing terms, by striving to be "world champions--whether in soccer or in matters of democracy."[5]

Third, and this point is closely related to the second, the tragic legacy of the Holocaust led to a consensus among the democratic forces in the Federal Republic to guard against a revival of right-wing extremism and pro-Nazi sentiment. Examples of this consensus were the campaign of SPD Chairman Kurt Schumacher against anti-Semitism and right-wing radicalism,[6] and Adenauer's successful efforts to have the *Sozialistische Reichspartei* (Socialist Reichs Party), a neo-Nazi party, declared unconstitutional in 1952.[7] This unwritten accord between the democratic forces is also evidenced by two milestones in the history of the West German parliament: the vote on the Reparations Treaty of 1953 with Israel and the decision to abolish the statute of limitations for genocide and murder in July 1979. Finally, even during the critical years 1985/86, when Kohl and U.S. President Reagan paid their highly controversial visit to the military cemetery at Bitburg and hitherto respected German historians denied the singularity of the Holocaust, several positive signs surfaced.[8] Foremost among these was President Richard von Weizsäcker's speech commemorating the 40th anniversary of Germany's surrender at the end of the Second World War.[9] Clearly, these developments stemmed from the memory of the Holocaust, coupled with the determination not to repeat the mistakes of the Weimar years and to protect this second German republic from its domestic enemies.

Let me begin with the first point: U.S. and Allied policy for the occupation of postwar Germany and its relationship to the Holocaust. The work on formulating such a policy did not begin in earnest until August 1944, coinciding with the first American press accounts on the liberation of Majdanek.[10] Eventually, three agencies of the U.S. government--the Departments of State, War and the Treasury--drew up plans for the occupation. The most radical solution was proposed by Secretary of the Treasury Henry Morgenthau who, as a Jew, was particularly distraught by the news of the Holocaust. Clearly, the fate of millions of European Jews had a strong impact on the Morgenthau Plan, as the Treasury Secretary's proposal was quickly called. Morgenthau's best-known and most controversial suggestion was to destroy Germany's industrial capacity and to pastoralize the country. Unfortunately, the call for pastoralization was deemed so radical that it overshadowed other important aspects of the Morgenthau Plan such as the recommendation to give Germany a democratic government.[11]

Unlike the Departments of War and State, whose proposals for the treatment of Germany were at first much softer, Morgenthau hoped to accomplish the "complete and effective reform of German national character and society."[12] The Secretary wanted to eliminate what he perceived to be the German preference for authoritarianism and militarism by democratizing the Germans. Morgenthau was convinced that the German people's veneration of the military and its propensity for authoritarian government were the root causes of the two world wars and the Nazis' systematic murder of European Jewry. Consequently, Morgenthau concluded, the postwar world would only be peaceful and democratic if the Germans themselves were democratized.[13]

Although the Truman administration abandoned the Morgenthau Plan, official U.S. occupation policy for postwar Germany did reflect the Treasury Secretary's most important ideas. U.S. officials had decided that Germany was to be denazified, demilitarized, decartelized, decentralized, and democratized. These American priorities, collectively referred to as the five "D's," were adopted by the other major Allies at the Potsdam Conference in July 1945. U.S. policy-makers in particular were hoping that the implementation of the five "D's" would ultimately lead the Germans to embrace democracy and pluralism.[14]

Democratization was to be achieved through a process of reeducation intended to extirpate Nazism and to impress upon the Germans the tragic consequences of their society's failure to develop democratic institutions and traditions simultaneous with the Western powers.[15] In short, the Allied message was that Germany's militaristic and authoritarian past had not only permitted Hitler to rise to power but had also caused millions of Germans to serve his regime with utmost obedience. American occupation authorities believed that evidence of the annihilation of European Jewry and other Nazi crimes would make significant contributions to the reeducation of the Germans because it so graphically demonstrated the evil character of Nazism. This theory found practical application already during the closing weeks of the war when Allied troops were confronting thousands of German civilians with the gruesome sights of newly liberated concentration camps.

Not long after Nazi Germany's surrender, U.S. officials became more sophisticated in their approach and they began to use documentary films such as "KZ" and "Die Todesmühlen" for reeducation purposes. These documentaries depicted in graphic detail the atrocities committed in Nazi concentration camps. U.S. officials hoped that the use of these movies would accomplish several important goals. The two most significant aims were to instill in the German people a sense of collective guilt as well as an acceptance of Allied occupation policies that strove to destroy the remnants of Nazism and to democratize German society. In the end, the documentaries were ineffective. Surveys taken after showings of "Die Todesmühlen" in early 1946 indicated that most viewers continued to blame concentration camp atrocities on the Nazi leadership and did not hold the German people collectively responsible. Worse, some respondents pointed out that collective guilt was simply a "catchword of democracy" to give the Allies a free hand in postwar Germany. Clearly, such remarks indicated that this particular endeavor to use massive visual proof of the Holocaust and other Nazi atrocities to reeducate the Germans was not successful.[16]

While the attempt to employ documentaries for reeducation purposes failed, a second American program dealing with the legacy of Nazi crimes appeared to have more promising results. During and after the war, U.S. military courts had convicted and sentenced over 1,500 Germans for war crimes. Initially, the sole purpose of these proceedings was to punish those who had perpetrated the Holocaust, concentration camp atrocities, and crimes against Allied military personnel. Eventually, U.S. occupation officials found both war crimes trials and clemency useful for their campaign to reeducate the Germans. For example, in a letter to Protestant Bishop Theophil Wurm, a persistent critic of U.S. war crimes trials, U.S. Military Governor General Lucius D. Clay pointed out that "the evidence, introduced before the Courts, has demonstrated the evil which comes from abuse of power as could never have been demonstrated otherwise."[17] U.S. High Commissioner John J. McCloy used a similar line of reasoning when he granted clemency to 87 convicted war criminals on January 31, 1951. McCloy was careful to point out that he had applied "standards of executive clemency as they are understood in a democratic society."[18]

Clearly, both Clay's and McCloy's carefully-worded remarks were intended to convince the Germans of the evils of totalitarianism and the virtues of democracy since the latter system guaranteed due process of law even to the worst defendants. Apparently, the earlier trials of war criminals, including the Nuremberg Trial, had done just that. By the spring of 1947 a U.S. Military Government survey in the American zone found that 80 percent of the respondents believed that the war crimes trials had been just.[19] In another survey 30 percent indicated that they now knew about the "dangers of dictatorship," while 50 percent pointed out they had learned much about the "inhumanity of the concentration camps."[20] Yet, over time, public opinion in occupied Germany changed for the worse, and by the late summer of 1952 the Allied handling of war criminals received a dismal approval rating of 10 percent.[21] This negative development seems to have resulted largely from dissatisfaction about the continued occupation as well as growing self-confidence about Germany's future once it became obvious that the Cold War had put the country in the front line for the defense of the West. However, in light of the sharp attacks prominent politicians and church leaders directed at Allied war crimes trials, the survey also showed that the Germans had learned very little from the proceedings.

While Allied initiatives employing the Holocaust for reeducation and democratization efforts did not meet with the desired success, the legacy of this and other Nazi crimes was nonetheless relevant to the evolution of West German democracy. As I stated earlier, the memory of the Holocaust led to much international scrutiny of the German state and caused its democratic forces to cooperate closely on several key issues. That the Federal Republic's domestic development was being watched carefully became very evident in 1949 when the World Jewish Congress insisted that the Germans should construct constitutional and administrative barriers to prevent a revival of Nazism. The writers of the Basic Law, the Federal Republic's constitution, concluded the same. Thus, the Basic Law contained a provision declaring all political parties which threatened the democratic order unconstitutional. In addition, the German penal code now called for the punishment of those who encouraged racial hatred or the disparagement of religious communities. These provisions were clear indications that important lessons had been learned from the Holocaust and the experience of Nazism as a whole.[22]

During the early 1950s the West German government for the first time since the establishment of the Federal Republic directly confronted the legacy of the Holocaust. In March 1952, the state of Israel, the Conference on Jewish Material Claims against Germany and the Adenauer government began negotiations resulting in the Reparations Treaty of 1953. Initially, the agreement committed the Federal Republic to the payment of 3.5 billion marks to Israel and various Jewish organizations. The question of reparations was unpopular with most Germans (only 11 percent approved) and even with key members of Adenauer's cabinet.[23] Adenauer, who himself was morally committed to German-Jewish reconciliation, could not rely on his own Christian Democrats (CDU/CSU) or his conservative coalition partners, the Free Democratic Party (FDP) and the German Party (DP), to ensure parliamentary passage of the Reparations Treaty. He did, however, have the unqualified support of the opposition Social Democrats and their chairman, Kurt Schumacher, on this issue. Schumacher, normally a stern opponent of the chancellor's policies, was convinced that the Federal Republic's "moral and political rehabilitation" depended upon the successful conclusion of the reparations agreement.[24] Backed by Schumacher and the

SPD, Adenauer in the end had enough votes to ensure ratification of the treaty in the *Bundestag*.

Similar cooperation between the ruling Christian Democrats and the opposition SPD also caused the *Bundestag* to approve the first change in West Germany's statute of limitations for murder in 1965. Normally, the state had a period of 20 years to prosecute a murder case. This posed the danger that all murders committed during the Third Reich, including the killing of the Jews, could no longer be prosecuted after the twentieth anniversary of Germany's surrender on May 8, 1945. To ensure that Nazi crimes would be prosecuted in the future, approximately 50 CDU lawmakers introduced a bill in early 1965 calling for the extension of the statute from 20 to 30 years. At the same time, the Social Democrats proposed legislation to abolish the statute of limitations for murder and genocide altogether.[25]

The 1965 attempt to alter the statute of limitations ended in a compromise, giving West German authorities until December 31, 1969, to begin prosecution of crimes committed during the Nazi era which now carried the maximum punishment of life imprisonment. This compromise only postponed the inevitable, i.e. the abolition of the statute which finally occurred in 1979. Nonetheless, the *Bundestag's* 1965 initiative provided significant proof that the Federal Republic was making progress on its way to becoming a respectable democracy. In fact, the March 10 parliamentary debate on the CDU and SPD bills is widely viewed as one of the pinnacles in the legislature's history.[26]

The individual legislator who set the tone for this debate was Ernst Benda, a CDU deputy who was appointed to the Federal Constitutional Court in 1971. In his speech Benda established a clear linkage between the legacy of Nazi crimes now before the *Bundestag* and the Federal Republic's self-image as a democracy and a *Rechtsstaat* (nation of laws). Benda insisted that the concept of *Rechtsstaat* could no longer be limited to measures guaranteeing the rights of the accused such as the statute of limitations. Instead, he pointed out, a nation of laws must pursue justice, no matter how elusive this goal would prove to be. Implied in Benda's argument was that the Federal Republic could not call itself a democratic *Rechtsstaat* if its courts stopped punishing Nazi crimes simply because the statute of limitations had expired. Compared to the enormity of the crimes committed in Germany's name, the statute was a technicality which now threatened to obstruct justice. In short, German courts needed to continue addressing the criminal Nazi past so that justice could at least be approached since, as Benda admitted, it was unlikely that it could ever be entirely achieved.[27]

Benda's speech and the March 1965 *Bundestag* debate as a whole were carefully watched abroad, although Benda emphasized that this did not have an impact on his decision to seek an extension of the term of limitation for Nazi crimes.[28]

Twenty years after Benda's important speech, which hinted at but stopped short of defining the genocide of the Jews as singular, Richard von Weizsäcker unambiguously referred to the Holocaust as a crime "unparalleled in history."[29] Although he followed Adenauer's example by claiming that the German people were not collectively guilty,[30] the president accused the Germans of his generation of having willfully and conveniently ignored the truth before and during the war, only to plead ignorance and innocence in the post-war years. Von Weizsäcker implored his fellow-countrymen, both young and old, to remember the Holocaust, stressing that failure to remember would not only be an affront to the victims but detrimental to the Federal Republic itself.[31]

Von Weizsäcker's statements were all the more remarkable when one considers two important factors: his family's recent history and his party affiliation. His father, Ernst von Weizsäcker, had served the Hitler regime as a high-ranking official (*Staatssekretär*) in the foreign office. He was tried as a war criminal before an American military tribunal from November 1947 to April 1949, receiving a sentence of seven years.[32] During the trial Richard von Weizsäcker served as a counsel for the defense. In addition to having to come to terms with his father's past, von Weizsäcker knew his beliefs were unpopular with conservative members of the CDU/CSU, who objected to the president's view of the Holocaust as "unparalleled" in history and his description of May 8, 1945, as "a day of liberation" for "all of us."[33] Many Christian Democrats preferred to share the opinion of the historian Ernst Nolte who viewed the term "liberation" as misnomer in light of the Allies' collective guilt theory, Germany's territorial losses, the expulsion of several million ethnic Germans from Eastern Europe, and the hatred both Russians and Poles were bound to harbor after their experiences under Nazi occupation.[34]

The above episodes underscore the peculiar relationship between the Federal Republic and the Holocaust. On the one hand, the Germans were all too often callous, causing further grief for the victims who had managed to survive the slaughter. Such situations normally arose when the Federal Republic perceived the memory of the Holocaust as blocking its progress, and it then sought to rid itself of this shameful legacy. On the other hand, however, the Holocaust is also linked to West Germany's democratization. The Allies, and particularly the United States, were the first to employ the massive evidence of this Nazi crime in their attempts to reeducate postwar German society, a largely unsuccessful undertaking.[35]

After the Federal Republic gained semi-sovereignty in 1949, gradual improvements became noticeable. For example, those most dedicated to building a democratic and internationally respected German state arranged for the payment of reparations to Jewish organizations and Israel, although it must be pointed out that financial compensation falls short of true atonement. More impressive was the fact that Ernst Benda and those who supported his position--mainly lawmakers from the CDU and the SPD--established a direct link between West Germany's treatment of Nazi crimes and its self-acclaimed status as a democracy and a nation of laws. Clearly, Benda's call for a critical self-examination in this regard was an important milestone in the development of the Federal Republic, as was von Weizsäcker's conviction that the memory of the Holocaust is crucial for the German present and future. By causing democratically-oriented Germans to confront the Nazi past, the Holocaust in the end contributed to the new Europe as it emerged in 1990. The new Europe still has Germany at its center, but the latter is now a stable democracy and at present not a menace to its neighbors.

NOTES

1. J. Robert Wegs, *Europe Since 1945: A Concise History* (New York: St. Martin's, 1991), 338.
2. "Allies Sign Treaty To Free Germany," *The Commercial Appeal*, 13 September 1990, 1.
3. "Gar Nicht Auszuhalten," *Der Spiegel*, 7 January 1991, 57-58.
4. For example, see Anson Rabinbach, "The Jewish Question in the German Question," *New German Critique* 15 (1988), 159-92; and Jack Zipes and Anson Rabinbach, eds., *Germans and Jews since the Holocaust: The Changing Situation in West Germany* (New York: Holmes and Meier, 1986).
5. "Nie mehr Täter sein," *Der Spiegel*, 28 January 1991, 28.
6. Willy Albrecht, ed., *Kurt Schumacher: Reden-Schriften-Korrespondenzen 1945-1952* (Berlin: Dietz, 1985), 988-1006.
7. Dennis L. Bark and David R. Gress, *A History of West Germany*, 2 vols. (Oxford: Basil Blackwell, 1989), 1:295. In May 1951 this party managed to gain 11 percent of the vote during elections in Lower Saxony, causing grave concern for the West German government and the Allies who feared that Nazism was experiencing a revival.
8. There are numerous German books on the *Historikerstreit*. The best documentation is contained in Ernst Reinhard Piper, ed., *"Historikerstreit"-Die Dokumentation der Kontroverse um die Einzigartigkeit der nationalsozialistischen Judenvernichtung* (München: Piper, 1987). The most informative book in English on this subject is Charles S. Maier, *The Unmasterable Past: History, Holocaust, and German National Identity* (Cambridge, Mass.: Harvard University Press, 1988).
9. Press and Information Office of the Government of the Federal Republic of Germany, ed., *Remembrance, Sorrow and Reconciliation: Speeches and Declarations in Connection with the 40th Anniversary of the End of the Second World War in Europe* (Bonn: Press and Information Office, 1985), 57-72. Other encouraging signs were the critical responses of other German scholars and parts of the German press; see Jürgen Habermas, *Eine Art Schadensabwicklung* (Frankfurt: Suhrkamp, 1987), 11-17, 115-158; Hans-Ulrich Wehler, *Entsorgung der deutschen Vergangenheit? Ein polemischer Essay zum "Historikerstreit"* (München: Beck, 1988); and Rudolf Augstein, "Die neue Auschwitz-Lüge," in Piper, ed., *"Historikerstreit"*, 196-203.

10. "Nazi Mass Killings Laid Bare in Camp," *The New York Times*, 30 August 1944, 1.
11. Henry Morgenthau, Jr., *Germany Is Our Problem* (New York: Harper, 1945), 16-17, 48-49.
12. Warren Kimball, *Swords or Ploughshares? The Morgenthau Plan for a Defeated Germany, 1943-1945* (New York: Lippincott, 1976), 59.
13. John Morton Blum, *From the Morgenthau Diaries*, 3 vols. (Boston: Houghton Mifflin, 1967), 3:327.
14. Paper presented by James F. Tent at the 1991 American Historical Association meeting in New York.
15. Michael H. Kater, "Problems of Political Reeducation in West Germany, 1945-1960," *Simon Wiesenthal Center Annual* 4 (1987), 99.
16. Brewster S. Chamberlin, "Todesmühlen. Ein früher Versuch zur Massen-'Umerziehung' im besetzten Deutschland 1945-1946," *Vierteljahrshefte für Zeitgeschichte* 29 (1981), 420-436.
17. Clay to Wurm, 19 June 1948, RG 338, The U.S. Army in World War II, U.S. Army Europe (henceforth: USAREUR), Box 464, Bishop Wurm File, Washington National Record Center, Suitland, Maryland.
18. Public Relations Division, U.S. High Commission for Germany (HICOG), 31 January 1951, USAREUR, Box 461, Execution of War Criminals File.
19. Anna J. and Richard L. Merrit, eds., *Public Opinion in Occupied Germany: The OMGUS Surveys, 1945-1949* (Urbana: University of Illinois Press, 1970), 161-62.
20. Ibid., 122-23.
21. "Current West German Views on the War Criminals Issue," 8 September 1952, Reactions Analysis Staff, Office of Public Affairs, HICOG, RG 338, USAREUR, Box 469, News Clippings File.
22. Thilo Vogelsang, *Das geteilte Deutschland* (München: dtv, 1985), 169. Also, see the Basic Law's Article 21 and paragraphs 131 and 166 of the *Strafgesetzbuch*.
23. Michael Wolffsohn, *Ewige Schuld? 40 Jahre Deutsch-Jüdisch-Israelische Beziehungen* (München: Piper, 1988), 22-29. Among the opponents in the cabinet were Justice Minister Thomas Dehler (FDP), Finance Minister Fritz Schäffer (CSU) and Transport Minister Hans Seebohm (DP).
24. Albrecht, ed., *Kurt Schumacher*, 1006.
25. Adalbert Rückerl, *NS-Verbrechen vor Gericht* (Heidelberg: Müller, 1982), 176.

26. Ibid., 177.
27. Presse-und Informationszentrum des Deutschen Bundestages, *Zur Verjährung nationalsozialistischer Verbrechen. Dokumentation der parlamentarischen Bewältigung des Problems 1960-1979*, Schriftenreihe *Zur Sache* 3/80 (Bonn: Druckhaus Bayreuth, 1980), 157.
28. Ibid., 154.
29. Press and Information Office, ed., *Remembrance, Sorrow and Reconciliation*, 61.
30. For Adenauer's refusal to admit collective guilt, see Wolffsohn, *Ewige Schuld?*, 23.
31. Press and Information Office, ed., *Remembrance, Sorrow and Reconciliation*, 61-63.
32. Norman E. Tutorow, ed., *War Crimes, War Criminals, and War Crimes Trials: An Annotated Bibliography and Source Book* (Westport, Conn.: Greenwood, 1986), 475-476. The court eventually commuted the sentence to time served.
33. Press and Information Office, ed., *Remembrance, Sorrow and Reconciliation*, 59.
34. Bark and Gress, *A History of West Germany*, 1:12. Nolte gained considerable notoriety for the views he expressed during the *Historikerstreit*.
35. Allied war crimes trials thus shared the fate of denazification as a whole, which was also rejected by most Germans. As time progressed, surveys results showed that the percentage of respondents supporting Allied denazification efforts was dwindling by the late 1940s. See Kater, "Problems of Political Reeducation," 103-105.

Writing After: Literary and Moral Reflections of the Holocaust

Efraim Sicher

This essay is not concerned with literary representation of the Holocaust but with the moral and artistic problem of the contemporary Jew who writes *after* an event which surpasses the limits of human imagination. The inhumanity to which the perpetrators and victims descended is scarcely bearable in an artistic medium, indeed must not seem bearable if truth is to be preserved. Apart from the harrowing records of camp inmates and other witnesses which leave their trace on the collective memory of the next generation, the Holocaust bears tremendous moral weight upon those who live in its aftermath. Life continues as if nothing had happened, but this very complacency must challenge the integrity of the artist.

To borrow George Steiner's terms, those who live *after*--whether or not they lived during and whatever their nationality or location--are in a sense survivors. They must face the moral responsibility of the governments and organizations which collaborated with the Final Solution by complicity or silence.[1] They must face the breakdown in codes of human behavior in so-called civilized society. They cannot escape the complexes of Judeo-Christian relations, whether we speak of reconciliation or revisionist denial, bearing the burden of guilt or wiping the slate clean, ritualizing the suffering into a new religion or justifying it.[2] I would like to give a few examples of the literary treatment of living in the aftermath of the Holocaust in order to indicate the complexity and irresolubility of a dilemma that undermines the literary text. The Holocaust becomes a burden and a haunting presence, while writing is at the same time a means to survival and a means to exorcism, a self-therapy, or, as Israeli psychiatrist Henry Szor has called it, *Wiedergutmachung* ("making good again"), a debatable use of the term for the reparations paid to victims of Nazism by the West German government; indeed, some of the writers to be discussed later in this essay would strongly deny the possibility of any "making good."[3]

WRITING AND SURVIVAL AFTER

In my book on contemporary Jewish writing in Britain,[4] I argued that there has been a significant reappraisal of Jewish themes, primarily under the impetus of the Holocaust, or rather its delayed impact on public consciousness, especially in the wake of the Eichmann trial and Hannah Arendt's *Eichmann in Jerusalem* (1963), the first major postwar confrontation between Jew and German. Arendt questioned the moral position of those who brought Eichmann to justice, for the trial took no account of Jewish complicity in the machine of mass-murder. And what meaning did justice have in a crime so monstrous?

For Arendt the trial was an attempt to publicly expiate guilt and to find a scapegoat for all Nazi crimes against the Jews, instead of seeing Eichmann as part of a crime against humanity inflicted on the Jews. The community's need to expiate guilt through a scapegoat is a theme of C.P. Taylor's play *Happy Days Are Here Again* (1965). This is one of the themes present in a prize-winning novel by Bernice Rubens, *The Elected Member* (U.S. title *Chosen People*, 1969) and it may be seen to inform one reading of Harold Pinter's *The Homecoming* (1964). The hidden guilt and shame of the Jewish family in these works present a dubious picture of their supposed moral stance and sacred memory, suggesting that Jews are not immune to extreme behavior or the universal aberrations of the human psyche. That assumption raises serious questions about good and evil as absolute categories.

In his play *Good* (1981) C.P. Taylor explored the conscience of an S.S. officer attached to Eichmann's outfit who remains, to the end, a "good" person; in fact, his neuroses suggest everyman on the psychiatrist's couch, and we are reminded of our own complicity in the cultural genocide and postcolonial wars perpetrated against the peoples of the Third World, as well as our compliance with a nuclear holocaust, the "final solution to end all final solutions." The playwright feels compelled to bring this warning to the public consciousness because of his own awareness that had the Battle of Britain gone the other way he too would have been a victim of the camps.[5] A literature professor, Halder, is conscripted to the Nazi euthanasia program. His specialization in literature is significant not just for the Faust theme (suggested by his student mistress), but also because it is a novel justifying euthanasia which he wrote to "write out all that guilt" for his treatment of his mother, who suffers from senile dementia. A Jewish friend Maurice serves as secret confessor and at the same time as a hysterical gauge of the persecution of the Jews. While obscenities and self-hate are the only language with which Maurice can respond to Nazism, Halder's decision-making capability breaks down and he develops a pseudo-psychological justification for joining the Nazis and for joining his mistress Anne. These are strategies of survival and self-interest which denigrate the Jew-Marxist humanism as "complicating" the simple logic of Nazism. Halder hears bands playing at the time the Nazis come to power and this imagined music accompanies his own long march from alarm to compliance and complicity. At the gates of Auschwitz he still thinks he is hearing Schubert in his head, but this time it is real, for the camp inmates are made to play while the gas chambers perpetrate the barbaric work of a music-loving nation.

George Steiner's novel *The Portage to San Cristóbal of A.H.* (1981), published the same year as the first performance of *Good* and itself adapted for the stage by Christopher Hampton, goes a step further and gives Adolf Hitler, tracked down by Israeli secret agents in the South American jungle, the opportunity to justify himself. Exploiting the spy-thriller qualities of the capture of Eichmann and persistent rumors about the whereabouts of Mengele, Steiner composes a polyphony of inner voices that respond in a familiarly postmodernist discourse to the capture of the leader of the Third Reich, the thought of whom is to some so obscene as to be sacred. However, several voices, including those of the Israelis are recognizably inauthentic. Moreover, the occasional false note seems to betray a discourse that speaks of Hitler as an Anti-Christ, prophesized by one "Nathaniel of Mainz" (presumably Steiner is thinking of Nathan of Gaza, a kabbalist and disciple of the false messiah Shabetai Tsvi). The long demented speech of Lieber that takes up the whole of chapter six speaks of an antitheology, in which the Word of the Creation is matched by the negation of the Word, "its backside of evil," "the night side of language." This hellish speech is almost unspeakable.

> But there shall come a man whose mouth shall be as a furnace and whose tongue as a sword laying waste. He will know the sounds of madness and loathing and teach it to others. He will know the sounds of madness and loathing and make them seem music.[6]

He will know the word that will unsay creation. That mystical fantasy comes in a litany of victims of Nazism whose sufferings are left to the unimaginable ellipses in Lieber's ravings, but are too imaginably obscene, leaving the impression of six million acts of perverted depravity, rather than a mass murder machine that committed six million acts of inhumanity with the systematic banality of bureaucratic procedure (Himmler did order the murderers not to lose their "decency," to kill without weakening or committing excesses). The mention of one Nathaniel Steiner among the victims provides a clue, perhaps, to George Steiner's own identification with the authorship of this particular apocalypse, and it is in keeping with the peculiar logic behind it that Hitler makes the last speech that closes the book. Hitler defends himself by arguing that he learned the fanatic teaching of the master race from the Jews, that his practice of extermination could be judged no worse than that of Stalin and the Jewish-supported Bolsheviks, that the Holocaust allowed the establishment of the State of Israel and the consequent unjust treatment of the Arab refugees. But the premise that Hitler derived his ideas from a Jewish apostate more than anything points to the most preposterous claim of Steiner's novel, that the esoteric cipher of Biblical verses mixed with Christian sources and heretical thoughts could represent an identifiable Jewish voice. I am not sure how much this detracts from Steiner's more serious conclusion that there can be no conclusion, no final judgement, or that at least it is not in the hands of men. But the philosophy behind that assertion leaves only speculation and a deconstruction of the Word that inevitably reduces evil almost to a play on words.

There is, of course, a danger in representing evil to the extent that it becomes all too human and even excusable. Hyam Maccoby, one of Steiner's more reasoned critics, has complained that in playing the Devil's advocate Steiner runs the risk of putting convincing arguments in Hitler's mouth which, apart from being quite untypical of his erratic racist demagoguery, might be misread as valid.[7] In fact, A.H. repeats some of Steiner's own arguments in *In Bluebeard's Castle* that anti-Semitism was rooted in Gentile resentment at the exacting moral demands of Jewish monotheism. According to Steiner's Freudian thesis, the Jews are regarded as the guilty agents of Culture, for society would like to return to the "silence of the jungle." Alvin Rosenfeld, on the other hand, admires Lieber's speech as successfully locating a register that mediates between the extremes of exclamation and lamentation. The craziness of Lieber is that of Ernie Levy and Mr. Sammler who have seen hell and know what was done to mankind; Lieber represents the Jewish consciousness "possessed by historical memory at its most lacerating. To bear the burden of such memory is to carry a weight of experience almost too heavy for words to express."[8] Lieber needs Hitler; the Jew-Nazi *döppelgang* is indispensable to his identity. Yet when it comes to the direct representation of Hitler at the end of the book, Rosenfeld objects to the introduction of the essayist's *speculation* into the *incarnation* of the idea; it achieves the very opposite of laying the ghost to rest and Steiner could have foreseen that.[9] Indeed, the revisionist expropriation of the Hitler cult in recent years illustrates the tremendous difficulty and responsibility of any writer or historian in conjuring up the name and image of the leader of the Third Reich.[10]

REFUGEE SURVIVAL AND WRITING

The clearest example of writers who personally bear such difficulty and responsibility are refugees who were born in Germany and came as children to England before the outbreak of war.[11] Those who came as children often lost close relatives, sometimes all, and grew up in a strange, unchosen land, feeling guilty they had not been *there*, as Karen Gershon has written in "I Was Not There":

> The morning they set out from home
> I was not there to comfort them
> the dawn was innocent with snow
> in mockery--it is not true
> the dawn was neutral was immune
> their shadows threaded it too soon
> they were relieved that it had come
> I was not there to comfort them

> One told me that my father spent a day in prison long ago
> he did not tell me that he went
> what difference does it make now
> when he set out when he came home
> I was not there to comfort him
> and now I have no means to know
> of what I was kept ignorant

> Both my parents died in camps
> I was not there they were alone
> my mind refuses to conceive
> the life they must have known
> I must atone because I live
> I could not have saved them from death
> the ground is neutral underneath

> Every child must leave its home
> time gathers life impartially
> I could have spared them nothing since

> I was too young--it is not true
> they might have lived to succour me
> and none shall say in my defence
> had I been there to comfort them
> it would have made no difference.[12]

Being alive the poet has not even the knowledge of what she has been deprived: "and now I have no means to know/of what I was kept ignorant."

The Bread of Exile (1985), Karen Gershon's fictionalized autobiography, epitomizes the agony of the lack of memory which drives the poet back to Germany to reclaim loss. The child's parting from parents is itself tinged with guilt, since nobody could envisage they would never be seen again. The outward journey is remembered as a kind of adventure, a transit to a temporary refuge, and thereafter the English language is a "raft of words" to escape from childhood to an unenviable refugee status among hostility and misunderstanding.[13] The danger in Germany after Kristallnacht was not fully appreciated and the child's parents were disparaged for not being able to keep their children, while on the other hand the child was constantly being reminded how lucky she was to have been given a place when so many were left behind. In Germany being a Jew was relearnt by assimilated German Jews, while in England after the outbreak of war the Jewish refugee invited suspicion and hatred as a German enemy alien. Separation from a brother or sister, internment, evacuation, curfew and travel or residency restrictions reinforced the trauma. Inge, Gershon's fictionalized self, prevaricates a number of fantasies to deal with her repressed desire to be free, including an incestuous infatuation with her alter-ego brother, who at once realizes the wish to be heroic and the wish to reunite with the victims of the Final Solution by smuggling himself back into Germany to join the transport to death. A further source of betrayal of parents is the temptation to overidentify with the Aryan, the English baby Georgie, and another the more insidious missionizing of the prim Miss Pym.

The alternation of identities (Jew/Nazi, male/female, victim/torturer) comes out more forcefully in Gershon's novel *The Fifth Generation* (1987), also based on her own experiences. Barbara, a *Kindertransport* survivor, works in a home for disturbed children as a means of atonement for having survived. There she meets Luke, a Gentile, whom she marries in a mistaken attempt to escape her past, reasoning that being a Jew matters only to Hitler and to continue being a Jew is to perpetuate racism. She refuses to read books about the Holocaust out of a fear that the victims may make claims on her. Some of the children in the home have survived a

Nazi lamp shade factory and the couple adopt one of them, Peter Sanger, named for the initials stamped on his left buttock that mark him as an offcut, a reject, as Abel. But the initials turn out to be also the mark of Cain when it is revealed that he may be the son of Hitler. A number of suicidal and sadomasochistic desires are enacted here, an expression of the unleashing of Nazi perversion and the normalization of thinking of oneself as a lamp shade (not metaphorically as in Sylvia Plath's poem). The fantasy of not being a Jew robs the boy once more of his parentage (his foster parents) as well as complicating his need to create real parents "dead and dung." "He felt like Cain, cursed to seek refuge and flee again and find a home nowhere, penalized for trying to strike roots."[14] The return to Germany in search of identity--the missing home, the missing family, the missing childhood,--or as an act of defiant survival is recurrent in fiction and real life, and here it is a kind of private *Wiedergutmachung*, a claim to reparation that would somehow exorcise the haunting past which bequeaths the guilt "to the fifth generation."[15]

In his novel *Reparations* (1981), Rudolf Nassauer exacts a literary and moral form of reparations by describing wealthy Jewish bankers in Frankfurt from their dispossession under the Nazis to the vengeful dispossession of the Germans by their heirs after the war (in property rackets reminiscent of Fassbinder's notorious play and in Machiavellian funding of the Baader-Meinhoff gang). Tobias, a German Jewish refugee growing up in England, finds the puzzle of his personal history falling into place with the revelations of Belsen and Auschwitz after the war:

> A mustiness lingered over his memories, he saw everything like superbly trimmed gardens left to overgrow, the tendrils of creepers climbing up columns and lovers' nooks until they were hidden like forgotten tombs. He saw himself stretched on a rack, one moment he was tied to it, the next he was holding on to the torturer's apparatus, fearing to let go in case he would float out of the orbit of sanity.[16]

The violent rage unleased in him has to do both with thirst for retribution and sadomasochistic longing that goes back to the demonic forebodings of Nazi terror from 1931 onwards when the family watched with fascination the cruelty of which they were the victims. England has nothing to hold him and he breaks with his wife to be sucked up by Germany. The battle for reparations is a merciless demand for restitution of the status quo ante, with the Jews as bosses, and for the restitution of loss, the cynical catchword being "A la recherche du temps perdu." Only when they feel they have sufficiently exorcised the devil do Tobias and his cousin Julius leave Germany.

Efraim, the eponymous narrator of Alfred Andersch's German novel *Efraim's Book* (1969), also returns from England to his native Germany. In search of the illegitimate daughter of his English friend and employer, he discovers not just the guilty memories of others, but also the absent "trace" of his own past. Efraim writes a novel about his search for his identity and career between bouts of memory and self-searching on a typewriter in hotel rooms or his ex-wife's flat in London. He returns to Berlin as an English journalist and the geography of Berlin and Rome intersects with the absence of these places in his past. The new Berlin slang and the German which he writes form a psychological no-man's land divided by the Berlin Wall, a new Ghetto wall, blocking out his childhood. When he visits his former home, he evinces little desire to evict the new residents, but merely feels the frustrated hopelessness of restitution of more than financial or property rights, the restitution of his past.

Fibich and Hartmann in *The Latecomers* (1988) by British Booker prize-winner Anita Brookner embody different responses to survival. Having come to England as children, they escaped their family's fate in Germany. Fibich, like his English wife Christine Hardy, was deprived of childhood and affectionate parents. Neither he nor his friend and business associate Hartmann remember their German past. They "came late" and find it surprising that they have survived so well and so long, earning themselves comfortable homes and families. But while Hartmann smothers the absence of memory in daily comforts and *savoir-faire*, a "damage limitation" policy, Fibich cannot be at ease, even on his psychoanalyst's couch. After many years Fibich decides to return to Berlin in search of his past. He finds there a foreign city whose sounds and sensations confirm his psychological and geographical displacement and where he discovers he is anchored only in the need of his wife and son for him. Returning to England, he witnesses a reenactment at the airport of the isolated traumatic scene in his memory, a mother fainting at her child's departure. The scene results in a near breakdown but also in an emotional release expressed in a notebook he leaves for his son Toto. The novel ends with Fibich leaving his son a note that speaks of winning a battle of the mind and includes an atheistic prayer for a blessing on Toto, rather different from the prayer for the soul of Elya Gruner at the close of *Mr. Sammler's Planet*. Like Bellow's novel, however, Brookner's sensitive verbal portrait of a shattered personality sums up a world devoid of moral or existential certainties, though missing here are the quirky idiosyncrasies of character and sharp vision we associate with Mr. Sammler.

Unlike the camp inmates, whose lives are a memorial to what happened, whose writings, as Elie Wiesel testifies, are a remembering, the child refugees do not even have the memory with which to commemorate their loss. Their guilt at being alive makes their writing a *kapara* (penance) without remission. They have been, moreover, doubly cut off from German culture, for they are not simply exiles: their native tongue has denied them in more than one sense. In 1966 Michael Hamburger declared he was writing "for the horror-stricken. For those abandoned to butchery. For survivors. We learnt language from scratch, those people and I."[17] Hamburger's poem on Eichmann, "In a Cold Season" (in his collection *Weather and Season*, 1963), is one of several which record the delayed reaction to the personal trauma of Nazism. Hamburger has said that the poem failed because it was meant to do good, not just be good. It was meant to penetrate the complacency that mercy was somehow inferior to justice, for the Jews to whom mercy was denied should have accorded it: "Retribution only buries the stench."[18] The men and women whom Eichmann had killed were to him no more than words on official papers.

Words cannot reach him in his prison of words: Whose words killed men because those men were words.[19]

The poet could not bring himself to add one more death, Eichmann's, to the six million, because to silence the murderer of words does not flesh one word. Therefore to pity Eichmann, who had no pity, for the sake of those who died for lack of pity, is to affirm the human in his victims by sparing the human in him: "Dare break one word and words may yet be whole."

Following T.W. Adorno's dictum that there can be no poetry after Auschwitz,[20] Hamburger has called the making of language as an aesthetic object "a harmless but ludicrous and childish occupation."[21] But not only is poetry possible, it is necessary. In a world, as Sartre remarked in *What is Literature?*, that can do very well without literature and still better without man, poetry is the sole means to a human existence. If Celan's *Todesfuge* sounded to Adorno incongruously and even obscenely lyrical, it speaks nevertheless, or perhaps more so, because the lyricism disturbs.

Hamburger's poem "Treblinka" (in *Ownerless Earth*, 1973), is prefaced with the words, "A Survivor Speaks." These are literally the words of a survivor of the camp, Richard Glazar, who witnessed the first night in November 1942 that the bodies were burned while in the barracks a Warsaw opera singer sang the Yiddish song based on the verse in Psalms:

> "My God, My God,
> Why has Thou forsaken us?
> We have been thrust into the fire before,
> But we have never denied Thy Holy Law."[22]

Yet these words which preface Hamburger's poem and which claim the possibility of speech after surviving an experience that must render dumb are charged also with the anguish of the poet who was not there. The vividly imaged rainbow flare over the camp where the corpses are burned resembles the coat of many colors of Joseph, the "chosen" son and scapegoat victim of his brother's jealousy. The voice of the opera singer drives away cold and fear, gushing as blood from a wound with the cry of Jesus on the crucifix, "Eli, Eli. . . ." That, too, is a question of the silence of God, but one which was used to justify two millennia of persecution of the Jews:

> Long we'd been dirt to be wiped off, dust to be dispersed
> Older than he, old as the silence of God.
> In that light we knew it; and the complaint was praise,
> Was thankfulness for death, the lost and the promised land,
> The gathering up at last, all our hundred hues
> Fierce in one radiance gathered by greater darkness,
> The darkness that took our kings, David and Solomon
> Who living had burnt with the same fire;
> All our hundred languages gathered again in one silence.[23]

As for Karen Gershon, who spoke of nature's indifferent neutrality, life is qualified by death, the sure knowledge of mortality and the final, determining silence. In Germany there remain not even gravestones to mark the exiled poet's origins ("The Search," in *Weather and Season*, 1963), and in the confrontation with the Christian culture in which he writes there is no return home, no homeland to which to return.

Hamburger has translated the Holocaust poets Nelly Sachs and Paul Celan, but he is also well-known for his translations of Holderin and Rilke. What of that liberal humanism, the premise of European civilization, which was the culture of Nazi Germany? Steiner would say that when great literature or music is enjoyed down the road from the death camp or in the death camp itself the only option is silence.

> We come after. We know that a man can read Goethe or Rilke
> in the evening, that he can play Bach and Schubert, and go to his
> day's work at Auschwitz in the morning.[24]

Steiner does not argue that writers should stop writing, in accordance with Adorno's declaration, but in *Language and Silence* he asks whether they are writing too much, whether language has become mediocre, inhumane, illiterate. . . . The devaluation of the word is more apparent since the manipulation of the German language for the murderous purposes of Nazism, yet the mass media continue that semantic sanitization and obfuscation. The belief that the Humanities necessarily humanize was placed in doubt by the bestiality of the twentieth century, to which the universities offered little moral resistance. Literature and sadism can coexist: the SS officer in the concentration camp may have been reading Rilke very well indeed. Nevertheless, Steiner believes it to be the role of the critic after Auschwitz, in the age of bestiality, to preserve the values of humane liberalism by showing what to read and how to read it. The possibility of humaneness lies in the cathartic power of literature. The Anglo-Jewish poet Jon Silkin is far less optimistic than Steiner about the civilizing role of literature, but he is more convinced that poetry is not merely written out of a mimetic urge, that it can change individuals, "for just as we cannot assume that the concentration camp officer wasn't reading Rilke 'well,' we may also question whether he was reading "properly." There is no way of knowing. There is only the parallel and endlessly disturbing coexistence of cruelty which is worse than barbarism, with art."[25] Living *after* irrevocably alters our appreciation of the literary past. We must reread Keats, just as modern Jewish writers come to English literature with a peculiar rereading of Yeats, T.S. Eliot, Pound and the modernists, and just as Silkin would have us reread the First World War poets, in particular Isaac Rosenberg and Wilfred Owen.

Owen spoke of the pity that was in the word and his poetry revealed a cruelty that preluded the Holocaust. But can poetry do justice to an unspeakable cruelty of the magnitude of Auschwitz? Certainly Silkin had to overcome apprehensions in writing his celebrated poem "Death of a Son" that he might be desecrating the memory of the child's death.[26] Yet the fact that he and others have made poetry out of the deaths of six million speaks for itself. Auschwitz has rendered useless many basic moral and semantic values and the poet must find a language not debased, must fight the continuing devaluation of language and morality by the mass media which employ vulgarity and parascientific jargon, as did the Nazis and other totalitarian regimes, to obfuscate live issues. The violence of the Holocaust is a possibility to be guarded against and it requires incredible courage and gift to render imaginable the unimaginable, to make readable the unbearable--indeed, what must not seem bearable!

SURVIVAL AND DESTINY

In his discussion of the modern Jewish situation Rabbi J.B. Soloveitchik has written that the meaning of the Holocaust is ultimately unknowable. To be and to act after Auschwitz are in Judaism questions of an *ex-post facto* decision-making situation (*halakha lema'aseh*). Soloveitchik makes a basic distinction between *yi'ud* and *goral*. The latter is necessary existence, the former willed existence, purposeful and target-oriented. This was the choice facing Jonah when he fled God's appointment to a prophetic mission and it was to free-willed destiny that he had to return in recognition of the special Divine relationship with the people of Israel. In Soloveitchik's *yi'ud* it is the shared destiny of Israel that defines the modern Jew's universal vocation. To deny this is to flee "individual freedom" as Jonah fled and to submit to some necessary fate,[27] to a fate as absurd and meaningless as the burden of Sisyphus in Camus' existentialist parable. By contrast, other Jewish thinkers have seen in Auschwitz a break in the covenantal tradition or at least at challenge that redefines it, as in Fackenheim's "614th commandment."[28] A.J. Heschel's parallel (in *Man in Quest of God*, 1954) of the giving of the Law at Sinai when the midrashic mountain of history is over the heads of the people suggests, however, a renewal of the covenant at Auschwitz that also involves free-willed choice under existential coercion.

Traditional Judaism responded to the apparently hopeless fate of European Jewry by commitment to survival, by sanctifying life (*kiddush hekhaim*) just as previous generations had died as martyrs (*kiddush hashem*). It was humanity which died at Auschwitz, not God, whose presence was concealed (*hester panim*). Yet the secular Jewish writer has responded to survival as meaningless in a world lacking moral direction. This breakdown in man's dialogue with God questions the Jew's continuing covenantal relationship with Him through Abraham and at Sinai, yet it paradoxically draws on the Hebrew covenantal tradition, through the motifs and *topoi* of the *'aqedah*, the doubts of Job or the lament for destroyed Jerusalem (the *khurban*).[29] At the same time the modern Jewish writer insists on the uniqueness of the Holocaust and attempts a new paradigm of Jewish history and human experience.

The result is a literature that denies literariness, while confirming Aristotle's claim that literature, rather than history, was the means for comprehending human life *in extremis*.[30] It is a literature that speaks of the unspeakable. Its language is a language of silence. The ensuing dialogue is an agonized search for individual destiny in ways that may contradict the moral imperative of Soloveitchik's vision of communal responsibility in national destiny. This is because the Holocaust is viewed by George Steiner and others as a disjuncture in theology as in language.[31] No longer is it a question of the Divine discourse speaking the language of man, an axiom of Judaism, but the negation of meaning in language and the apparent absence of an addressee. Even time and space have become somehow nameless, blank. In Aharon Appelfeld's fictional universe, for example, there is a before and an after, but camp experience forms a determining lacuna in the narrative time-space continuum; Appelfeld's survivors carry the Holocaust within them as a void the fragments personality and time into an existential zone predating actual deportation, a supratemporal zone which overrides political, theological and personal questions of survival and destiny. This is something that a story like "Bertha" has in common with the "drama of the absurd" of Beckett and Pinter, besides the elusive symbolism in the Kafkaesque tradition of modernism, and something it has in common with the surrealism of some contemporary Israeli prose (Amos Oz' *My Michael*, A.B. Yehoshua's *Three Days and a Child* or David Shachar's *Jerusalem Fantasies*) which transcends the personal and communal crises of the everyday threat of death and betrayal to get at the essence of being.[32]

A distinction has to be made here between Israeli and Diaspora writers. For Israelis the Holocaust is present in the collective consciousness and the national calendar as part of the transition from destruction to redemption. In terms of political history, the rising of the phoenix from the ashes retroactively links the establishment of the state with the destruction of the major Jewish communities in Europe and justifies the existence of the sole refuge of Jews from continuous anti-Semitism; in existential terms, the constant military threat to Israel maintains the possibility of repeated genocide and highlights the unwillingness or incapability of the outside world to prevent it. These are lines of thought that are very much at the center of artistic and ideological controversy in Israel today. What is clear, however, is that the exilic past cannot be deleted from the nation's historic memory, as was attempted in the early days of the State when a new Sabra culture was in the making. When a boy liberated from Nazi Europe erases German words from the kibbutz classroom blackboard in Uri Orlev's *Lead Soldiers* he is effectively protesting the normalization of the new state and fulfilling the biblical injunction of remembrance to erase the name of Amalek, never to forget.

The Diaspora writer is conscious of all of these problems, of course, but he has chosen not to live in Israel, has chosen not to "slam the door on Europe." Both Saul Bellow's *To Jerusalem and Back* (1976) and Clive

Sinclair's *Diaspora Blues* (1987) make fundamental criticisms of Israel's political stance, but the advantage claimed of being an outsider must remain dubious. There is another factor, though, that of Hebrew, in which most Diaspora writers are not at home. Hebrew has taken over from Yiddish as the principal cultural language of the Jews and the demise of Yiddish makes the destroyed East European heritage a referential lost homeland to an extent to which it is not in the Israeli mind.

The search for literary identity is therefore a search in cultural and historical memory for personal destiny, as when Philip Roth has Franz Kafka escape early death and deportation in Nazi-occupied Prague and fell to obscurity in Roth's own New Jersey childhood (in *Reading Myself and Others*). When the Anne Frank of the Diaries is transported to the imagination of *The Ghost Writer*, she is K., who "without having done anything wrong . . . was arrested one fine morning." Reading oneself and others is to be Joseph K./Anne Frank and to grapple with the personal destiny and communal responsibility inherent in survival. Sanford Pinsker has argued that Roth's *Ghost Writer* describes both a modern indwelling of texts and a "Rescue" of the lost East European past akin to Cynthia Ozick's rescue of Bruno Schulz in *The Messiah of Stockholm* (1987).[33] However, in "redeeming" Anne Frank, Zuckerman ultimately fails to confront the finality of the Holocaust and delivers a slap in the face of the well-dressed crowds who attend the Broadway spectacle of *Anne Frank's Diaries*. That humor should emerge from Zuckerman's guilt feelings is a painful irony.

A different working out of personal and literary destiny is to be found in the Anglo-Jewish poet and novelist Elaine Feinstein's *The Border* (1984), a novella built around a Viennese poet called Hans Wendler and his physicist wife Inge who are caught in a web of sexual passion and betrayal as Hitler's shadow darkens across Europe. The borders of betrayal prove thin, as does the border between Vichy France and Spain where the last drama of survival and death is played out in the same hotel in which Walter Benjamin killed himself. The novella is written under the sign of Benjamin's own writings and fate, and one cannot help thinking that Feinstein is writing out her own thoughts on poetry and silence, not without some guidance from the spirits of her beloved Osip Madelstam, Paul Celan and Marina Tsvetaeva.

Another Anglo-Jewish poet who has recently written on the destiny of the Jewish people is Jon Silkin. *Footsteps on a Downcast Path* (1984; reprinted in *The Ship's Pasture*, 1986) is a tunnel vision of Jewish history from the Roman destruction of Jerusalem to the Warsaw Ghetto. Like Schwarz-Bart (in *Last of the Just*), Silkin sees the York massacre of 1190 (described in his earlier poems "The Coldness" and "Resting Place") as the beginning of the long road to Auschwitz. Here the persecutions of the Jews, including their expulsion from England, are a sexual violence that rack the speaker in a Danteesque diorama (presumably the Tel-Aviv Diaspora Museum) as he struggles with Mephistopheles, but he survives to the strange reality approaching redemption in modern Jerusalem. Silkin's Jerusalem in his earlier *The Psalms and Their Spoils* (1980) was a response to Blake and here the messianic city merges with Yehuda Amichai's "Venice of God" (in "Jerusalem, Port City"), the fantasies of David Shachar, kabbalistic sources and European modernism to suggest a different kind of landscape to that of T.S. Eliot's *Wasteland*. It is a lethal universe where genocide and bestiality are natural to the human condition, where suffering must be reckoned with neither as meaningful nor as negative theology, but where one must be thankful for survival, where survival is a kind of poetry.

Jewish writers in English in particular have to face the hostile stereotype of the Jew in the Christian culture in which they are writing, a stereotype exploited by the Nazis. Emanuel Litvinoff's "To T.S. Eliot" is an angry reply to the author of "Burbank with a Baedeker: Bleistein with a Cigar." Litvinoff claims identity with Bleistein and with the "protozoic slime" of Eliot's Shylock, with the partizans in the sewers under the Warsaw Ghetto and the ashes of children in Treblinka. Litvinoff chides Eliot: "You had a sermon but it was not this."[34] The playwright Arnold Wesker has rendered his anger at English literary anti-Semitism in a new, post-Holocaust version of Shylock. *The Merchant* (1977; revised version, 1983) is not a rewriting of Shakespeare's *Merchant of Venice* but a presentation of historical anti-Semitism from a Jewish point of view. Shylock defends his Bond not because he is bloodthirsty, but because he is obliged to defend the reputation and integrity of the Jewish community. His decision to insist on the Bond binds him to the destiny of the community--Soloveitchik's *yi'ud*,--though he sacrifices Antonio, his friend in Wesker's version. That existential decision is an indictment of a society which could contemplate the reality of the Jew cutting the flesh from a Christian, which could itself contemplate the cutting and incineration of human flesh. In insisting on the Bond, Shylock becomes what Sartre calls in *Anti-Semite and Jew* an "authentic Jew" who does not run away from his situation but accepts his destiny, thereby claiming his liberty and rendering the anti-Semite impotent. Just as he sees anti-Semitism binding Jew and non-Jew into a situation of guilt, Sartre sees a similar condition on the writer, who cannot escape the moral commitment that comes with the writing act.[35]

Cynthia Ozick, Saul Bellow, Edmond Jabès and George Steiner deserve separate studies[36] but these few examples which space allows of second-generation writing suggest that it is impossible for any contemporary Jewish artist to ignore the existential predicament of personal and literary destiny while retaining artistic integrity. Several recent critics agree that the context of the Holocaust is inescapable for the modern Jewish writer.[37] Citing the examples of Isaac Bashevis Singer's *The Slave* and Bernard Malamud's *The Fixer*, Alvin Rosenfeld declares, "All novels about Jewish suffering written in the post-Holocaust period must implicate the Holocaust, whether it is expressly named or not."[38] The impact of the Holocaust on literature is barely legible. But the disjuncture of human discourse at Auschwitz cannot be "made good." Our theory and history of language and of culture have undergone imperceptible yet irradicable revision.

NOTES

1. George Steiner, "A Kind of Survivor," *Language and Silence: Essays, 1958-1966*. (Harmondsworth: Penguin Books, 1969), pp. 119-135. Steiner's own identity is filled with the shadows of the "Central European heritage" not generally shared by American Jews; Gershon Shaked has probed those shadows of identity among German Jewish writers in his collection of essays *The Shadows Within: Essays on Modern Jewish Writers* (Philadelphia: Jewish Publication Society of America, 1987). Shaked's comments on Saul Friedländer's inability to come to terms with the cultural and moral situation in Israel and his wished-for European identity may be applied also to Steiner, who likewise writes out of a persecution by the past.
2. See Robert Alter, "Deformations of the Holocaust," *Commentary*, 71, 2 (1981), 48-54.
3. On exorcism and *Wiedergutmachung* see Efraim Sicher, "The Burden of Remembrance: Second Generation Literature," *Jewish Book Annual*, 48 (1990), 26-41.
4. Efraim Sicher, *Beyond Marginality: Anglo-Jewish Literature after the Holocaust* (Albany: State University of New York Press, 1985).
5. C.P. Taylor, "Author's Note," *Good* (London: Methuen, revised edition 1983).
6. *The Portage to San Cristóbal of A.H.* (New York: Simon and Schuster, 1981), p. 45. The mystery of Steiner's anti-creation theology may be traced to the chapter on "Language and Gnosis" in his book on language and translation *After Babel: Aspects of Language and Translation* (New York: Oxford University Press, 1975) and to Gershom Scholem's *Major Trends in Jewish Mysticism*, as well as to some of the writings of Walter Benjamin and his own remarks on Treblinka and the Word in *Language and Silence*.
7. "George Steiner's Hitler: Of Theology and Politics," *Encounter* 58, 5, (1982), 27-34. Saul Friedländer sides with Maccoby when he agrees that nothing could justify elevating Hitler into a metaphysical principle and fears that Steiner's pseudo-Hitler is closer to contemporary fantasies of Nazism than historical realities; indeed, he notes that the presentation of Hitler as a secular messiah adopting Jewish ideas of race and salvation is found both in Steiner's novel and in Syberberg's *Hitler, A Film From Germany* (*Reflections of Nazism: An Essay on Kitsch and Death* [New York: Harper & Row, 1984], pp. 111-115). Not all share Maccoby's view. Robert Boyers has defended

Steiner as the author of a political novel who has portrayed honestly the various viewpoints of the world's nations, each of which had its own vision of Hitler (*Atrocity and Amnesia: The Political Novel since 1945* [Oxford: Oxford University Press, 1985], pp. 156-172.) Bernard Bergonzi, who earlier had harsh words for *In Bluebeard's Castle*, extolled *The Portage* as a powerful and vivid story which highlights the difficulty of retribution. To wreak physical vengeance is to make Hitler into a scapegoat for the world's sins, in effect washing the world of its guilt through another crucifixion whose blood would again have been carried by the Jews ("George Steiner: On Culture and on Hitler" in his *The Myth of Modernism* and *Twentieth-Century Literature* (Brighton: Harvester Press, 1986), pp. 161-171).

8. Alvin Rosenfeld, *Imagining Hitler* (Bloomington: Indiana University Press, 1985), pp. 87-88.
9. *Imagining Hitler*, pp. 83-102.
10. Hitler's "trial" in the South American jungle can be traced to the survival myth and the revenge fantasies of popular fiction, among them Ira Levin's *The Boys from Brazil* and Herbert Liebermann's *The Climate of Hell*; the source for the converted Jew Grill's supposed influence on Hitler is a West German book called *Adolf Hitler--Begründer Israels* (1974) (Rosenfeld, *Imagining Hitler*, pp. 96-97). Joseph Lowin has noted that the closing speech contradicts the last words attributed to Hitler in the bunker, spurring on Germany to continue the war against the Jews ("Steiner's Helicopters," *Jewish Book Annual*, 41 (1983-1984), pp. 48-56).
11. The story of the ten thousand children who were brought out of Germany on the *Kindertransporte* is told in Karen Gershon (ed.), *We Came as Children* (London: Gollancz, 1966) and in Barry Turner, . . . *And The Policeman Smiled* (London: Bloomsbury, 1990). See also Gerhard Hirschfield (ed.), *Exile in Great Britain: Refugees from Hitler's Germany* (Leamington Spa: Berg Publishers/Atlantic Highlands, NJ: Humanities Press, 1984) and Marion Berghahn, *German-Jewish Refugees in England: The Ambiguities of Assimilation* (London: Macmillan, 1984).
12. *Selected Poems*, (London: Gollancz, 1966), p. 11. Reproduced by permission of the author.
13. A similar story of guilt for leaving parents behind and for the impossible burden of finding sponsors to save them is told in Lore Segal, *Other People's Houses* (New York: Harcourt, Brace and Ward, 1964). Always made to remember she lived in "other people's houses,"

she cannot feel like other British or American Jews who accept life's normalcies without alarm, "but I, now that I have children and am about the age my mother was when Hitler came, walk gingerly and in astonishment upon this island of my comforts, knowing that it is surrounded on all sides by calamity" (p. 312). Lore Segal was fortunate in having her parents flee in time to England, as was Eva Figes, whose poetical autobiography *Little Eden: A Child at War* (London: Faber, 1978) tells what it was like to fight an intermittent private war against one's own vulnerability, self-recriminations and ignorance. The guilt is mixed with blame apportioned to parents for both marking out their children's fate as Jews and for keeping silence on the true situation in an effort to protect them. When the newsreels from Belsen at the end of the war blurted out the horrific truth, "I told myself it was unfair, how was I supposed to know, and at the same time I felt it was all my fault, (her mother's) unhappiness, my unreasonableness, even the death of those I loved. From now on there was no escape from the burden of guilt" (p. 130).

14. *The Fifth Generation* (London: Gollancz, 1987), p. 80. Discussing the relation of memory to fiction, Lore Segal relates how she went back to her family's prewar home in her native Austria and found the past superimposed on the present, so that her father became transformed in her imagination into a Nazi ("Memory: The Problems of Imagining the Past," in *Writing and the Holocaust*, ed. Berel Lang, New York: Holmes and Meier, 1988, pp. 58-65).

15. The effect of the Holocaust on the third and fourth generations of survivors has been underscored by Gershon in a 1990 television documentary for the British network Channel Four, "Stranger in a Strange Land." Gershon's family is dispersed among different countries and languages; one daughter, Naomi, has relived her mother's refugee experience by moving to Israel and marrying an Ethiopian rescued by Operation Moses (see her comments, Naomi Shmueli, "Meurav yerushalmi," *Maariv*, 9 May 1989, Independence Day supplement, 7).

16. Rudolf Nassauer, *Reparations* (London: Cape, 1981), p. 147.

17. Hamburger cited by Stephen Spender in his introduction to Abba Kovner and Nelly Sachs, *Selected Poems* (Harmondsworth: Penguin Books, 1971), p. 17.

18. 1964 interview in J. Sonntag, ed., *Jewish Perspectives: 25 Years of Modern Jewish Writing (A Jewish Quarterly Anthology)* (London: Secker and Warburg, 1980), p. 88.

19. *Collected Poems* (Manchester: Carcanet, 1984), p. 129.

20. Adorno's statement has been so often misrepresented that it is worth quoting his remarks directed at literary "engagement": "Dan Satz, nach Auschwitz noch Lyrik zu schrieben, sei barbarisch, möchte ich nicht mildern; negativ ist darin der Impuls ausgesprochen, der die engagierte Dichtung beseelt" (*Gesammelte Schriften* volume 11 [Frankfurt-am-Main: Suhrkamp Verlag, 1974], p. 422).
21. Stephen Spender, "Introduction," p. 17.
22. Recorded in Claude Lanzmann, *Shoah: An Oral History of the Holocaust (The Complete Text of the Film)* (New York: Pantheon, 1985), p. 14.
23. Hamburger, *Collected Poems*, p. 133.
24. *Language and Silence*, p. 15.
25. "Introduction," in Jon Silkin, ed., *Poetry of the Committed Individual: A Stand Anthology of Poetry* (Harmondsworth: Penguin Books, 1973), p. 21.
26. Communication to Kenneth Allcott, in K. Allcott, ed., *The Penguin Book of Contemporary Verse, 1918-1960* (2nd edition, Harmondsworth: Penguin Books, 1961), p. 383.
27. J.B. Soloveitchik, *Besod hayakhid vehayakhad* (Jerusalem: Orot, n.d.), pp. 397-398.
28. See Richard Rubenstein, *After Auschwitz* (Indianapolis, 1966); Arthur A. Cohen, *The Tremendum: A Theological Interpretation of the Holocaust* (New York: Crossroad Publishing, 1981); Irving Greenberg, *Voluntary Covenant* (New York: National Jewish Resource Center, 1982); Emil Fackenheim, *To Mend the World* (New York: Schocken, new edition, 1989).
29. See David G. Roskies, *Against the Apocalypse: Responses to Catastrophe in Modern Jewish Culture* (Cambridge, MA: Harvard University Press, 1984).
30. G. Ramas-Rauch "Introduction," in G. Ramas-Rauch and J. Michman-Melman eds., *Facing the Holocaust*, pp. 3-5; cf. Lawrence Langer, *The Holocaust and the Literary Imagination* (New Haven: Yale University Press, 1975), pp. 14-20. For a discussion of the problem in Hebrew literature see Alan Mintz, *Hurban: Response to Catastrophe in Hebrew Literature* (New York: Columbia University Press, 1985).
31. George Steiner, "The Long Life of Metaphor: An Approach to the 'Shoah,'" *Encounter*, 68, 2 (1987), 55-61. Reprinted in Berel Lang, ed., *Writing and the Holocaust* (New York: Holmes and Meier, 1988), pp. 154-171. For another treatment of the disjunction of language which touches on failing discourse as a means to representation of

Auschwitz in Celan, Sachs and Jabès see Susan E. Shapiro, "Failing Speech: Post-Holocaust Writing and the Discourse of Postmodernism," *Semeia*, 40 (1987), pp. 65-91.
32. Gershon Shaked explains that the Holocaust made the surrealist nightmare of Kafka's novels and stories only too real; the resulting rereading of Kafka translates Kafkaesque situations to the uprootedness of Appelfeld's survivors and to the anxieties of Israel under siege in A.B. Yehoshua (*The Shadows Within*, p. 17).
33. Sanford Pinsker, "Jewish-American Literature's Lost-and-Found Department: How Philip Roth and Cynthia Ozick Reimagine their Significant Dead," *Modern Fiction Studies*, 35, 2 (1989), pp. 223-235.
34. *Notes for a Survivor* (Newcastle: Northern House, 1973), unpaginated.
35. This is my own reading of the play. Wesker in fact does not himself subscribe to the traditional community and has advocated his Shylock as the "free spirit" of Judaism, defying the state and resisting authority or the crippling urge to conform. His Shylock is, in Wesker's view, a more genuine response to the "banality of evil" than Christopher Hampton's stage adaptation of George Steiner's novel (Arnold Wesker, *Distinctions*, London: Cape, 1985, pp. 245-283).
36. See Alan Berger, "Holocaust Survivors and Children in *Anya and Mr. Sammler's Planet*," *Modern Language Studies*, 16, 1 (1986); Berel Lang, "Writing-the-Holocaust: Jabès and the Measure of History," in Lang, ed., *Writing and the Holocaust*, pp. 245-260; Joseph Lowin, "Steiner's Helicopters," *Jewish Book Annual*, 41 (1983-1984), pp. 48-56. "In the Shadow of the Holocaust," a special issue of *Studies in American Jewish Literature*, 9, 1 (Spring 1990), includes articles on Bernard Malamud, Cynthia Ozick, Holocaust poetry and the theme of loss in the American Jewish family.
37. See Alan Berger, *Crisis and Covenant: The Holocaust in American Jewish Fiction* (Albany: State University of New York Press, 1985); D. Bilik, *Immigrant-Survivors: Post-Holocaust Consciousness in Recent Jewish American Fiction* (Middletown: Wesleyan University Press, 1981); Sidra Dekoven Ezrahi, *By Words Alone: The Holocaust in Literature* (Chicago: University of Chicago Press, 1980), pp. 176-216; Efraim Sicher, *Beyond Marginality: Anglo-Jewish Literature after the Holocaust* (Albany: State University of New York University Press, 1985), pp. 153-167; Berel Lang (ed.), *Writing and the Holocaust* (New York: Holmes and Meier, 1988); Randolph L. Braham (ed.), *Reflections on the Holocaust in Art and Literature* (New York: Columbia Press, 1990); Jonathan Morse, *Word by Word: The*

Language of Memory (Ithaca: Cornell University Press, 1990). The compelling force of collective memory of the Holocaust is attested to by Art Spiegelman's *Maus* and its sequel, David Grossman's *See Under Love*, Dan Ben Amotz' *Remembering and Forgetting*, Anne Roiphe's *A Season for Healing*, Steven J. Florsheim (ed.), *Ghosts of the Holocaust: An Anthology of Poetry by the Second Generation* (Detroit: Wayne University Press, 1989) and David Rosenberg (ed.), *Testimony: Contemporary Writers Make the Holocaust Personal* (New York: Random House, 1989).

38. *A Double Dying: Reflections on Holocaust Literature* (Bloomington: Indiana University Press, 1980), p. 60.